THE GREEK MYTHS

THAT SHAPE THE WAY

WE THINK

THE

Greek Myths

THAT SHAPE THE
WAY WE THINK

RICHARD BUXTON

Frontispiece: Heinrich von Füger, *The Creation of Man by Prometheus*, 1790

First published in the United Kingdom in 2022
by Thames & Hudson Ltd, 181A High Holborn,
London WC1V 7QX

First published in the United States of America in 2022
by Thames & Hudson Inc., 500 Fifth Avenue, New York,
New York 10110

The Greek Myths That Shape the Way We Think
© 2022 Thames & Hudson Ltd, London
Text by Richard Buxton

Designed by Matthew Young

British Library Cataloguing-in-Publication Data
A catalogue record for this book is available from
the British Library

Library of Congress Control Number 2021943193

ISBN 978-0-500-51880-9

Printed in China by Shanghai Offset Printing
Products Limited

Be the first to know about our new releases,
exclusive content and author events by visiting
thamesandhudson.com
thamesandhudsonusa.com
thamesandhudson.com.au

Contents

An Inexhaustible Resource

The stories we know as 'the Greek myths' took shape some 3,000 years ago in the Aegean world, at a time when what would become its characteristic form of organization, known as the *polis* (city-state), was in the process of development. After their modest beginnings, in a network of small communities, the reach of the tales underwent an extraordinary expansion. At first they were assimilated into the wider Mediterranean and Near- and Middle-Eastern contexts of the Hellenistic kingdoms that resulted from and consolidated Alexander's extraordinary victories. When these kingdoms succumbed in their turn to Roman might, the Romans reshaped Greek myths for their own purposes. In the centuries that followed the Fall of Rome, the tales were adapted to the late antique, medieval and Renaissance frameworks of European culture, eventually to be carried still farther in the wake of westward and eastward European exploration and conquest. Ultimately, they have far transcended the sphere of European domination, to achieve global resonance as compelling imaginative vehicles of thought and feeling.

Today it is hard to think of an intellectual debate, moral dilemma or political crisis to which this or that Greek myth has not been applied profitably. When a hypothesis was formulated in the 1970s to suggest the reciprocal influence of organisms and their non-organic environments, Gaia, the Greek goddess of the Earth, provided the obvious designation. When, one fine morning in the mid-2010s, a British prime minister took it into his head to organize a plebiscite to determine whether the United Kingdom should remain in the European Union, many commentators detected an analogy with the hapless, reckless Pandora, who released all the troubles of the world when she opened her box (although, in the form of the myth told by the Greeks, it was a large storage jar, not a box). Without their mythical forerunners, the *Titanic* ocean liner, the *Apollo* space programme, the *Amazon* multinational corporation, the *Nike* brand of sportswear, *Ajax* disinfectant, *Hermès* silk scarves, and the Athens-based *Heracles General Cement Company* would have had to search elsewhere for their names. In contemporary business projects, advertising and marketing, Greek mythology seems still to be the go-to treasure trove when it comes to a choice of name. Add to this the significant presence of Greek myths in virtually every contemporary artistic medium, from plays and poems to comic books and video games, and it becomes clear that the ancient stories still retain a power that belies their antiquity.

This durability has not been uncontested. At various times and for various reasons the mythology of classical antiquity – that which the poet Philip Larkin notoriously dismissed as the 'common myth-kitty' – has been roundly repudiated.[1] One ground for such rejection has been a sense of outrage at the myths' alleged immorality, as evidenced already by the Christian convert Clement of Alexandria (2nd–3rd century CE), who was scandalized by, among many other things, the idea that the goddess Aphrodite could be said to have been generated from the severed penis of the sky god Ouranos.[2] Ridicule has been another common reaction. In 1712 Joseph Addison mocked the routine recourse by contemporary poets to 'our Jupiters and Junos' ('downright puerility, and unpardonable in a poet that is past sixteen'); a decade later, the French philosopher Bernard de Fontenelle characterized the myths as 'a mass of chimeras, day-dreams, and absurdities'.[3] A more recent gambit has been to stigmatize them, along with the study of the two languages in which they were originally told, as the privileged property of an outmoded, self-congratulatory cultural elite, especially in Europe and North America. Nevertheless, in spite of such criticisms, the myths have endured. The explanation goes far beyond the social cachet that an allusion to a myth might be thought to confer, in view of the high status that 'the Classics' have traditionally enjoyed. Far more significant is the myths' astonishing potential for chameleon-like adaptability, thanks to the breadth and profundity of the questions that they raise. Greek myths are thought experiments meaningful for virtually everyone, regardless of their economic circumstances or cultural background. The aim of this book is to demonstrate this on the basis of a series of case studies. Before that, to set the scene, we shall look back to the world of ancient Greece, in order to review the principal contexts within which these experiments were first conducted, and to highlight the most important themes that they were used to explore.

The contexts of myth-telling

Myths were embedded in ancient Greek society. They were told in the home by grandparents, parents and nurses to children, who also learned to recite them at school. They were painted onto decorative vessels ('vases') used for all manner of domestic purposes. They were cited by poets, orators, philosophers and historians as examples of moral conduct to be followed or avoided, and as records of real and significant past events. They were matters of the utmost seriousness, and yet at the same time could be imagined in contexts of hilarity and even gross obscenity. No part of human life was untouched by myths.[4]

They were, in particular, inextricably connected with religion. The battle between the heroic Lapiths and the semi-equine Centaurs was sculpted on the marble metopes of the south flank of the Parthenon on the Athenian Acropolis (a metope is a rectangular space on a temple frieze). Demeter's quest for her daughter Persephone, abducted by Hades, the god of Death, was evoked on stone reliefs and ceramic vases found at the site of the 'mystery' cult practised at Eleusis. Images of the infernal ferryman Charon and the god Hermes, jointly charged with conveying the souls of the dead to the Underworld, appear regularly on vases known as *lekythoi*, which were placed as offerings containing olive oil at the tombs of the deceased. In addition, myths were narrated during ritual events celebrated to honour the gods, a prominent example being the festival of the City Dionysia at Athens, at which the tragedies – virtually every one of them based on a myth – were performed for Dionysus. Last and certainly not least, the gods and heroes whose exploits are evoked by the myth-tellers are mostly the very same gods and heroes who were the objects of worship in sanctuaries the length and breadth of the Greek world.

This embeddedness did not diminish when Greece succumbed to the military might of Rome. Pausanias' meticulous account of his travels through the Hellenic landscape – the *Description of Greece*, written during the 2nd century CE – contains in virtually every paragraph a description of a place, building or sacred object to be found at a particular location, and linked in one way or another to the world of myth. One example among thousands concerns the founder-hero of a small community in Laconia:

> At the place called Arainon is the tomb of Las, with a
> statue standing upon the monument. The local people
> say that this Las was their founder, and that he was killed
> by Achilles, who landed in this country to ask Tyndareus
> if he could marry Helen. But the truth is that it was

Patroclus who killed Las, and that it was Patroclus who was wooing Helen.[5]

By means of the introductory phrase 'the local people say ...', a statue placed on a grave in the southern Peloponnese and visible to Pausanias' own eyes is implicitly linked to events believed to have taken place before the Trojan War, when a number of Greece's greatest heroes asked Tyndareus for permission to marry Helen (Tyndareus was the husband of Helen's mother, Leda, though most myth-tellers regarded Helen's true father as Zeus). Since Greek mythology was a topic as far removed as it could possibly be from fundamentalist doctrinal rigidity, Pausanias feels free to correct his informants ('but the truth is ...'); yet his version, like theirs, assumes a connection between events long ago and a contemporary sacred site. The tale of Helen's wooing, like countless other myths, was updated and reaffirmed by being embedded in a sacred place.

What – for the Greeks – were the myths about?

First, the myths were about the family. Countless Greek tales involve this apparently universal human institution, dramatizing the intense feelings that can be aroused within it. In Homer's *Iliad*, the intergenerational emotional bonds uniting Troy's ruling family – Priam the father, Hecuba the mother, Hector the son, Andromache the daughter-in-law, and their son Astyanax – embody an ideal of living that counterbalances the unforgiving dislocations of war produced by the Greeks' invasion. In the *Odyssey*, similarly strong, reciprocal ties link Odysseus to his father, Laertes, and his son, Telemachus. Among the gods, too, parent–child relationships can be a powerfully loving force, as in the case of Demeter and Persephone: the mother withholds all fruitfulness from the world until she gets her beloved daughter back (at least temporarily). More numerous, however, are myths that conceive parent–child relationships as conflictual: Kronos castrated his father Ouranos, and was in turn overthrown by his son Zeus; Oedipus killed his father and cursed his sons; Medea and Heracles killed their children; Agamemnon slaughtered ('sacrificed') his daughter Iphigenia. Sibling relationships might be no less fraught. Rivalry for the throne of Mycenae between the brothers Atreus and Thyestes led to a ghastly act of revenge: Atreus murdered Thyestes' young sons, cooked them and fed them to their unknowing father at a banquet. Between sisters there was usually more solidarity. When King Tereus raped his wife's sister and tore out her tongue to try to silence her, she wove her testimony into a tapestry that she sent to her sister; the two of them subjected Tereus to a horrific, cannibalistic punishment similar to that suffered by Thyestes. As for relationships between couples, these appear in varied and often extreme forms, with disruption within marriage being a favourite theme. Helen's adultery with the Trojan prince Paris led her cuckolded husband Menelaus to instigate the Greek expedition to besiege Troy. When Agamemnon brought the enslaved Trojan princess Cassandra back from Troy to share his bed, his wife, Clytemnestra, had already taken a lover: a poisonous cocktail of infidelity. Nor was adultery restricted to mortals. Zeus was serially unfaithful to his wife, Hera, while Aphrodite's affair with Ares led to the notorious episode in which her husband, the craftsman god Hephaestus, magically fastened the blissful lovers to their bed in a near-invisible net. By contrast, Odysseus' relationship with his wife Penelope, as explored in Homer's *Odyssey*, looks perfect at first sight – and yet the couple were reunited only after the hero's lengthy sexual adventures with Calypso and Circe, and his (chaste) dalliance with the eminently marriageable princess Nausicaa. The psychology of relationships between the sexes is one of the most complex and potent motifs in the myths.

A second major theme is the encounter of mortals with the alien and the strange – in a word, with that which is 'other' (the term is, it has to be admitted, a piece of academic jargon; but it is a very *useful* piece.) In one common pattern, a hero – a special kind of mortal whose behaviour challenges the boundaries of what humans can achieve – confronts a physically monstrous or awesomely hybrid adversary: Perseus and the snaky-haired Gorgon Medusa; Bellerophon and the lion/serpent/goat Chimaera; Odysseus and hideous Scylla, with her six heads and her loins encircled with baying dogs. The capacity to overcome such dangers is one mark of the hero. Yet it is not always monsters who are the embodiments of strangeness: strangeness also resides within the very personalities of the gods. Dionysus, in particular, is a divinity who visits *ekstasis*, 'ecstasy' – literally, the state of 'standing outside' – on those who fall under his influence; he is the quintessential outsider god, whose power goes far beyond wine, extending instead to a general capacity to invade human consciousness. 'Otherness' is a feature of many other gods, too, for instance semi-goatish Pan and sexy Aphrodite (the incarnation of erotic passion as a kind of madness), as well as Zeus himself. When Zeus' lover Semele insists that he make love to her in all his glory, the ruler of the gods does so accompanied by, or perhaps even in the form of, the thunder and the lightning, thus incinerating her; he is both marvellously desirable and unfathomably strange. Myths of alterity raise all kinds of questions about what distinguishes the human from the non-human.

Another pervasive motif concerns origins. Myths explain how things are by narrating how they came to be: this is mythology as aetiology (the study of causes). 'How things began' is, to take the ultimate perspective, a matter of cosmology. It all started with primordial Chaos ('Gap'), and then with Gaia ('Earth') and Ouranos ('Sky'), the primeval couple from whom the rest of the gods were born in a sequence of generations. Their births could be vividly memorable, as with Athena's emergence from Zeus' head when Hephaestus split it open with an axe, or Aphrodite's birth from the bloody, seminal foam that oozed into the sea from Ouranos' severed genitals. The landscape too had its origins, which were sometimes accounted for in myths: the island of Rhodes emerged from below the sea, to be snapped up by Helios as the favourite territory over which he would be patron. The presence of human beings is another feature of the world that needs to be explained and, once more, myths of origin do the job. After the Flood, Deucalion and Pyrrha – the Greek Noah and his wife – found themselves in a depopulated world. They cast stones behind them, and these turned into people: human beings were thus the children of meta-morphosed earth. Individual human communities too have their origins, and myths give such communities legitimacy in narratives that often (as with the stones of Deucalion and Pyrrha) symbolize the importance of the before/after distinction through the notion of transformation. Thus the people of Boeotian Thebes claimed descent from the Spartoi ('Sown Men'), who sprang fully armed from the earth into which a serpent's teeth had been planted: this tale of a subterranean origin graphically expresses the Thebans' sense of being rooted in their territory ('autochthony'). Finally, many of the customs and rituals of human life were anchored in and thus sanctioned by aetiological narratives. Most famously, the practice of animal sacrifice was said to have derived from a foundational moment when the Titan Prometheus divided up the carcass of an ox at a meal once shared by men and gods. The tasty meat that this myth allotted to humans – much more appetizing than the portion that was left for the gods – would continue to be theirs for ever afterwards in real-life religious ceremonies.

Politics is another important focus. Politicians in search of legitimacy regularly found it in the world of myth. When the 6th-century BCE despot ('tyrant') Peisistratus returned to Athens after a period of exile, he did so riding in a chariot in the company of 'Athena' – otherwise known as Phye, a tall and beautiful local woman whom Peisistratus had dressed up in full armour. The implication was that the city's patron deity was offering Peisistratus her backing. When Augustus appropriated Apollo as his personal patron, consolidating the relationship by building a temple to the god directly adjacent to his own house on the Palatine hill in Rome, he was following a time-honoured precedent that identified a hotline to the gods as a fail-safe source of political authority. Nowhere is this more evident than in the inconceivably lavish Grand Processions mounted in Alexandria by the Hellenistic ruler Ptolemy Philadelphus, featuring gorgeous mythological tableaux depicting Dionysus, his bacchants and his satyrs. The megalomaniac Roman emperor Commodus claimed a different mythical aura when he portrayed himself as Heracles, complete with club, lionskin and a handful of golden apples of the Hesperides. States as well as individual leaders drew on the emblematic power of myth, often through the images used on coins: Helios in Rhodes, Asclepius in Kos, Athena and her iconic owl in Athens; the list is almost endless. Power looks better if authorized by tradition, and myths are an ideal source of that tradition.

A particularly intricate theme in Greek myth revolves around the dilemmas and paradoxes of choice. The classic case is that of Orestes, whose mother, Clytemnestra, murdered her husband, Orestes' father, Agamemnon. Should Orestes leave his father's death unavenged or – as Apollo's oracle commanded him – kill his mother? Hardly less agonizing was the dilemma of Antigone: ought she to leave her (traitorous) brother unburied or defy the edict that forbade the burial – an edict issued by the ruler of the *polis*? Another group of mythical explorations of choice involves the notion of destiny (or 'fate'). Often such explorations feature prophecies and oracular predictions. Seers such as Teiresias and Phineus accurately predict the future; but does that mean that the humans whose actions they predict have no freedom of choice? Apollo's oracle at Delphi, and Zeus' at Dodona, figure in numerous narratives; but do their predictions render meaningless the deeds of the protagonists whose futures they anticipate? Here is a nest of conundrums, whose complexity is neatly summarized in an episode involving Agamemnon. When a goddess ordered him to sacrifice (i.e. slaughter) his daughter Iphigenia if he wanted to secure a favourable wind for his fleet's voyage to Troy, he 'put on the yoke of Necessity' (to quote the chorus of Aeschylus' play *Agamemnon*). He put the yoke on: a self-chosen act; yet the yoke belonged to Necessity – so he presumably had no option but to put it on. Ordinary mortals (as opposed to seers) recognize their 'destiny' only retrospectively, when it is too late to affect it. For the gods, too, destiny is something in which they may find themselves implicated – and the question whether *they* can alter destiny is a source of yet more paradoxes. A moving example of a god's involvement in the interrelationship between choice and fate occurs in the *Iliad*, where the sea nymph Thetis foresees that her beloved son Achilles is destined to die young, immediately after the death of his arch-rival, the Trojan warrior Hector. Although she knows that it will hasten Achilles' death, she asks Hephaestus to make new armour for him – armour in which he will kill Hector.

Apart from any connection with ideas of destiny, relationships between humans and gods are the centrepiece of countless myths, and they constitute our final theme. Sometimes these relationships are sexual, as with Aphrodite's union with Adonis, Dionysus' with Ariadne, and Zeus' with women too numerous to list, as well as with beautiful Ganymede, the young prince of Troy abducted by Zeus. While a modern sensibility might well feel uneasiness at the idea of a relationship founded on an abduction, Greeks tended rather to stress the honour that a god paid to a mortal by 'carrying them off'. Not that such liaisons always ended happily. Whereas Ganymede's role as Zeus' wine steward was sealed by the boy's immortalization, the abduction of the mortal Tithonus by Eos, goddess of Dawn, led only to a scenario in which, while Eos retained for ever her divine youthfulness, Tithonus just got older and more shrivelled.

Many stories stress not the proximity of humans to gods but the gulf between them, narrating what happens when humans overstep the boundaries that should confine them. The virgin goddess Artemis was accidentally surprised by the hunter Actaeon while she was bathing naked in a spring; she turned him into a stag, and his own hounds tore him apart. Arachne tried to out-weave Athena, and was transformed into a spider for her temerity. When Pentheus, king of Thebes, rejected the worship of Dionysus, the god drove the women of the city insane, including Pentheus' own mother; as the uncanny power of the god overwhelmed them, they tore the king's body apart with their bare hands. Perhaps the most important aspect of divine–human relationships is the sheer intensity of the gods' involvement in human affairs. To the gods, it matters who wins and who loses on the battlefield at Troy; it matters whether Jason and his Argonauts succeed in their quest for the Golden Fleece. The gods intervene on one or other side of the action according to their preferences and whims. The attitudes and behaviour of the gods towards mortals – and vice versa – are an indispensable and fundamental part of Greek mythology.

After antiquity

Our brief thematic review has already hinted at the amazing potential of Greek myths to convey ideas and inspire feelings about humanity's place in the world. The rest of this book will examine how this potential has been actualized, both in Greco-Roman antiquity and in the post-classical tradition. About this tradition, three general points are worth emphasizing at this stage.

First: diversity. The range of contexts within which the myths have been re-imagined since the Greco-Roman period is astonishingly wide. Written texts have been fundamental, and they are of many kinds. One major branch of the textual tradition involves allegorical interpretations, designed to display the interpreter's virtuosity. Myths were typically explained as allegories of natural phenomena or as moral or political *exempla*: key players in the medieval and early modern periods were Giovanni Boccaccio (*Genealogy of the Pagan Gods*), Natale Conti (*Mythologies*) and Francis Bacon (*The Wisdom of the Ancients*). Much more recently, psychological analysts such as Sigmund Freud, Carl Jung and their successors have adopted a not dissimilar strategy, designed to unmask submerged or archetypal meanings beneath the narrative surface. Alongside such expositions are an incalculably large number of literary works in which authors have (often brilliantly) revisited mythological forerunners, whether in epic, pastoral, novel, tragedy or comedy, and whether in Symbolist, Expressionist, Modernist, Postmodernist, Feminist, Post-colonialist or other -ist mode. A different type of context involves physical objects. Wedding chests, maiolica pottery, garden sculpture, tapestries, frescoes – the decorative mythological images evidenced in such visual and tactile media pervaded the Renaissance, and can still be seen in museums, galleries, public spaces and private houses throughout the world. Sounds are no less significant than sights: new seams of myth narration have been opened up in orchestral music, popular song, opera, ballet and cinema (though Greek myths had already featured in silent movies). Video games and comic books are already making a significant mark, and in the future there will surely be other, still newer contexts that, as yet, only someone with the foresight of Prometheus could anticipate. Perhaps the most important absentee from our list of modern contexts is religion, together with its rituals; in the modern world there is nothing comparable to the embeddedness of myths in the practices and beliefs of sacred cult. Yet about the seriousness of many modern takes on Greek mythology – even if it is not a *sacred* seriousness – there can be absolutely no doubt.

Second: messiness. The felt presence of Greek mythology at any one time or place is certain to be uneven. Even if a myth is alluded to in a company name or product brand, this does not imply that all (or indeed any) of those who have dealings with the company, or buy the product, could supply details about the myth that underlies the name; at the very least, different people will have different degrees of awareness about such details. The same unevenness will presumably have applied to guests at a dinner party in Renaissance Florence who were eating from a plate portraying Leda and the Swan; some of the diners might have given you chapter and verse from an ancient text, whereas others might just have been titillated by the improbable and risqué sex act without knowing any of the background. Again, when Real Madrid fans flock to the Fountain of Cybele in the centre of the city to celebrate a victory, just down the road from the Fountain of Neptune where the Atlético de Madrid fans congregate, knowledge about the two divinities is likely to be – to say the least – unevenly distributed among the supporters.

Another sort of messiness concerns historical development. It is all too easy to trace an apparently convincing, single genealogical line from, say, the account of Odysseus' wanderings in Homer's *Odyssey* (perhaps 8th–7th century BCE) to Simon Armitage's poetic dramatization in *The Odyssey: Missing Presumed Dead* (2015): Homer influenced B, who influenced C ... who influenced Z, who influenced Armitage. Or to make a similar claim for the progression from the *Theogony* of the poet Hesiod (perhaps 8th–7th century BCE) to the movie *Clash of the Titans* (2010; dir. Louis Leterrier). However, traditions rarely work as straightforwardly as this; certainly the tradition of re-presentations of Greek mythology does not. It may be that a writer or artist using a mythological theme in 1900 had in mind only one previous model going back no more than a few years. Or it may be (by contrast) that a writer or artist deliberately ignores all the intervening stages of myth transmission, to go back to 'the original' of, say, 700 BCE. Each case is different. The tradition is unruly and complicated, and all the more fascinating for that.

Third: novelty. New media evolve, others recede; myths are adapted to changing contexts and fulfil different needs. In one period, certain myths strike a resonant cultural chord; in another period, the very myths that used to be flavour of the month will seem irrelevant or trite. The ubiquitous, sumptuous and often frankly pornographic nudes of Renaissance painting – the Venuses, the Ariadnes, the Danaës – could not reappear with the same effect in the early 21st century; thanks to a fresh awareness of the politics of gender, the goalposts for the expression of erotic fantasy have moved. Representations of the gods have been particularly sensitive to changing cultural circumstances. Since the 17th century, myths focusing principally on divinities (e.g. the Judgment of Paris) have tended to decline in prominence (though it is true that Nietzsche turned Apollo and Dionysus into the conceptual tools he needed). In compensation, other myths have gained ground, particularly when they deal with the family (Medea, Oedipus, Orpheus/Eurydice), with politics (Antigone), or with that which is threateningly strange or alien (the Amazons; Heracles' encounters with monstrosity). Yet the gods still have their imaginative niche: as we shall very soon see, Prometheus is perhaps the prime example, even if his significance as a god is paradoxically heightened by his role as a champion of humanity against the gods.

So the tradition from which we are about to select our examples is diverse, messy and constantly renewed. But, most of all, it is alive. It is time to turn to the first instance of that life.

Prometheus

Few characters in Greek mythology have enjoyed such a diverse afterlife as Prometheus. At times in the post-classical tradition he has featured as a kind of Christ figure, subjected to a crucifixion-like torment rendered all the more terrible by the victim's certainty – his name means 'Forethought' – that his agony will continue for aeons. At times he has shone out as the heroic foe of tyranny, rebelliously brandishing the torch of freedom in the face of despotic cruelty. At times he has been lauded as the bringer of fire, the gift that enabled humankind to develop its productive, technological and socially progressive capacities. At times he has been seen not just as humanity's helper, but as its very creator. At times, notwithstanding his various heroic roles, what has been stressed is his capacity for tricky deception. Throughout these re-imaginings, his abiding characteristic has been his closeness to humanity, coupled with the dreadful anguish which that closeness costs him. To show how all this has come about – and to help us to identify issues that the Prometheus story can be deployed to think about *now* – we start by listening to three voices that speak to us from classical antiquity: those of a poet, a playwright, and a philosopher.

Prometheus in antiquity

The first of these voices takes us back to the beginnings of the extant Greek mythical tradition – a period that, some would say, predates even the composition of the great Homeric epics. In his *Theogony*, an impressive account of the genesis of divine power in the cosmos, the poet Hesiod (perhaps 8th–7th century BCE) relates a sequence of episodes leading up to the establishment of Zeus' sovereignty. A significant part of the narrative centres on the activities of the Titans, divinities whose authority preceded and sometimes conflicted with that of Zeus and the other Olympians. One of the Titans was Prometheus, the son of Iapetus (another Titan) and the Oceanid Clymene. Though a good deal of the *Theogony* describes acts of god-on-god violence, it is deception rather than force that lies at the heart of the Prometheus story. Twice the crafty Titan cheated Zeus in order to benefit humanity by depriving the gods of their due. (*Why* Prometheus should have befriended humankind is never spelled out, and remains intriguingly enigmatic.) One trick took place at a foundational event in the development of Greek religious practice: the original sacrifice of a slaughtered animal to the gods. Prometheus divided the carcass into two portions: one looked unappetizing because it was wrapped in the stomach (which, however, concealed the meat); the other looked tempting because it was wrapped in glistening fat (which, however, concealed inedible bones). Zeus' deliberate choice of the option that seemed preferable, but really wasn't, is puzzling: perhaps the best way for Zeus to demonstrate Prometheus' duplicity was to carry the implications of that duplicity into action. At all events, that choice inaugurated the custom whereby, ever afterwards, it would be humans who enjoyed the tastier cuts at a sacrifice, leaving the gods with nothing but the upwardly rising savour of burnt offerings.

Furious at the attempted deception, Zeus withheld fire from human beings, plunging them back into a state of nature. Prometheus countered with his second trick, which once more played artfully with the boundary between inside and outside: he filched fire back again from the gods by concealing it in a stalk of fennel, and restored it to the human race. Doubly incensed now, Zeus punished Prometheus as well as humanity. Upon humankind he bestowed the first female, moulded from earth by Hephaestus and seductively adorned by other Olympians; she was delectable on the surface, but destructively scheming within. (Fortunately not all Greek myths display such blatant misogyny.) Zeus thus gave Prometheus tit for tat, deftly counteracting his adversary's two exploitations of the inside/outside polarity with one of his own. As for the punishment of Prometheus, Zeus could not kill him (he was immortal), but he did the next best thing. He bound him fast in a remote wilderness, pinioning him with shackles driven through a rock. There an eagle feasted every day on the captive's liver; each night the liver regenerated, pristine for the next day's ghastly banquet. The eagle was Zeus' sacred bird: it was as if, by proxy, Zeus himself were lacerating and devouring his adversary. Only if Zeus' own will were to change would the torture be ended. And so it would turn out, when, in the far distant future, Zeus' son Heracles shot the eagle: the supreme god's lust to punish was eventually outweighed by his desire that his son should win renown.

Hesiod modified his *Theogony* narrative in another major poem, the *Works and Days*. There, the destructive woman is named as Pandora, who is sent to mortals by Zeus and, against Prometheus' strong advice, is foolishly welcomed on their behalf by his slow-witted brother Epimetheus ('Afterthought'). Notoriously, Pandora had a large storage jar, which she opened, allowing the contents – evils and sicknesses – to fly out into the world. The memorable detail that Hope (a personification of the emotion of hope) stayed in the jar when Pandora replaced the lid is thought-provokingly ambiguous. Does hope therefore remain as a constantly accessible resource for mortals? Or does the fact that she/it is still confined in the jar mean that it is out of their reach?[1] However we resolve this dilemma, the upshot of the Prometheus–Pandora episode is to leave humans in a state of affliction. Whatever Prometheus' good intentions, his interplay with Zeus leaves neither himself nor his human protégés with much to look forward to. In the case of humankind, what lies in store for them is a life of hard grind. *... necesse est?*

Our second voice, perhaps even more resonant than that of Hesiod, can be heard in *Prometheus Bound*, the mighty tragedy attributed to the playwright Aeschylus (5th century BCE; some modern scholars have doubted Aeschylus' authorship, though it was never questioned in antiquity).[2] The drama opens with the brutal pinioning of Prometheus to a desolate Scythian crag by the gods Bia (Violence), Kratos (Strength) and – albeit reluctantly – Hephaestus. The audience is spared nothing of the ghastly process of total immobilization:

> STRENGTH. Now drive straight through his chest with all
> the force you have
> The unrelenting fang of the adamantine wedge.
> HEPHAESTUS. Alas! I weep, Prometheus, for your
> sufferings.
> STR. Still shrinking? Weeping for the enemy of Zeus?
> Take care; or you may need your pity for yourself.
> *[Hephaestus drives in the wedge]*
> HEPH. There! Now you see a sight to pain your eyes.
> STR. I see Prometheus getting his deserts.[3]

Adamant is an unimaginably hard substance. Only something like that would do the job (much like the kryptonite that might have destroyed Superman).

Static though the stagecraft is, the narrative scope of the play nevertheless extends across tens of thousands of years. It reaches

[handwritten margin notes: "re 'angsty'" / "tragedy"]

back into the past, as Prometheus recalls everything he has given to humanity: fire, reason, astronomical lore, mathematics, writing, medicine, divination ... But it is the future that dominates; for this is a tragedy of foreknowledge. Prometheus' piercing mind compels him to anticipate every last drop of suffering that awaits him. This differentiates him utterly from mortals, as he points out to the chorus of Oceanid nymphs who come to witness his plight:

> PROMETHEUS. I caused men no longer to foresee
>   their death.
> CHORUS. What cure did you discover for their distress?
> PROM. I planted blind hopefulness within them.
> CHOR. Your gift brought them great blessing.[4]

No such blissful ignorance for Prometheus. Yet he is not totally helpless, for he knows a secret – something he may be able to use to bargain with. Zeus, he enigmatically reveals, is planning a union from which will be born a son more powerful than his father. Given my help, argues Prometheus, Zeus could avoid being overthrown. (Later sources spell this out: the proposed union is with the sea nymph Thetis, and Zeus will escape the danger by marrying her to Peleus instead – their offspring being Achilles.)[5] But, for now, such eventualities are irrelevant. Zeus' henchman, the torturer's apprentice Hermes, threatens Prometheus with an even direr punishment if he refuses to reveal the secret: the eagle, and the self-regenerating liver. The Titan's response prefigures the reaction of every subsequent resistance hero faced with the contemptible lackey of a ruthless dictator 'Do your worst.'

Our third voice takes us to political philosophy. In his dialogue *Protagoras*, Plato (5th–4th century BCE) constructs a thought experiment about the origins of human society. In so doing he offers a new take both on the interaction between Zeus and Prometheus, and on the Prometheus–Epimetheus relationship. In this version, after the gods have created all living creatures, they instruct Epimetheus and Prometheus to endow those creatures with the skills they need in order to survive. Epimetheus makes the allocations to all the other animals but forgets humans. Prometheus intervenes by stealing fire for humankind, giving them various techniques and means of self-protection into the bargain. Even so, human life is still precarious, since it lacks social cohesion. Far from being angry at Prometheus' intervention, Zeus sends Hermes down to Earth to supply humans with the qualities of respect and justice, to alleviate the disharmony. Plato's intriguing reworking of the myth thus removes both Hesiod's vision of the downward trajectory of human life, and Aeschylus' moral antithesis between the tyrant and the rebel.

Already in Hesiod, Aeschylus and Plato, most of the main contours of Promethean mythology are visible. In particular, all their narratives associate the Titan with origins: the inaugural animal sacrifice, the genesis of fire, the dawn of human culture. But one important feature, an even more fundamental aspect of origins, is absent: the role of the Titan as the creator of humankind. Though earlier writers allude to the theme, this act of primordial transformation is consolidated in *Metamorphoses*, the magnificent and vastly influential work of the Roman poet Ovid (43 BCE–c. 18 CE). The Ovidian Prometheus mixes earth with rainwater and from the mixture moulds 'an image of the all-governing gods', standing erect and gazing towards the heavens.[6] A variant on the same theme, less well known than that in Ovid but more emotionally impressive, can be found in one of Aesop's fables, where the clay used by Prometheus was said to have been mixed with *tears*. This is a poignant expression of the Titan's embodiment of creativity and suffering, and also a way of suggesting that the very essence of humanity is a mixture of those same two qualities.[7]

All the main episodes in the literary record recur in visual representations. The most dramatic scene is that of the Titan's horrible exposure to the remorseless beak of the eagle, an episode memorably conveyed on a Laconian cup in the Vatican Museums (see below). Among images of Prometheus' rescue by Heracles is that on an Attic *krater* (see p. 28, above) showing the hero in the act of shooting the eagle. Later in antiquity we find representations of the scene that, because of its depiction of the act of creation, will exercise a powerful hold over the medieval and early modern minds: the fabrication of humanity. One variation on the story can be seen on an Etruscan scarab gem (see p. 28, below), portraying Prometheus making a human torso. A more substantial image is that on a marble sarcophagus in the Prado in Madrid (see p. 29); here, Prometheus creates a human figure, upon whose head Athena places a butterfly (in Greek *psuche* means 'butterfly' and also 'soul').

Attributed to the Arkesilas Painter, Prometheus and Atlas, Laconian *kylix*, 560–550 BCE.

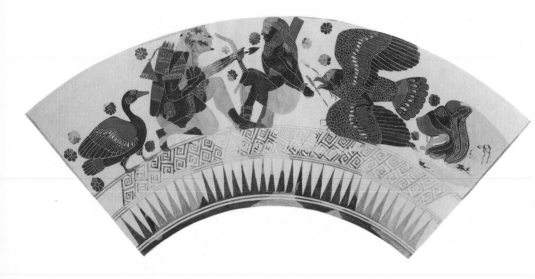

Attributed to the Nettos Painter, Heracles,
Prometheus and the eagle, Attic *krater*, c. 625–575 BCE.

Etruscan scarab gem engraved with the image
of Prometheus, 3rd–2nd century BCE.

Prometheus does not always appear in such an authoritative light. In the *Birds* of Aristophanes (produced in 414 BCE), he creeps nervously onto the stage carrying a parasol to avoid being observed from above by Zeus. He has good reason to be worried. He is acting as an adviser to the birds, who have founded in the sky their own utopian city, which is blocking the Olympian gods from receiving the rising savour of sacrificial offerings. But that's Aristophanes. His dramatization of the Prometheus–Zeus stand-off sits perfectly within the gloriously irreverent conventions of Athenian comic drama, but it does not represent the predominant attitude in antiquity, nor is it the attitude that will resonate in the thoughts and feelings of most later hearers and retellers of the myth. How, then, did these post-classical 'receivers' adapt the variegated constellation of Promethean mythology that they inherited?

Prometheus models the first man, Roman sarcophagus, *c.* 185 CE.

A medieval and Renaissance Titan

In an excellent monograph on Promethean mythology in and since antiquity, Carol Dougherty begins her discussion of the reception of the myth with the portrayal of the noble, rebellious hero during the Romantic period.[8] This choice of starting point expresses an important truth, yet at the same time it might mislead. Romanticism was certainly the setting within which Prometheus would achieve unprecedented iconic status, but an awful lot of cultural water had passed under the bridge before that. From late antiquity till the Renaissance, the Prometheus who dominated the imagination was not the Byronic insurgent but the creator, the fabricator, the 'anthropoplast' – the moulder and then the animator of human beings.

Within the overall late-antique project of the incorporation of classical ('pagan') mythology into a Christian worldview, the case of Prometheus constituted a particular conundrum. How could you square his role as creator with that of the God who formed Adam and brought him to life? For the Carthaginian Christian writer Tertullian (c. 160–c. 240 CE), there could be only one answer: the *verus Prometheus*, the 'true Prometheus', was the omnipotent Lord God who made humanity from earth.[9] A century later, another North African Christian writer, Lactantius, adopted his own gambit for sidelining Prometheus' challenge to the Lord's act of creation: what Prometheus invented was merely the art of making *statues*; the only true creator of real human beings was the Christian God.[10] The process of humanizing Prometheus, while at the same time acknowledging his prodigious gifts, was con-tinued by Augustine (354–430 CE), who argued that Prometheus was a mortal who was 'esteemed the best teacher of wisdom'.[11] Throughout the medieval period Prometheus' human rather than divine status, alongside his sculptural prowess, continued to be highlighted. An influential instance is the 12th-century writer Petrus Comestor, who gave alternative explanations of the myth

Prometheus, detail of illustration from Maso Finiguerra's
The Florentine Picture-Chronicle, folio 13, c. 1470–75.

that Prometheus created human beings: either he made *autom-ata* – statues that walked – or he brought civilization to human-ity.[12] A vivid representation of the 'anthropoplastic' Prometheus, incorporating the notion of the Titan as astrologer, appears in the so-called *Florentine Picture-Chronicle* (see previous page), a series of drawings by Maso Finiguerra (c. 1470–75). Underlying all these approaches is the idea of Prometheus as prefiguring the Christian Creator, but not calling that Creator's unique status into question.

The approaches we have just looked at can be brought under the broad heading of 'euhemerism', the term scholars apply to a mode of interpretation that reads the gods as based on ordi-nary human beings and their deeds as reflections of actual, real-world events. (Euhemerus was a Greek writer who pioneered this approach.) A parallel perspective, equally important in the medieval period, is allegorical: here, the interpreter's goal is to uncover the true meaning that underlies the apparent one. A classic example occurs in the vast 14th-century mythographical treatise *Genealogy of the Pagan Gods* by the great Italian humanist and writer Giovanni Boccaccio. Boccaccio starts from ancient accounts (by Servius and Fulgentius) that report that Prometheus' virtuosity in fabricating inanimate man attracted the attention of Minerva (Athena), who guided him up to the sky so that he might find what he needed to complete his work.[13] There he con-nected a fennel stalk to the chariot wheels of the sun god Phoebus, captured fire, and brought it back to Earth to spark into life the human he had created. So much for the myth: now for what Boccaccio sees as the allegory. Guided by wisdom (= Minerva), Prometheus takes from the sky the clarity of truth (= fire) and inserts this into the body he has created, so rendering human-kind rational instead of brutish. As for the punishment in the Caucasus, this represents, according to Boccaccio, an allegorical way of referring to Prometheus' withdrawal into solitude, where he was troubled by sublime and deep thoughts – the meaning

Giant fennel in Crete.

supposed to underlie the torn-by-an-eagle narrative. Allegorical interpretation of Prometheus had a long and intricate history, and he did not always come out on the morally superior side. In his hugely influential work *Mythologiae*, the 16th-century Italian mythographer Natale Conti saw Prometheus as symbolizing the heresy of Protestantism, as opposed to the heraldic eagle adopted as an emblem by the Holy Roman Empire.[14]

A paradoxical aspect of Prometheus is the way he can be *Passio* portrayed as either coolly authoritative or utterly helpless. Representations of him bestowing life on his human creation belong to the first category; images of his anguish when attacked by the eagle belong to the second. Sometimes the two scenes are juxtaposed, as on the panel of a *cassone* (chest) painted by Piero di Cosimo: to the left, the Titan purposefully and reverently applies his torch to ignite the heart of his statuesque human, while to the right Mercury binds Prometheus' contorted body to a tree, as the eagle waits hungrily above (c. 1515; see pl. 11).[15] More often [an artist will opt for one of the scenes and ignore the other.] But in any case there is an implied narrative link between the two episodes: *because* Prometheus created humanity, *therefore* he was punished. Occasionally the link is of a more literal kind, for sometimes Prometheus appears wearing or holding a large ring.[16] The key to such images lies in a rare ancient tradition according to which the Titan had to wear a link of the chain that bound him to the rock, since Zeus had sworn to punish him for all time; the presence of the ring demonstrated the continuity.[17] Indeed, for the Italian humanist Polydore Vergil, Prometheus was the inventor of rings.[18]

Ring of power archetype

In the 16th and 17th centuries the theme of Prometheus' punishment attracted many major artists. Occasionally the Titan retained his dignity: clothed, upright and relatively unconcerned.[19] Much more often, artists rivalled each other in evoking the torments of the tortured victim, whose body lies twisted and sprawling on the ground. A powerful example is Rubens' oil on canvas of *c.* 1611–18, now in the Philadelphia Museum of Art (see pl. 1). Rubens spares us little of the cruelty of the scene: not only is the eagle's beak graphically doing its terrible work, but one of the talons seems to be gouging an eye. Yet the bird itself is magnificent, seeming to be, thanks to perspective, as large as Prometheus. It dominates the action, effortlessly justifying its role

scapegoat

cf. Nietzsche

Henry Fuseli, *Hephaestus, Bia and Kratos Securing
Prometheus on Mount Caucasus*, c. 1800–10.

as the symbol and agent of the supreme god.[20] Numerous later artists would give their own versions of the chastisement of the Titan, none more grimly than Henry Fuseli, who visualized the opening scene of Aeschylus' tragedy in all its stark horror (see previous page). The major difference from *Prometheus Bound* is that, in Fuseli's terrifying image, the Titan lies supine as opposed to being forced to remain upright (c. 1800–1810).

A Romantic and proletarian hero

Given the role of hope, blind or otherwise, in the Prometheus–Pandora nexus of motifs, it is no coincidence that the Prometheus myth assumed particular significance during and immediately after the French Revolution, when libertarian optimism blossomed following the fall of the *ancien régime*, only to wither again in the wake of the Terror and to become, at best, problematic during the Napoleonic Empire. However, it was not in France that the myth of the noble, rebellious Titan reached its apogee, but in Germany and England.

J. W. von Goethe engaged repeatedly with the myth in various genres of his writing, perhaps most memorably in the hymn 'Prometheus' (c. 1773), which encapsulates the protest of the fist-shaking rebel against his divine oppressor. It celebrates humankind in defiance of the gods, and at the end salutes the role of the creative artist on a note of triumphantly humanist self-assertion (the last word in the German original is 'ich'!):

Here I sit, forming mortals
In my own image,
A race after my likeness,
To suffer and weep,
And rejoice and take delight,
And heed your will no more
Than I![21]

36

Prometheus was no less central to the artistic imagination of Byron than he was to that of Goethe. '[Aeschylus'] *Prometheus,*' Byron wrote, 'has always been so much in my head, that I can easily conceive its influence over all or anything that I have written.'[22] The Prometheus he has in mind is not the Hesiodic trickster but the Aeschylean rebel against the injustice of tyranny, prepared to put up with anything in pursuit of his ideals – not a bad model, either, for a long-suffering, revolutionary poet forced to endure the carping of his critics in the face of his yearning for eternal fame. These lines from the ode 'Prometheus' give the gist of it:

> Titan! to thee the strife was given
> Between the suffering and the will,
> Which torture where they cannot kill;
> And the inexorable Heaven,
> And the deaf tyranny of Fate,
> The ruling principle of Hate,
> Which for its pleasure doth create
> The things it may annihilate,
> Refused thee even the boon to die:
> The wretched gift Eternity
> Was thine – and thou has borne it well.[23]

'Prometheus' was published in 1816, the year in which Byron, Percy Bysshe Shelley and Shelley's wife, Mary, spent a torrentially inclement but artistically memorable summer in the Villa Diodati near the shore of Lake Geneva. Like Byron, both the Shelleys made landmark contributions to the afterlife of the Prometheus myth.

In the case of Percy Bysshe, the relevant work is the lyrical drama *Prometheus Unbound* (1820), at once a reworking of Aeschylus and a radical rethinking of Aeschylean principles. Whereas the Greek play had begun at the very outset of Prometheus' torment, Shelley takes us 30,000 years into the future, with the Titan in precisely [the same immobile and tortured plight.] Yet not every-thing has remained the same. Whereas Jupiter/Zeus is still the prisoner of his own evil, Prometheus' mentality has changed. He has revoked the curse that he hurled at the supreme god of Olympus, and now aspires to an idealized world in which tyranny and vengeance will be replaced by freedom and equality. As for hope, in this new and optimistic vision both Prometheus and the humankind that he champions will [enjoy it – and not 'blindly'.] Bliss would it be in *that* dawn to be alive.

Significantly less blissful is the prospect for humanity out-lined in Mary Shelley's epoch-making novel *Frankenstein, or The Modern Prometheus* (1818). At the most obvious level, the central Prometheus-equivalent in the story is indeed Victor Frankenstein, whose hubristic, Faust-like scientific knowledge enables him to fabricate an artificial human and then to 'infuse a spark of being into the lifeless thing that lay at my feet'.[24] But the Monster he creates recalls other aspects of Promethean mythology, Aeschylean and Platonic rather than Ovidian and Aesopic. For the Monster's own narrative tells how his partial progression out of a state of nature was inspired by the moment when he came across a fire abandoned by wandering beggars. He is fascinated by fire, and learns by experience its properties, its benefits, how to preserve it, and eventually its role in sustaining social life and its simultaneous capacity to destroy.[25] As has been well pointed out, 'Mary Shelley's meditation on the creative process reveals the dark underside to the visionary dreams of remaking man that fuelled the imagina-tion of Romantic mythmakers.'[26] When she and Percy sat at home by the warmth of a fire, the sight of its flames must have sparked interesting conversation.

Promethean heroism took a radically new turn later in the 19th century and beyond, as the god became associated with the nexus of ideas that linked the "progress" of industrial technology to the promotion of socialist ideals. In the preface to his doctoral

Margin notes:
Promethean paralysis

Things Change nonetheless

Consciousness regained

psychic change amid fatal circumstance generates a sort of cheap hope

Pyroma-nia

This is why the revolutionary is wont to destroy rather than create (prideful egoism)

Cartoon by Lorenz Clasen (?), Karl Marx as Prometheus, 1843.

thesis, Karl Marx famously described the Titan as 'the most emi-
nent saint and martyr in the philosophical calendar'.[27] Before
long, Marx himself would be acting the role of Prometheus, when
the banning of his periodical *Rheinische Zeitung* gave rise to a cartoon (see previous page) depicting the theorist chained to a printing press while his liver was being pecked out by the (Prussian)
eagle; at his feet a group of Oceanids, reminiscent of Wagnerian
Rhinemaidens, pleads for his release. No longer the isolated and
individual hero as conceived by Byron or as re-embodied in the
person of Victor Frankenstein, Prometheus can now be celebrated
as a collective and socially engaged figure, concerned above all for
the "wellbeing" of humanity. The image of the suffering proletarian
hero persisted into the time of the German Democratic Republic,
as in Heinz Czechowski's poem 'Prometheus' (1963), in which the
Titan is chained to a cauldron in a factory and fends off the eagle
with a stirring rod.[28]

Prometheus our contemporary

In accounts such as those of Hesiod and Aeschylus, Zeus retained
his authority as a deity regarded by a contemporary audience not
just as dominant thanks to poetical tradition, but as a living power
and object of religious cult throughout the ancient Greek world.
Much the same went for the Jupiter who figured in Roman trans-
positions of the myth. But as soon as the religious underpinning
of the myth evaporates, the Zeus–Prometheus conflict sheds any
theological connotations and mutates into a political confrontation between a ruthless dictator and a noble freedom fighter. The
moral contours of the polarity become much clearer.

A striking modern example is the extraordinary film *Prometheus*
(1998), written and directed by the Yorkshire poet Tony Harrison.[29]
Searing in its social realism and dazzling in its use of rhyme and
dialect, the work embraces the declining coal industry in Britain,
the politics of Communist Eastern Europe and, above all, the

ambiguity of fire. In *Prometheus*, fire is a destroyer of the environment and of people (Auschwitz, Dresden), yet also the sustainer of the means (cigarettes) by which the film's Prometheus equivalent – the chain-smoking, cancer-ridden, foul-mouthed ex-miner known simply as Old Man – indicates his refusal to give in to and his contempt for Zeus (the boss) and his smooth-talking underling Hermes. Cigarettes are the film's fennel stalks, and what they contain takes its grim toll:

> HERMES. When forms of fire get men destroyed
> Zeus is more than overjoyed ...
> You'd think that he'd be satisfied
> with Europe's toll of genocide.
> But when he hears the children wheeze,
> those brought up near plants like these ...
> children coughing, little tots
> with nebulizers in their cots,
> cancer and asthma, if we wait,
> might, thinks Zeus, part compensate.[30]

But the Old Man has his answer:

> That bloody Zeus that you kowtow to
> but a man like me will never bow to!
> Power stations fuelled by t'pits
> blow smoke at you immortal shits.[31]

[handwritten margin note: Athesiam, perhaps, has roots in such deistic blaming... but still does it not at least admit the "immortal shits"?]

Harrison's uncomfortable, dystopic vision finds room for moments of dark optimism along the way. It ranks among the most impressive achievements of a brilliant poetic career.

Prometheus is still a name to conjure with. It has been invoked to endorse, among other things, an exclusive brand of cigar accessories (see overleaf), a company of high-end property developers, and 'an open-source systems monitoring and alerting toolkit'.[32] An internet search also came up with this:

Empower your maintenance and operations with a suite of integrated solutions that extend and enhance the functionality of your EAM, ERP, or CMMS. Bring alignment, consistency, accountability and visibility to every person and department who plays a part in your asset management success. *This* is the Prometheus platform. This is the face of integrated, full-circle enterprise asset management.[33]

What this might conceivably mean in plain English is anyone's guess, but it is clear that the name of the Titan is being invoked in order to surround the relevant product with an aura of knowledge and power.

As well as those working in business marketing, politicians too get in on the act. In September 2019 the then prime minister of the United Kingdom, Boris Johnson, made a speech to the United Nations in the course of which, unburdened by false modesty, he likened himself to the heroic Prometheus. One of his key policies,

God of Fire cigars.

he argued, was being remorselessly pecked at by his nefarious political opponents, just as Prometheus' liver had been devoured by the eagle. During Johnson's classical education at Eton and Oxford, his teachers will presumably have brought to his attention an alternative angle to the myth, according to which Prometheus had a history of trickery and deceit. Since serial duplicity was, at least in the opinion of his critics, not just an incidental feature of Johnson's political career but its guiding principle, he wisely avoided mentioning that particular Promethean trait in his speech. To be fair, he was perfectly entitled to do so: after all, there is no such thing as a definitive version of a myth. However that may be, there is no question of Johnson being especially associated with Prometheus: the allusion forms part of a wider pattern. The handlers, image-makers and speechwriters who fabricated this politician's personal brand blended two elements: the Man in the Street (habitually photographed wearing a hard hat and high-visibility jacket or a butcher's apron, or holding a beer glass) and the Brainy Toff (all those classical allusions). Seen in this light, the function of Johnson's constant references to The Classics was to counterbalance the persona of the 'lovable clown' by imparting gravitas – a nostalgic echo of an era when budding empire-builders were taught Homer and Virgil at the same few schools, and much of the map was coloured pink.

Alongside the reuses of Prometheus by advertisers and politicians, there have been developments in various artistic media. A smart and amusing example is *The Last Hero* (2001), the twenty-seventh novel of Terry Pratchett's *Discworld* fantasy series.[34] For Pratchett, the Prometheus myth is part of a game to be played with the reader – and the game is rollicking good fun. Though Prometheus does not appear by name, his identity is evoked in the person of the first hero of the Discworld, 'Fingers' Mazda, said to have stolen fire from the gods and given it to mankind, receiving for his pains the traditional, rock-chained incarceration and daily ripping by an eagle. The name 'Mazda' points to the ancient Iranian god Ahura Mazda (Pratchett revels in syncretistic humour). Eventually the Silver Horde – a group of elderly heroes led by Cohen the Barbarian – plan to return fire, and more than fire, to the gods by exploding their mountain home with Agatean Thunder Clay. After changing their minds about the plan to blow the gods up, the Horde avoid the prospect of death by stealing the horses of the Valkyries (syncretism again, this time borrowing from Germanic mythology). At last, thanks to Cohen's gesture of giving him back his sword, the fate of long-suffering Mazda comes full circle:

> And in a place on no map the immortal Mazda, bringer of fire, lay on his eternal rock.
>
> Memory can play tricks after the first ten thousand years, and he wasn't quite sure what had happened. There had been some old men on horseback, who'd swooped out of the sky. They'd cut his chains, and given him a drink and had taken it in turns to shake his withered hand.
>
> Then they'd ridden away, into the stars, as quickly as they'd come.
>
> Mazda lay back into the shape his body had worn into the stone over the centuries. He wasn't quite sure about the men, or why they'd come, or why they'd been so happy. He was only sure, in fact, about two things.
>
> He was sure it was nearly dawn.
>
> He was sure that he held, in his right hand, the very sharp sword the old men had given him.
>
> And he could hear, coming closer with the dawn, the beat of an eagle's wings.
>
> He was going to *enjoy* this.[35]

The Miller books lack this Criterion... her books are pure shit.

The colossal sales of Pratchett's fantasy books confirm that, when [engagingly re-imagined,] myths can still be tremendously popular. *is popular a good thing?* This continues to be the case. In 2015, the Philadelphia Museum of Art joined forces with a local publisher specializing in comics to produce *Prometheus Eternal*, an anthology exemplifying the influence of Rubens' classic vision of the myth on a number of leading contemporary cartoonists and illustrators of comic books.[36] A few years earlier, Ridley Scott's movie *Prometheus* (2012), the fifth in the *Alien* franchise, had brought the name of the Titan before a far larger public. The plot explores the interrelationship between aliens, gods and humanity, in the context of an interstellar expedition – on the spaceship *Prometheus* – to search for a group of (?) godlike extraterrestrials (the 'Engineers') who may have been responsible for originally creating human beings on Earth. Thanks to this movie, huge numbers of cinema-goers have been shown that at least the name of Prometheus – and perhaps more than that, via the notion of human origins – provides food for thought.

Prometheus as creator of humanity, as cheating deceiver, as defiant political prisoner, as tortured martyr, as technologist, as champion of the industrial proletariat – these are just some of his roles. Much more rarely has stress been placed on his role as the embodiment of forethought. This is surprising, since 'forethought' is just what his name means. Arguably this aspect of his character may reach greater prominence in the future. Think of developments in modern medicine, which bring us ever closer to a day when a doctor may be able to tell a patient not just that they have less than a year to live, but that (unless they fall under a bus) they may have 178 days and 15 hours to live. What could a human being do with that kind of foreknowledge? Alternatively – turning that medical example on its head – think of an individual, a family or a society optimistically formulating medium- and long-term plans a month or two before the onset

45

of a pandemic. Could it be that the 'blind hopes' conferred on humanity by Prometheus may have something to be said for them after all? The implications of the idea of foreknowledge are complex and profound. The myth of Prometheus offers one way of tackling them.

Blind/false hopes often lead to neuroses and anxiety. What the author is considering is not foresight qua foresight: for hindsight allows him to conceive of examples and hypotheticals whereby fearful fretting about the future seems to have a causal relation to actual future outcomes (only considered as past events).

CHAPTER 2

Medea

At first sight it is hard to think of two mythological characters more unlike each other than Prometheus and Medea. Prometheus: male; a deity locked into a mighty struggle with other gods about sovereignty over the cosmos; starring in a general narrative about the origins and progress of human beings; immobile on his mountain top. Medea: female; sometimes attributed with divine qualities, but more often envisaged as embroiled in her all-too-human passions; inscribed in a series of destructive relationships as, constantly mobile, she shifts from one family group to another. Yet Prometheus and Medea do have one thing in common, something rooted in their names. Both incorporate the Greek verb *mēdomai*, meaning 'I plan', 'I contrive', 'I devise'. If Prometheus is He Who Thinks in Advance, Medea is She Who Plans.

Always on the move

Medea was the granddaughter of the sun god Helios and daughter of Aietes, king of Aia – a realm usually identified with Colchis near the eastern shore of the Black Sea. Events in Aia are wonderfully evoked by the epic poet Apollonius of Rhodes in his *Argonautica* (3rd century BCE), and we shall broadly follow his account. Aia was special because it housed the fabulous Golden Fleece, a talisman that Aietes guarded jealously (it belonged originally to a miraculous flying ram, which had airlifted a brother and sister to safety

47

as they escaped from their wicked stepmother). When Jason and his fellow Argonauts arrived in Aia to seize the Fleece, Aietes set him a series of impossible-seeming tasks in order to earn the prize. He had to overpower and yoke fire-breathing bulls, sow the earth with a serpent's teeth, and slaughter the men who germinated and sprang up fully armed. Even if he negotiated those trials unscathed, he had then to evade the lethal snake that guarded the Fleece. All this he accomplished – thanks to Medea.

Part of Apollonius' narrative focuses on the magical potions and charms used by Medea to ensure Jason's triumph. She renders him temporarily invulnerable by anointing him with 'the drug of Prometheus', a plant with a flesh-like root that grew where the eagle-gored Titan's blood fell to Earth (perhaps there is less symbolic distance between Medea and Prometheus than one might have thought).[1] She also neutralizes the Fleece's snaky guardian by sending it to sleep with her trademark mixture of incantations and drugs (see opposite). (Sorcery ran in the family: she was the niece of Circe, the divine enchantress with the scary ability to metamorphose her victims into animals.)[2] But why did Medea want to help Jason at all, treacherously contravening her father's wishes? The reason was simple: she had fallen desperately in love with him after Eros had pierced her with his passion-arousing arrow. And that threw Medea into all kinds of erratic (and erotic) movement:

> For a long time she remained there in her ante-chamber:
> shame would not allow her to go further. Then she
> turned around and went back in again, but then came out
> again, and then hid away inside again; her feet carried her
> this way and that, all to no purpose.[3]

Her heart – as Apollonius tells us in his most famous simile – flutters and dances like a sunbeam reflected from the trembling surface of water freshly poured into a bucket.[4] In the lead-up to Jason's contests, her emotions oscillate similarly:

Medea drugs the serpent, *krater* from Ruvo, Puglia, 4th century BCE.

> At one moment she thought that she would give him the
> drugs as charms against the bulls; then she would not,
> but would herself face death; then she would not die
> and would not give the drugs, but with calmness would
> endure her misery just as she was.[5]

But she does not die, and she does give Jason the drugs, making
her departure from home inevitable. In spite of the anguish that
this separation brings her, Medea has no option but to abandon
Aia, boarding Jason's ship, the *Argo*, as it sails back to Greece. Her
preference for her lover over her father becomes even more bru-
tally irrevocable at one point on the voyage, when the pursuing
Colchians, including her brother Apsyrtos, catch up with them.
Luring Apsyrtos into an ambush, she averts her eyes as Jason murders him. That is Apollonius' version of events. In a gruesome

variant, Medea herself kills Apsyrtos, dismembers his corpse and throws it into the sea for the Colchians to retrieve, thus delaying their pursuit.[6]

A notable feature of many ancient narratives about Medea, not just that of Apollonius, is the sense of movement that so often engulfs her: as we have already seen, her behaviour habitually exemplifies restlessness, oscillation and turmoil (except in brief moments of uncanny stillness when she is exercising magical control).[7] But her career also involves movement of a more literal kind, when she is forced into repeated displacements from one geographical location to another. The *Argo*'s home port was Iolkos (modern Volos), which, after the perils of the voyage to Greece from Colchis, is Medea's next destination.

It was the dynastic situation at Iolkos that had provoked the Argonautic expedition in the first place. King Pelias had quarrelled about the throne with his half-brother, Jason's father, Aison. Seeing Jason as a potential threat, Pelias had sent him away on Mission Impossible: to seize the Golden Fleece. While Jason was away, Pelias (according to one version) threatened to kill Aison, who chose the path of suicide by drinking a fatal draft of bull's blood; another version held that Aison remained alive, but that his power was usurped by Pelias.[8] In any case, the story resumes with the *Argo* back home, and it is a story that focuses on Medea's sorcery. She convinced the daughters of the ageing Pelias that they could rejuvenate him if they chopped him up and put him in a cauldron of boiling water laced with appropriate herbs (to demonstrate her skills, she had successfully rejuvenated either an old sheep or Jason's father, Aison; see opposite). But in the case of Pelias Medea deliberately chose herbs that were ineffective, leaving his daughters as perpetrators of a horrible act of collective homicide. Having metaphorically torn apart her own family in Colchis, she had now literally butchered another family. There was nothing for it but to become a migrant once more, heading south towards Corinth.[9]

Attributed to the Copenhagen Painter,
Medea rejuvenating a sheep, Attic *hydria*, 480–470 BCE.

What happened there is dramatized in the greatest work of art ever devoted to this constellation of myths: Euripides' tragedy *Medea* (431 BCE). When the play opens, Medea is already reduced to the role to which later tradition so often consigns her: that of a marginalized outsider, a non-Greek in a foreign land. Jason, by contrast, is doing rather well. Having cast Medea aside, he is now betrothed to Glauce, daughter of the Corinthian king Creon. Creon knows what Medea is capable of, and proposes to banish her and the two sons she has had by Jason. After successfully persuading Creon to grant her just one day in which to make plans for her exile, Medea employs the time to annihilate everything dear to Jason. Using her sons as innocent couriers, she sends Jason's bride-to-be a golden coronet and a lovely dress; but when Glauce puts the coronet on, it exudes a stream of skull-melting fire, while the dress is steeped in a fiendish poison that devours her body, and also that of Creon as he embraces his dying daughter. Next Medea punishes Jason further by murdering their two sons, in order both to hurt him unbearably and to prevent someone else from killing the boys to avenge Creon (see pl. III). This is not, however, the only version of the myth. The sources agree that the children died, but there is disagreement about how and why. One version has it that they perished accidentally as Medea tried to make them immortal;[10] another relates that it was the Corinthians who killed them.[11] Euripides' tradition-defining version (of which he may himself have been the originator) establishes for ever the figure of 'Medea the filicide'.

But the act of murder comes at dreadful cost to its perpetrator. Before committing it, Medea suffers another episode of tormented oscillation, as she alternately determines to kill the children, then relents, then steels herself again. Yet in the end the decision can only go one way. Once the deed is done, the outcome follows automatically: to abandon this place too. She flies off on her serpent-powered chariot, taking the corpses of her children with her, thus denying Jason the chance to bid them a last farewell at their tomb (see overleaf). The Euripidean Medea is both an unattainably distant, quasi-divine figure and an agonizingly conflicted human being.

Other myth-tellers pick up the story where Euripides left it. Two more migrations await Medea. From Corinth she moves to Athens, alone this time – Jason is just a bad memory. She has been offered asylum by the Athenian king Aegeus as a *quid pro quo* for promising to cure him of his childlessness, for he has no legitimate heir.[12] Medea succeeds in integrating herself so well that she marries Aegeus and bears him a son called Medos, a name that symbolizes the centrality of the mother, rather than of the father, to the child's existence. But the unexpected arrival of an anonymous young stranger prompts Medea to resume her career as a serial poisoner. As she realizes but Aegeus does not, the newcomer is Theseus, Aegeus' long-lost son by another woman. When her plot to remove this potential threat to her own status fails, she migrates yet again, this time back to Colchis. As the mythographer Apollodorus relates, she 'discovered that Aietes had been deposed by his brother, Perses. She killed Perses and restored the kingdom to her father.'[13] Full circle: in her end is her beginning. Or perhaps not quite ... We hear, exceptionally, of a variant according to which, after death, Medea married Achilles in the Elysian Fields.[14] Not that that would have persuaded those who maintained that Medea was a goddess and could not have died. In Greek myth, there is almost always 'another story'.

Before we leave the Medea myth as the Greeks told it, it will be useful to reflect on the picture as a whole.[15] Two prominent themes are the emotional pressures of repeated migration and the pain of betrayal (of Aietes by Medea, and of Medea by Jason). Perhaps less obvious, but no less important, is the motif of intergenerational succession between males. The dynastic conflicts between Aison and Pelias, and between Aietes and Perses, constitute one kind of example; another concerns Aegeus' inheritance – will it

Medea escapes, Faliscan red-figure *krater*, 4th–3rd century BCE.

pass to Medos or Theseus? Throughout all this there persists the image of a strong and dangerous woman, capable of exerting extraordinary power over others – and even over time itself, by magically effecting rejuvenation. It is impossible to draw a simplistic moral from her career (does any Greek myth generate a simplistic moral?). But one striking fact merits particular scrutiny: Medea remains apparently unpunished for her serial acts of violence. This can be read in different ways. If we stress Medea's quasi-divine superiority – well, gods and goddesses can occupy a moral territory outside that which is available to mortals, and that includes carrying out with impunity actions that for mortals would lead to inevitable punishment. If, by contrast, we stress Medea's humanity – well, at least in the real world, not every crime leads to punishment. But in any case, during her sequence of migrations Medea does suffer psychologically, and repeatedly so, in spite of her manipulative mastery. She is resilient, resourceful, deceitful and dangerous, but also vulnerable: an outsider who at times takes centre stage and acts with tremendous dominance. It is a heady and paradoxical mixture, and it will have a fascinating imaginative afterlife.

For the Romans, Medea remained one of the most emotionally powerful characters in the entire mythological repertoire. Ovid tells her story repeatedly in various genres of his poetry, notably in an imaginary letter from Medea to Jason in his collection known as *Heroides* ('Heroines'). Another influential Medean voice belonged to the tragedian Seneca (*c.* 4 BCE–65 CE), who wrote a *Medea* in which the cruelty and distress exceed anything in Euripides: as the drama ends, the departing murderess hurls the corpses of the children out of her flying chariot and down upon their father below, prompting him to exclaim:

Go through the lofty spaces of high heaven, and bear witness, where you ride, that the gods do not exist.[16]

Here is just another Medean paradox: the very fact that Medea can make this kind of supra-normal escape suggests that she herself has something divine about her. There is also her reliance on the goddess Hecate, whose real presence she invoked earlier in the play to ratify her own sorcery. Seneca's Jason may feel and speak as if the gods do not exist – understandably enough, in the face of his dreadful personal suffering – but the truth may not be so simple.

Medea figured in the visual as well as the written life of Rome. At one point in his poems Ovid mentions the intriguing fact that Roman domestic houses might contain, among other controversial subjects, paintings of Medea 'with murder in her eyes' – a look that we can still see on surviving representations (see overleaf).[17] One way of reading such images is to see them as bearers of a (male-oriented) message: look what happens when a dangerous woman gets out of control.[18]

Medea contemplates killing her sons, fresco from the
House of the Dioscuri, Pompeii, 62–79 CE.

After antiquity

Medieval and Renaissance retellings diversify and complicate the story of Medea as it had been told by the Greeks and Romans. Depending on where the emphasis is placed in each new version, the meanings of the myth can shift in unexpected and sometimes contradictory directions.

Let us listen first to a remarkable pair of vernacular Tuscan/Venetian tales from the late 13th century.[19] On the return voyage from Colchis, Jason leaves Medea high and dry on an island, much as Theseus faithlessly abandoned Ariadne on Naxos. But soon the narrative takes a quite un-Ariadne-like turn. Jason has left Medea pregnant with twins. She gives birth to them with no one to help her, after which she somehow survives for three years living off roots and grass. Eventually a passing ship rescues her and conveys her to where Jason is now living, married to the daughter of the local king. Medea's terrible revenge surpasses anything in the classical tradition. Not content with murdering her sons, she feeds their hearts to their unwitting father and, for good measure (in the Venetian version), nails the rest of their bodies to his bedroom door (this time the reader can hardly avoid recalling Procne, who punished her brutal rapist-husband by feeding him their son). Ghoulishly aggressive though Medea's crime may be, she cannot escape the emotional trauma of committing filicide. Rejecting the possibility of further migration, she throws herself onto the upright blade of a sword.

Contrast *this* Medea with the woman envisioned by Christine de Pizan (1364–c. 1430), one of the most fascinating literary figures in the whole of medieval Europe. Born in Venice, she moved to Paris when her father received an appointment there as court astrologer. Christine has become a trailblazer for modern feminists – justifiably so, given her blend of personal qualities and literary gifts: she supported herself and her children by her writing after her husband died of the plague. She returned repeatedly to the theme of Medea, whom she found to be not only learned but also deeply understandable as a woman. In one of her works, *The Book of the City of Ladies*, Christine explored both these aspects of the heroine in two separate passages:

> An extremely beautiful lady with a tall, slim body and a very lovely face, Medea was the daughter of Aietes, king of Colchis, and his wife, Perse. In learning she surpassed all other women, for she knew the properties of every plant and what spells they could be used for. Indeed, no art had been invented that she had not mastered ... The king's daughter, Medea, was so struck by Jason's good looks, royal lineage and impressive reputation that she thought he would make a good match for her. In her desire to show her love for him, she resolved to save him from death, for she felt such compassion that she could not bear to see a knight like him come to any harm. She thus freely engaged him in lengthy conversations and, in short, taught him various charms and spells that she knew would help him succeed in his quest for the Golden Fleece. In return, Jason promised to take no other woman but her for his wife, swearing that he would love her for evermore. However, Jason broke his word. After everything had gone just as he had planned, he left Medea for another woman. She, who would have let herself be torn limb from limb rather than play such a false trick on him, fell into utter despair. Never in her life did she experience happiness or joy again.[20]

A myth-teller's particular choice of episode is decisive for the overall moral impression that the character creates. Medea is the perfect example. She is, after all, uniquely mobile, and this mobility is exactly what enables her story to signify so many different things. Such 'episode dependence' is especially noticeable in one particular material context of Renaissance visual art: the *cassone*. *Cassoni* were wedding chests that contained the bride's *trousseau*; in 15th-century Florence they were conveyed through the streets from the house of the bride's father to the house of her new husband, as part of the wedding celebration. Remarkably – at least at first sight – one of the myths that decorated such chests was that of Jason and Medea.[21] One can think of a dozen episodes in Medea's career that, if prominently displayed, would have left Florentine wedding guests feeling distinctly uneasy about the future of the real-life couple whose happiness they were toasting. But it was precisely the wedding ceremony of Jason and Medea that was evidently felt to be a different matter: a king's daughter united to a chivalric young hero. That, at any rate, seems to be the logic of a painting by Biagio d'Antonio (see p. 60, above), in which the joining of the mythical couple's right hands symbolizes the moment at which future bliss is anticipated.

But Medea's darker side had not been forgotten. Only slightly earlier than Biagio's painting are manuscript illustrations emanating from the court of Philip the Good, duke of Burgundy. In one, Medea is bleeding Aison's skull as a prelude to rejuvenating him (see p. 60, below); in another, parts of Apsyrtos' body float grotesquely in the sea between the *Argo* and the Colchians' vessel, with Medea presiding inscrutably over the scene (see p. 61); in a third, Medea's fiery dragons inflict carnage at the wedding feast of Jason and his new bride.[22] The context – and hence the representation – is a world away from a celebratory Florentine *cassone*. The illustrations come from manuscripts of Raoul Lefèvre's prose romance-biography *L'Histoire de Jason* (1460), a work that aimed to praise its hero and exculpate him from accusations of misconduct. It presented Jason's love for Medea as a product of enchantment, and suggests that he was right to abandon her because of her wickedness.[23] Jason's integrity needed to be preserved: after all, hadn't Duke Philip established an order of chivalry bearing the name of the Golden Fleece?[24]

Attributed to Biagio d'Antonio, *The Betrothal of Jason and Medea*, c. 1486.

Medea bleeding Aison, miniature from Raoul Lefèvre's *L'Histoire de
Jason extraite de pluseurs livres et presentée a noble et redouté prince Phelipe,
par la grace de Dieu duc de Bourgoingne et de Brabant*, 15th century.

Medea's visual story has continued in fits and starts until the present day. There are notable landmarks along the way, invoking different aspects of her mythical profile. The conflicted mother who protectively embraces her children while grasping the dagger that will end their lives appears in Eugène Delacroix's famous oil painting of 1838 (p. 63). Thirty years later, Frederick Sandys opted for the isolated, wild-eyed sorceress, complete with toads, dragon, and an ambiguous liquid being poured into a burner (p. 62). Another ten years on, and we have *The Murder of Pelias by his Daughters* by Georges Moreau de Tours, in which the hapless old man is about to be stabbed to death ('rejuvenated') by his deluded daughters, one of whom looks as if she has just come from a soft-porn photo shoot. (Sexual titillation justified by an impeccable classical pedigree – how many tens of thousands of European artworks find their rationale in this combination!) In the background, a baleful Medea surveys the scene.

Apsyrtos dismembered, miniature from Raoul Lefèvre's *L'Histoire de Jason extraite de pluseurs livres et presentée a noble et redouté prince Phelipe, par la grace de Dieu duc de Bourgoingne et de Brabant*, 15th century.

Frederick Sandys, *Medea*, 1866–68.

Eugène Delacroix, *Medea*, 1838.

But in the Medea tradition as a whole, visual representations play second fiddle to dramatizations on stage.[25] The reason must surely lie in the continuing impact of Euripides' tragedy, supplemented by its Senecan reworking; these two classic plays have dominated the post-Renaissance re-imagining of this cluster of myths. The litany of major dramatists to have addressed the stories is impressive: Pierre Corneille, Franz Grillparzer, Jean Anouilh, and literally dozens of other playwrights and composers of operas, ballets and other music-based productions (see pl. IV). All these artists have been inspired by the destructive human conflicts embedded in the Euripidean plot.

The history of European culture being what it is, the vast majority of those who have remade Medea's mythology have been male. But over recent decades things have changed significantly, especially in the area of playwriting. In tandem with developments in feminist thought, women writers have discovered in Medea an icon through whom to explore issues of gender, patriarchal power and exclusion. Two prime locations for these explorations have been Ireland and Italy.[26]

In October 1998, the audience in the Abbey Theatre in Dublin sat down to watch the première of *By the Bog of Cats*, by the award-winning playwright Marina Carr. The drama is set squarely in an Irish context. Hester Swane is a traveller – an outsider. She has lived for fourteen years with her partner, Carthage Kilbride; they have a seven-year-old daughter. Carthage now plans to throw forty-year-old Hester over and marry a girl half her age, the daughter of a wealthy landowner. Hester's vengeance begins when she burns down Carthage's house, and ends when she knifes her daughter to death, 'altruistically' protecting her from the consequences of abandonment by her mother. Although the work is explicitly based on Euripides' tragedy,[27] the ending takes us far from the Greek model – though not from a number of other, more recent retellings of the myth (such as those by Corneille and Anouilh).[28]

Instead of embarking on a career of change and movement, Hester immobilizes her fate for ever by committing suicide.

To describe Carr's drama as 'a woman's view of Medea' would be grossly patronizing: there are as many different 'women's Medeas' as there are women who have re-imagined her. Wholly distinct in tone and plot from Carr's version, but no less thought-provoking, is Maricla Boggio's Italian *Medea* (1981), predating Carr's drama by a couple of decades.[29] Like several of Boggio's other works, it takes the classical tradition as its starting point – not just Euripides and Seneca, but the classical *tradition*, since the play's central character quotes the words of a number of postclassical Medeas along the way. But Boggio's vision is emphatically situated in the feminist movement of the 1980s. This Medea comes to terms with her husband's unfaithfulness not by murdering her younger rival, but by striking up a bond of gender solidarity with her: the gift of a dress from one to the other – in Euripides, a dress that brought about ghastly suffering – becomes a symbol of affection between the two women, an affection that infectiously extends to other women too:

> I gave it to you
> and it was a spontaneous gift
> spontaneously accepted ...
> You were wearing a pair of blue jeans; over them
> you put on the white dress
> and immediately you became a little girl,
> and you danced with joy
> while the other women joined the dance
> and sang.[30]

This is a far cry from Euripides, Seneca or any other ancient source – or most other modern sources, for that matter. However, one thing that Boggio's Medea does have in common with her classical predecessors is mobility, but in quite a new sense. Boggio's heroine moves, grows and develops *psychologically*. In the past she had chosen to undergo repeated abortions, so that her 'Jason' (whom she describes as 'my eldest child') would not have to share his wife's attention with the demands of a young family. Putting such male-directed concerns behind her, she now places solidarity with other women at the top of her priorities – and incidentally rejects the idea of killing her living children. Boggio's version confirms the truth that Greek myths can still be located at the epicentre of the most pressing contemporary social debates.

In re-creations such as those by Carr and Boggio, Medea's goddess-like aspect has no place in the socially realistic stories being told: no feature of active contemporary belief corresponds to such a category of being. There are, however, other modern retellings in which Medea's more-than-human eeriness translates into a character imbued with a differently supernatural quality: that of a ghost. Here the leading form of artistic expression has been cinema. Perhaps the best-known example is *The Others*, directed by the Chilean-born Spanish cineast Alejandro Amenábar (2001). The location is a lonely mansion on the island of Jersey; the time is soon after the end of World War II. The central character, Grace (played by Nicole Kidman), is the mother of two young children, a boy and his elder sister. Since Grace's husband has not returned from the war, she has to cope on her own, a task rendered more difficult by the children's strange allergy to daylight. Not only that: the house they are living in seems to be haunted by a group of ghostly intruders. Only as the plot unfolds does it emerge that the true ghosts are Grace and her children; those whom they regard as intruders are the ordinary human beings who have come to live in the house as its new owners. The reason why Grace's children have become ghosts is the event that brings the plot close to the classical model: Grace herself killed the children by smothering them. But differences from the classical Medea plot are no less apparent. Grace killed the children not from a desire to inflict

Film still from Alejandro Amenábar's *The Others*, 2001.

revenge on her husband or to protect them, but out of despair ('Mummy went mad,' says her daughter), after which Grace committed suicide. What their current status as ghosts has done is to give Grace a second chance to look after them; this she does, as a religiously devout mother concerned for their wellbeing and education. What is more – and here is another difference from the 'classic' plot – she shows no inclination to move. On the contrary, as the film ends, she affirms that she and the children will never leave the house, since that is where they belong.

More explicitly horrific in its deployment of the supernatural is *The Curse of La Llorona* (dir. Michael Chaves, 2019), based on a Mexican legend about a woman who drowned her children in a fit of jealousy prompted by her unfaithful husband and then drowned herself. Subsequently she comes back as a malevolent spirit who preys on the children of other women, seizing and then murdering them. Here the Medea myth blends into that of Lamia, the mythical woman who became a child-devouring monster after losing her own children. As in *The Others*, the Medea figure is a *revenante*, remaining in place after committing her murderous acts rather than migrating elsewhere, and elsewhere, and elsewhere again.

As will already have become evident, there is no shortage of modern Medeas. What should also be evident is that it is her profile as filicide that has forged ahead of every other aspect of her ancient mythical profile. The child-killer who has a justifiable defence to be made on her behalf: this is what has come to fascinate contemporary audiences in the theatre and the cinema. And contemporary readers too: Toni Morrison's disturbing, controversial and multi-award-winning novel *Beloved* (1987) narrates the story of a black woman, Sethe, who killed her young daughter to protect her from a life of slavery. Here again the plot involves the supernatural, in the shape of the character known as Beloved, apparently the reincarnation of the daughter Sethe killed. The novel's powerful realism is grounded in fact, being inspired by the story of a 19th-century African-American woman who escaped slavery, was recaptured and killed her child to prevent the girl from being

Thomas Satterwhite Noble, *The Modern Medea*, 1867.

forced back into captivity (see opposite). If slavery is the ultimate category of the 'other', *Beloved* offers the ultimate exploration of a Medea in that condition.

Our attempt to follow Medea's progress through all her movements – and, more rarely, her immobility – has concerned itself predominantly with retellings in various artistic media. But spare a thought also for unsung heroines: those working as academics. They too have played a significant part in 'thinking with Medea', two in particular. Both are distinguished Hellenists; both are women and mothers. Professors Patricia Easterling and Edith Hall have shown brilliantly how contemporary statistical research about the social and legal facts surrounding infanticide can throw light on, and in turn be illuminated by, the myth of Medea as killer of her children. More than forty years ago, Easterling drew attention to the weakness of the argument, advanced by some (male) classicists, that the conduct of the Euripidean Medea is something no sane or civilized person could comprehend. Statistics prove otherwise: in the data highlighted by certain studies, a large proportion of murder victims are children, and a large proportion of these are killed by a parent – an act often followed (unlike in Euripides) by the suicide of the murderer.[31] Hall went further, citing studies of maternal filicide that formulate a pattern quite astonishingly like that of Medea: a woman married once, with children in her sole care, suffering from social isolation and desirous of exacting revenge on the husband.[32] Contemporary issues of motive, law and social responsibility can find a focus in, and even draw inspiration from, a myth that is anything but dead.

These are serious matters, and they merit serious analysis. But, as we have said and will repeatedly say again, Greek myths are supple and variable, capable of conveying an extraordinary range of meanings according to the context of narration and the purposes of the narrator. Not every 'use' of the Medea myth need refer to infanticide. Medea is a name to conjure with, but not necessarily to kill with: Greek mythological names can often simply be invoked because of the culturally impressive aura they bestow. We meet this everywhere in the world of commercial naming. 'Medea' designer bags are the brainchildren of the Italian twin sisters Giulia and Camilla Venturini; the classical allusion they embody presumably conveys a sense of generalized female empowerment, with a *frisson* of danger thrown in. In fact, the model in one of the publicity stills shows more than a hint of the Maria Callas look (from Pasolini's 1969 film *Medea*), as if what lay behind the label was a famous (one might say, legendary) reinterpretation of the ancient myth rather than the myth itself. Be that as it may, the image confirms that Brand Medea sells. More importantly, one hopes, it makes you think.

Maria Callas in Pier Paolo Pasolini's *Medea*, 1969.

CHAPTER 3

Daedalus and Icarus

Prometheus is a god. In spite of her vulnerability, Medea, too, has divine attributes. By contrast, the two mythical characters we look at next are unambiguously mortal, with many of the weaknesses that can characterize human beings, though also, in the case of the elder of the pair, some astonishing skills into the bargain. Daedalus and Icarus were father and son, a relationship that constitutes the central dynamic of their story. A strong affective bond united them, yet there were also tensions that precipitated the son's downfall. Daedalus, unlike Icarus, has far more to his rich and varied mythical biography than that single and literally catastrophic episode. But it is Icarus, not Daedalus, whose image has proved to be the more symbolically resonant.

Daedalus was renowned as an architect and maker of statues; his very name means 'cleverly or artistically made'. He was hardly less prodigiously gifted than divinities such as Hephaestus, Athena and indeed Prometheus, all three of whom were supreme in artisanship. Daedalus' origins were Athenian, but he had to leave his home city (for a reason we shall come to later) and migrated to Crete. Eventually (for another reason we shall come to) he had to escape once more, this time either to Cumae, near Naples, or to Sicily, where his ingenuity shone undimmed. But his artistic prowess extended well beyond these locations: works attributed to him could be viewed in many parts of the world to which Greek culture extended. One source of his inspiration lay in Egypt, where the construction of a pharaoh's tomb allegedly influenced the design of the Cretan labyrinth that Daedalus would famously create.[1] The location and manner of his death are uncertain, though his last journey may have been a return to Athens.[2]

In contrast with Daedalus' career of multiple virtuosity and serial movement, Icarus' story is simpler and more tightly focused. Ancient myth-tellers were interested in neither his childhood (which they passed over in silence), nor his adulthood (he did not live long enough to have one). All that mattered was a single, devil-may-care escapade during his adolescence, when he joined his father on that breakout from Crete. For Medea, airborne conveyance on a serpent-drawn chariot was a feature of her progress throughout her career. For Icarus, the capacity to fly was something momentary, enabled by his father's brilliant but, in this case, ultimately lethal inventiveness.

The Greek and Roman sources

Virtually every classical myth differs from every other according to the profile of the ancient sources through which it is transmitted – a point easily overlooked if one relies solely on modern mythological dictionaries or the equivalent internet sites, where the individual contours of the evidence for each myth often get ironed out into a deceptively smooth and continuous narrative. In the case of Daedalus and Icarus, their mythology has to be pieced together from a broad range of diverse sources, which are best examined case by case.

First, there are a couple of brief mentions in the works of the two greatest epic poets of antiquity. In the *Iliad*, Homer refers to the circular dancing-place that Daedalus made for the Cretan princess Ariadne, so already in the 8th–7th centuries BCE Daedalus was famous as an architect associated with the Cretan royal family.[3] Then there is a poignant moment in Virgil's *Aeneid* (29–19 BCE), where Daedalus is said to have built at Cumae a temple that depicted scenes relating to the Minotaur. Daedalus would also have sculpted a golden image of the fall of Icarus, Virgil adds: but twice the hands of the grieving father dropped ineffectually and prevented him from working.[4] Next on the list of sources comes Pausanias' account of his travels through Greece (2nd century CE). In several passages about memorable artefacts he had seen at various locations, the author records the presence of archaic wooden statues ascribed to Daedalus; he also provides snippets of information about the sculptor's mythical biography.[5]

More substantial is a group of references in the huge 'universal history' written by Diodorus Siculus (1st century BCE). The narrative begins with an account of Greek and non-Greek mythology, in the course of which the historian has a good deal to say about Daedalus. One of Diodorus' prominent themes is the knowledge that distinguished Greek travellers to Egypt – philosophers, politicians, and religious or mythical figures such as Orpheus – gained from their visits there. Daedalus was another to be inspired by his visit to Egypt; at Memphis, for example, he was credited with having built part of the temple of Hephaestus that featured a wooden statue of the artist himself carved by his own hands. What distinguished his statues from the works of earlier artistic tradition was, relates Diodorus, their amazingly lifelike quality: eyes open, legs apart as if striding, arms expressively extended. But genius can have its downside if it resents the presence of great skill in others. While under Daedalus' tutelage in Athens, the sculptor's young nephew Talos threatened to outdo his teacher by designing three brilliantly innovative tools: the potter's wheel, the serrated saw, and the compass for drawing circles. In a fit of jealousy Daedalus killed the young pretender (according to one version he pushed Talos off the Acropolis) and was duly condemned in court.

Like many another murderer in Greek mythology – Medea for one – Daedalus managed to escape and to continue his career elsewhere. From Athens he headed for Crete, where he completed two extraordinary commissions for King Minos and Queen Pasiphae. For Pasiphae he made an artificial cow in which she concealed herself in order to be impregnated by a magnificent bull sacred to Poseidon. (Her misdirected lust was a punishment inflicted by Poseidon, angry at Minos' refusal to sacrifice the magnificent animal in his honour.) The progeny of the scandalous union was the Minotaur, a ferocious bull–man hybrid that Minos ordered to be hidden away in an impenetrable labyrinth, the designing of which was Daedalus' second Cretan commission. But Minos was still furious at his craftsman-in-residence for fabricating the 'cow' that facilitated Pasiphae's indiscretion. So when Theseus slew the Minotaur, Daedalus had to leave Crete in a hurry, taking his son with him. Diodorus records contrasting versions of how father and son eluded capture: either they fled by ship, and Icarus drowned when he fell overboard (plausible but dull), or they left by air (far more exciting):

> Daedalus, despairing of making his escape by any boat, fashioned with amazing ingenuity wings that were cleverly designed and marvellously fitted together with wax; and fastening these on his son's body and his own he spread them out for flight, to the astonishment of all, and made his escape over the open sea that lies near the island of Crete. As for Icarus, because of the ignorance of youth he made his flight too far aloft and fell into the sea when the wax that held the wings together was melted by the sun, whereas Daedalus, by flying close to the sea and repeatedly wetting the wings, made his way in safety, marvellous to relate, to Sicily.[6]

This bald narrative leaves out almost all that is moving in the story. To supply the sweep and energy of the episode and the raw emotional climax to which it leads, we need to invoke the soaring and dipping verses of a great poet – the next on our list of sources.

Thanks to his two renderings of the demise of Icarus, Ovid would prove to be the single most decisive shaper of the myth's post-classical tradition. In *The Art of Love* he links the aerial escape from Crete to the overall theme of the poem. Once you've caught your girl, says the poet, that's only half the battle: you still have to keep her. And that's tricky, because Amor, god of love, is a flighty god – as flighty as Daedalus, when Minos tried and failed to immobilize him. The connection between Amor and Daedalus is simple: wings. Whereas for Amor they belonged to his natural anatomy, for Daedalus they were an artful fabrication:

> Necessity is the mother of invention – though who
> would have thought that a human being could ever
> travel by air? The inventor created the equivalent of
> a bird's flying equipment by arranging feathers in a row,
> and binding the delicate structure together with linen
> thread. The bottoms of the feathers were then secured
> by dipping them in melted wax.[7]

In *Metamorphoses*, the culmination of Ovid's poetic genius, the father tries and fails to temper his son's impulsiveness:

> 'I warn you, Icarus,' [Daedalus] said, 'you must follow
> a course midway between earth and heaven, in case
> the sun should scorch your feathers, if you go too
> high, or the water make them heavy if you are too low.
> Fly halfway between the two ...'

> Now Juno's sacred isle of Samos lay on the left, Delos
> and Paros were already behind them ... when the boy
> Icarus began to enjoy the thrill of swooping boldly
> through the air. Drawn on by his eagerness for the
> open sky, he left his guide and soared upwards, till he
> came too close to the blazing sun, and it softened the

sweet-smelling wax that bound his wings together.
The wax melted. Icarus moved his bare arms up and
down, but without their feathers they had no purchase
on the air. Even as his lips were crying his father's name,
they were swallowed up in the deep blue waters which
are called after him. The unhappy father, a father no
longer, cried out: 'Icarus!' 'Icarus,' he called. 'Where are
you? Where am I to look for you?' As he was still calling
'Icarus' he saw the feathers on the water, and cursed his
inventive skill.[8]

There is a further twist in the Ovidian tale. As Daedalus was burying
his son, a partridge clapped its wings joyfully. The Greek word for
partridge is *perdix*, and Perdix was an alternative name for Talos, the
nephew whom Daedalus had pushed off the Acropolis in a jealous
fury. As the boy fell, Athena turned him into a partridge, which is
why the story is relevant to Ovid's *Metamorphoses*. Remembering
that fall, Ovid points out, the partridge is always frightened of
high places – one of many aspects of the myth of Daedalus and
Icarus that relate to the opposition between the high and the low.[9]

Daedalus' final port of call was Sicily. Once more – and here we let
Diodorus resume the tale – he found his talents in demand at a royal
court, this time that of King Cocalus of Camicus (near Agrigentum),
for whom he accomplished numerous feats of ingenious construction. One of the most notable was the building of a cliff-top city
virtually impregnable to outside attack; as with the labyrinth, the
winding passageways that led to its citadel were impenetrable for
a would-be intruder. But, as on Crete, it was Daedalus' very skill
that almost brought about his downfall. Minos had never relented
in his pursuit of his former architect, and the search led him to
Cocalus' court (this time it is the mythographer Apollodorus who
supplies the details).[10] In order to discover Daedalus' whereabouts,
Minos promised a huge reward to anyone who could pass a thread

Daedalus and Icarus, bas-relief from Villa Albani, Rome, 2nd century CE.

Icarus, bronze figure, *c.* 430 BCE.

through a spiral murex shell. As Minos well knew, only Daedalus would have the genius to fulfil the task, which amounted to a replication in miniature of the penetration of the Cretan labyrinth (Ariadne had given Theseus a ball of thread so that he could retrace his steps out of the maze). When consulted by Cocalus, Daedalus attached the thread to an ant, bored a hole in the shell, and let the ant do the rest. Now that the great craftsman had showed his hand, Minos demanded that Cocalus hand him over; but Cocalus refused to part with such a valuable asset. Minos never made it back to Crete: according to one version, Cocalus' daughters murdered him by pouring boiling water over him in the bath – the ultimate negation of the rule of hospitality. There may be a hint that Daedalus' ingenuity played a part in the murder, since among the inventions he was credited with in Sicily was a spa – a grotto heated by steam.

Our final literary source is the essayist and satirist Lucian (2nd century CE), who explored a variety of symbolic and allegorical aspects of Icarus' ascent and downfall. In two of his works, Lucian uses the notion of flying too high to point alternative morals. Either: the rich get above themselves and suffer the consequences. Or: if humble people enjoy a sudden elevation in fortune they may, equally suddenly, come to grief.[11] Elsewhere Lucian applies the same episode to knowledge rather than ethics. In the essay *On Astrology* Icarus is said to have been taught that arcane lore by his father, but when the boy abandoned reason he fell into 'a sea of unfathomable matters'.[12] In the dialogue *The Ship* (or *The Wishes*), Icarus' flight stands not just for knowledge but for knowledge as a source of power. When some friends discuss what each of them most desires, one of the group, a man called Timolaos, says he longs to possess a set of magical rings giving him the means to actualize the ultimate mortal dreams: eternal youth, freedom from pain, invisibility – and the ability to fly.[13] Thus equipped, he could travel anywhere, see the most astonishing marvels, discover everything that has always puzzled thinkers: the sources of the Nile, the existence of the Antipodes, the nature of the stars ... All in vain, says one of Timolaos' friends: 'You will suffer the same fate as Icarus. Your plumage will come off, you will fall from the sky and walk on the ground, and you will lose all those rings when they slip off your fingers.' Not that Icarus-like flight necessarily leads to disaster – at least in Lucian's satirical imagination. The dialogue *Icaromenippus* relates the incredible aerial journey undertaken by the philosopher Menippus. By attaching to himself an eagle's right wing and a vulture's left, he soared above the Earth in search of a new perspective on humanity. 'Imagine yourself', he tells his interlocutor,

> first descrying a tiny Earth, far smaller than the Moon looks; on turning my eyes down, I could not think for some time what had become of our mighty mountains and vast sea. If I had not caught sight of the Colossus of Rhodes and the Pharos tower, I assure you I should never have made out the Earth at all. But their height and projection, with the faint shimmer of Ocean in the sun, showed me it must be the Earth I was looking at. Then, when once I had got my sight properly focused, the whole human race was clear to me, not merely in the shape of nations and cities, but the individuals, sailing, fighting, ploughing, going to law; the women, the beasts, and in short every breed 'nourished by the fertile earth'.[14]

The achieving of such a view of the world might seem a classic illustration of the fatal perils of overstepping due limits, in the manner of Faust. But Lucian is not in the business of tragedy. Although Zeus clips Menippus' wings, he gives orders to Hermes to deposit the former airman back in his home city of Athens, unharmed and free to relate his Munchausen-like experiences to anyone who will listen.

Compared to the breadth and elaboration of the written tradition, artists homed in on a rather restricted number of iconographical schemata, but there are some visually arresting works nonetheless. One of the finest is a marble relief (2nd century CE) in the Villa Albani in Rome (see p. 77). It depicts a seated Daedalus engrossed in making an artificial wing; alongside him stands Icarus, Adonis-like in beauty, waiting for the job to be completed.[15] Dating from half a millennium earlier, a lovely bronze statuette represents the young man already winged and ready for take-off (see p. 78).[16] A recurrent image is that of the falling or fallen Icarus, a motif particularly popular in Roman wall painting.[17] One example comes from the House of the Priest Amandus in Pompeii, featuring the chariot of Helios, two boats full of watching fishermen, and two separate Icaruses: one at the top falling out of the sky, and one dead on the sea shore (see pl. v).[18] Another poignant painting from Pompeii also features the corpse of the doomed young man.[19] Also worth noting is the imagery of the episode that features the making of the artificial cow within which Pasiphae concealed herself. Here again, the motif was popular with Roman artists, as on a painting from Pompeii (see p. 82).[20] More unusual is a mosaic (2nd century CE) from the city of Zeugma in modern Turkey (see pl. vii) featuring both Daedalus and Icarus working assiduously as carpenters.[21] The bovine head in the bottom left-hand corner will presumably be the last item to be fixed in place. Finally we should mention representations from which Daedalus himself is absent but that depict his most famous design: the Cretan labyrinth, with the Minotaur at its heart. A mosaic from Conímbriga boils the icon down to its basics, featuring a rather non-threatening bull-man at the centre (see p. 83).

Underlying themes

One concept linking several episodes in Daedalus' story is his capacity to bridge gulfs, to cross boundaries, to link opposites. First, he commanded the boundary separating the animate from the inanimate: the artificial cow is one example, as are his trademark 'lifelike' statues (in one of Plato's dialogues, Socrates says that the statues run away if you do not tie them down).[22] Next, he could elide the

Daedalus and Pasiphae, fresco, House of the Vettii,
Pompeii, 1st century CE.

opposition between human and animal, as when he transformed
himself and Icarus into 'birds', or when he enabled Pasiphae to be
simultaneously a woman and a cow. The polarity between earth and
sky, too – or, more generally, that between above and below – is
another that he was able to mediate, thanks to the wings that enabled
the wearer to move between the two regions. Finally, he was master
of the opposition between inside and outside. The impenetrable
labyrinth, the impregnable citadel, the convoluted murex shell:
all these enigmas were ingeniously solved by the great designer.

The labyrinth with the Minotaur, mosaic from Conímbriga, Portugal, first half of the 3rd century CE.

If the linking of opposites is one key feature of Daedalus' mythology, equally fundamental is something far less abstract: the relationship between father and son. Many other Greek myths explore the same theme, coming at it from a variety of psychological angles. Sometimes the dominant sentiment is one of mutual respect and affection, as with Priam and Hector, or Odysseus and Telemachus. More often, parent and offspring are separated by an emotional distance, such as that which divided Oedipus from Eteocles and Polynices, the sons whom he cursed. Between Oedipus and his father, Laius, the distance expresses itself differently, in a momentary explosion of murderous violence brought about by ignorance, ill fate and the self-assertiveness that characterized this family. Between Theseus and Hippolytus the nature of the estrangement is different again: it arises through a tragic misunderstanding that leads father to curse son. In the case of the protagonists of the present chapter – by contrast with all the preceding examples – the emotional distance derives from the tension between paternal authority and youthful aspiration, generating a poignant blend of love and grief. A partially comparable case is the myth of Helios and Phaethon, in which filial heedlessness of the sun god's guidance led to the son's fatal chariot crash, caused by one of Zeus' thunderbolts. The main difference between the two myths is that Phaethon drove his father's chariot destructively close to the earth, whereas Icarus flew far above it. But in both cases it is the tremendous heat of the sun that brings about disaster, since managing that power is beyond the capability of any mortal.

Icarus' reckless exploit assimilates him, superficially at least, to a type of character found in many Greek myths: the hubristic overreacher who is punished for his or her rashness. The satyr Marsyas vaunted his musicianship above that of Apollo or Athena and was flayed alive for his arrogance. Niobe boasted that she had more children than the goddess Leto, Arachne that she was a superior weaver to Athena; both women suffered the punishment of metamorphosis. Icarus, too, got above himself (in his case, literally) and suffered the consequences. (One modern critical approach even interprets Icarus' flight as 'a rising against the sun god'.)[23] But the similarity is incomplete, since there is no element of misguided competition in Icarus' story. What he did was foolish, but it did not amount to a deliberate challenge to the gods. All the greater, then, is the sympathy that he earns.

Flying (too) high

The ideas implicit in the intertwined stories of Daedalus and Icarus have enjoyed a richly varied afterlife, but again and again the same set of questions recurs. What are the implications of 'flying high'? Is it a brave and glorious aspiration, or a reckless act that deserves to fail? Or could it be both glorious and reckless?

In medieval Europe, a prime context for rethinking the flight of Icarus was theology. The allegorical French treatise *Ovide moralisé* (early 14th century) represented Daedalus as the figure of God as creator, while Icarus stood for man, able to follow God to heaven thanks to his two wings, the right (the love of God) and the left (love of fellow man).[24] The key is to follow a middle course: flying too high means taking for granted that which God has given through grace; flying too low means loving the things of this world too much. Beyond the sphere of theology, the fate of Icarus came to be understood in a more general moral sense, as an allegory of the dangers of getting above oneself. Francis Bacon put it eloquently in chapter 27 of his *The Wisdom of the Ancients* (1609):

> The path of virtue goes directly midway between excess on the one hand and defect on the other. Icarus, being in the pride of youthful alacrity, naturally fell a victim to excess. For it is on the side of excess that the young commonly sin, as the old on the side of defect. And yet if he was to perish one way, it must be admitted that of two paths, both bad and mischievous, he chose the better. For sins of defect are justly accounted worse than sins of excess; because in excess there is something of magnanimity,—something, like the flight of a bird, that holds kindred with heaven; whereas defect creeps on the ground like a reptile.[25]

But it was not always a matter of morality: the myth of Icarus could also be applied to knowledge. In one of his essays, the Italian historian Carlo Ginzburg brilliantly analysed the ramifications of four words from St Paul's Epistle to the Romans (11:20): '*mē hupsēlophronei, alla phobou*', 'Do not think proud [literally 'high'] thoughts, but be fearful.'[26] As Ginzburg demonstrated, a thousand-year tradition of interpretation flowed from this concise exhortation. Thanks to a mistranslation in the Latin Vulgate edition of the Bible, Paul's words were repeatedly taken to apply not morally (the sin of pride) but cognitively (knowing too much). In spite of protests by such influential thinkers as Erasmus, Paul's maxim, understood in the sense of 'Do not seek to know more than you should', would be invoked to discourage unfettered speculation in a wide range of intellectual disputes, from theology and philosophy to the natural and political sciences.[27] The view of the monk and spiritual writer Thomas à Kempis (c. 1380–1471) was typical. Shun too great a desire for knowledge, he warned, since therein lay 'much fretting and delusion'; many aspects of intellectual knowledge were of little or no benefit to the soul.[28] And the very embodiment of the risks of such speculation was Icarus: woe betide you (his fate seemed to warn) if you go beyond the proper limits of enquiry. The idea was encapsulated in the vastly influential 16th-century book of *Emblems* by Andrea Alciati:

> Icarus, you were carried through the heights and the air,
> until the wax melted and cast you headlong into the sea.
> Now the same wax and the burning fire revives you, so
> that by your example you may provide sure teaching. Let
> the astrologer beware of predicting anything. For the
> imposter will fall headlong, if he flies above the stars.[29]

This was the fate of Faust, the legendary over-reacher whose intellectual arrogance led to inevitable downfall. In the words of the Prologue to Christopher Marlowe's *Dr Faustus* (c. 1592), the learning of this theologian and magician exceeded all,

> Till swoll'n with cunning, of a self-conceit,
> His waxen wings did mount above his reach
> And melting, heavens conspired his overthrow!

Yet that warning about the dangers of knowledge was not the whole story either. Icarus' flight came also to be associated with the *benefits* of knowledge. Symbolizing this sort of aspiration is the image of a poised and confident winged flyer, not plunging

In Aſtrologos.
EMBLEMA CIV.

Andrea Alciati, *In Astrologos* (Against astrologers), from 1621 edition of *Emblems*.

but gliding, as illustrated in the book of *Symbola varia* by Anselmus de Boodt (1686), bearing the Virgilian motto 'Nil linquere inausum': 'Leave nothing undared.'[30] And there was yet another way of reading Icarus' flight positively, indeed gloriously. In his sonnet 'Icaro cadde qui' ('Here Icarus fell'), the Neapolitan poet Jacopo Sannazaro (1458–1530) famously evoked the end of Icarus' career as a moment in which beauty transcended death, and ambition outweighed any sense of human limit:

> With such a fall well may he be content,
> if, soaring to the sky dove-like and brave,
> he with too fierce a flame was burnt and spent;

his name now echoes loud in every wave,
across the sea, throughout an element;
whoever in the world gained such a grave?[31]

When it comes to representations of high-flying in the visual arts, the most influential image is undoubtedly *The Fall of Icarus* attributed to Pieter Bruegel the Elder (c. 1555; see pl. VI).[32] Drawing on Ovid's account in the *Metamorphoses* yet at the same time diverging systematically from it, Bruegel's vision has inspired numerous spin-offs in modern times, in media as diverse as theatre, poetry, sci-fi cinema and rock music.[33] The painting is a study in indifference, a demonstration that everyday life can continue at its own rhythm oblivious of the intrusion of an explosive moment from the exotic world of myth. As in Ovid, three peasants put in an appearance: a fisherman, a shepherd and a ploughman. But whereas in Ovid these bystanders gawp in astonishment at the joint fly-past of Daedalus and Icarus, in Bruegel they entirely ignore the minor event at the bottom right of the image as Icarus disappears beneath the waves, head first and legs flailing. Of Daedalus there is no sign; any outpouring of fatherly grief would conflict with the dominant note of passionless tranquillity. Instead there is the ploughman, whose painstaking concentration on his task is the very embodiment of 'absence of excess' – an equivalent, it has been persuasively suggested, of the Ovidian Daedalus' warning to Icarus to maintain a middle path.[34]

W. H. Auden went to the heart of the matter in his poem 'Musée des Beaux Arts'. 'About suffering they were never wrong, The Old Masters', Auden begins. What 'the Old Masters' realized was that suffering takes place while ordinary people are going about their daily lives. While, in Bruegel's painting, the ploughman might have heard the splash of Icarus' fall, 'for him it was not an important failure'; and the sun kept shining in spite of it all. Auden was wrong about one thing, though: not all the 'Old Masters' saw it like that.

Francisco de Goya,
*Daedalus Watching
his Son Icarus Fall,*
c. 1825–28.

Honoré Daumier,
The Fall of Icarus, 1842.

Frederic Leighton, *Daedalus and Icarus*, c. 1869.

For some of them, suffering was front and centre stage. In a powerful drawing by Goya, for example (c. 1825–28), the open-mouthed horror on the father's face expresses the very opposite of apathy (see p. 89, above). And there was room for other moods too. A lithograph by Honoré Daumier (see p. 89, below) has enormous fun with the idea of Daedalus as astronomer (1842). A generation later, the artist Frederic, Lord Leighton found nothing to laugh about (see opposite); he saw only cool beauty and controlled heroism (c. 1869).

In 20th-century art it was Icarus, not Daedalus, who most often stole the artistic show, as in the striking paper cut-out by Henri Matisse (1944), in which the little red heart of passion contrasts with the falling black body, the brilliant blue sky and the fiery yellow sunbursts. But Daedalus has enjoyed his share of the limelight too, not least in the work of sculptors. In Eduardo Paolozzi's bronze statue *Daedalus on Wheels* (1994; see overleaf), displayed in the grounds of Jesus College, Cambridge, the robot-like figure is fully in keeping with the artist's general style, yet it is also peculiarly relevant to this particular subject, given the mythical connotations of Daedalus as master of the boundary between the living and the artificial. The wheeled platform that Daedalus stands on recalls the carts used in a bronze foundry:[35] the sculpted sculptor enacts the method of his own creation.[36]

Matisse and Paolozzi are just two out of dozens of 20th-century artists who re-imagined Daedaus or Icarus. Why should the mythical pair have come to special prominence at just this period? One reason lies in the development of air travel and the consequent imaginative interest aroused by the notion of flight.[37] Another relates to a renewed fascination with mazes, whether in puzzles or gardens or as sites for spiritual meditation.[38] To illustrate these trends we can cite two remarkable individuals. Each was psychologically attracted to this tale of aspiration and catastrophe, ingenuity and failure – perhaps because each, in his own way, exhibited an obsessive and hyperbolical personality.

Eduardo Paolozzi, *Daedalus on Wheels*, 1994.

Gabriele D'Annunzio (1863–1938) was a poet, novelist, Italian war hero, playboy, ultra-fastidious sexual predator, proto-fascist and would-be superman.[39] His exploits as an aviator (though not as a pilot) during World War I were the stuff of legend, enhanced by the wounds he received under fire, including the loss of an eye. At the Brescia air show of 1909 (the airport is still named after him) he recited a poem about Icarus to an audience of 50,000. For D'Annunzio, in his poetry, his novels and in his own life, flying high like Icarus was a way of attaining not just physical freedom but a superior, quasi-divine level of existence. As he put it in the novel *Forse che sì forse che no* (1910): 'The new instrument [i.e. aircraft] seemed to raise man above his fate, bestowing upon him not only a new dominion but also a sixth sense.'[40] The incarnation of the myth is the novel's protagonist Paolo Tarsis, lover of fast cars, fast aircraft and fast living. When Paolo plunges to his death in an air crash on a Sardinian beach, his downfall strikes a note not of ignominy but of glorious super-heroism. For D'Annunzio, as for Tarsis, the career of Icarus was the defining metaphor of his life.

Our other Daedalus-and-Icarus obsessive is Michael Ayrton (1921–1975), sculptor, writer and maze-maker *extraordinaire*. Has any other artist in history been so gripped by a single mythical *idée fixe* as Ayrton was by Daedalus and Icarus? He created hundreds of images of them, even outstripping Picasso's preoccupation with the Minotaur. In fact, Picasso not only influenced Ayrton but also aroused his artistic jealousy. One expression of this was Ayrton's own repeated creation of images of the Minotaur, a striking example being the bronze *Point of Departure* (1970), in which a triumphant Icarus soars above a cowering Minotaur (see overleaf). Ayrton's implied self-identification with Daedalus led him to design real mazes, and also to write the prize-winning novel *The Maze Maker* (1967), purporting to be an autobiography of Daedalus. For Ayrton, mazes constituted a fundamental dimension of existence:

93

Michael Ayrton,
Point of Departure, 1970.

'Such a total maze each man makes around himself and each is different from every other, for each contains the length, breadth, height and depth of his own life.'[41] Yet there was also an element of Icarus about Ayrton, as he sought to outdo his own gifted father, the poet and literary critic Gerald Gould (Ayrton chose to take the surname of his mother, the politician Barbara Ayrton). The psychological oscillation between Daedalus and Icarus comes across in two contrasting passages from Ayrton's fiction. First, rather simplistically, there is this extract from *The Testament of Daedalus* (1962):

> Icarus is more famous than I am, although he had no
> particular skill and could not be described as a maker of
> anything, except his own death, which he contrived in
> a vainglorious and very poetic manner. He is, however,
> more famous than I am and perhaps I resent that.[42]

Second, and more thoughtfully, there is this from *The Maze Maker*:

> I do not think I was an easy father for Icarus to have. I
> watched him too closely, hoping passionately to find in
> him my own particular virtues and have him surpass me
> in them.[43]

Icarus (more than Daedalus) remains a psychologically powerful image. In 1973 the controversial Los Angeles-based artist Chris Burden enacted an artwork named *Icarus*. For the performance, the artist lay naked on the ground, flat on his back. Assistants placed a sheet of glass on each of his shoulders, poured gasoline onto the glass, and ignited it.[44] The impression created was that of a human figure equipped with burning wings. After a few seconds Burden leapt up, causing the glass to crash to the floor. A decade later the heavy-metal rock band Iron Maiden released their own version of the tale:

> Fly and touch the sun, yeah, mmm
> Now the crowd breaks and a young boy appears
> Looks the old man in the eye
> As he spreads his wings and shouts at the crowd
> His eyes seem so glazed
> As he flies on the wings of a dream
> Now he knows his father betrayed
> Now his wings turn to ashes, to ashes his grave.[45]

In the business world, the concept of the 'Icarus paradox' has been coined to denote the way in which a firm may come to grief by remaining loyal to the winning formula that made it successful in the first place.[46] Coming to grief is not, though, the main concept that aviation groups have in mind when they adopt the ancient flyer for their logo, any more than it was for the similarly named predecessor of Olympic Airways that went bankrupt soon after it was established.[47] It is all too easy to mock such apparent misnomers: were these people really unaware (you might incredulously ask) that Icarus had a fatal crash landing? But such mockery, at least partly, misses the point. After all, one of the perspectives from which Icarus has been and can still be viewed is that of a young 'airman' whose exploits were bold and glorious. As always, the many-sidedness of Greek myths, their chameleon-like multiplicity, is one of their most potent characteristics.

1

Peter Paul Rubens, *Prometheus Bound*, c.1611–18.

11
Piero di Cosimo, *The Myth of Prometheus*, c.1515.

III
Attributed to the Ixion Painter, Medea killing her son, Campanian amphora, c. 340–330 BCE.

IV
Alphonse Mucha, *Médée*, poster for a performance by Sarah Bernhardt at the Théâtre de la Renaissance, Paris, 1898.

V

The fall of Icarus, fresco, House of the
Priest Amandus, Pompeii, *c.* 20 BCE–50 CE.

VI
Attributed to Pieter Bruegel the Elder,
Landscape with the Fall of Icarus, c.1555.

VII

Pasiphae, Daedalus and Icarus, Roman mosaic from Zeugma, 2nd century CE.

VIII

Miniature of Christine de Pizan and Minerva, from Christine de Pizan's *Le livre des faits d'armes et de chevalerie*, 1434.

CHAPTER 4

The Amazons

How do myths relate to events and people in 'the real world'? The question looks deceptively simple but is in fact enormously complicated. For one thing, the answer varies according to the myth being discussed. I suspect that few people nowadays will be much bothered to ask whether Prometheus or Medea or Daedalus and Icarus 'really existed'; if they do ask it, they won't gain much by doing so. But with the mythical women whom the Greeks and Romans called Amazons, things are – or seem to be – different. The possibility of a relationship between these female warriors and certain real-world ethnographic groups whom they allegedly resemble continues to be a burning issue. Was there, once upon a time, a matriarchal society, in which females as opposed to males held the reins of power? If so, do myths about the Amazons provide evidence for that society? Although these matters have been raised with particular reference to prehistoric archaeology, their ramifications extend far more widely. The idea of a society in which women exercise institutional power over men – even, more extraordinarily, the idea of an all-female society – all this takes us deep into the politics of gender.

We shall begin by trying to disentangle some of the intricate threads in the ancient myths about Amazons. After that we shall look at how those myths have been subsequently reused in order to think about the world. Our post-classical journey will take us from a remarkable proto-feminist writer of the Middle Ages, via a Spanish *conquistador*, to *Xena: Warrior Princess* and *Wonder Woman*. Along the way we shall try to dissect the implications of that super-tricky problem 'Did the Amazons really exist'?

Amazonian myths in antiquity

Three strands can be identified in myths that the Greeks and Romans told about Amazons. The first strand is ethnographical: the Amazons are imagined as a distinctive ethnic group poised somewhere in a no man's land (literally!) between myth and history/geography. The second strand consists of narratives about the exploits of individual Amazons such as Penthesilea, Hippolyte and Antiope in their interaction with Greeks and others. The third strand relates to one remarkable and ideologically formative event in the mythical past: the Amazons' invasion of Greece. We shall examine each strand in turn.

A good starting point for the ethnographical perspective is a passage from the historian Diodorus Siculus:

> Now in the country along the Thermodon river [in northern Anatolia, flowing into the Black Sea], as the account goes, the sovereignty was in the hands of a people among whom the women held the supreme power, and its women performed the services of war just as did the men. Of these women one, who possessed the royal authority, was remarkable for her prowess in war and her bodily strength, and gathering together an army of women she drilled it in the use of arms and subdued in war some of the neighbouring peoples. And since her valour and fame increased, she made war upon people after people of neighbouring lands, and as the tide of her fortune continued favourable, she was so filled with pride that she gave herself the appellation of Daughter of

Ares; but to the men she assigned the spinning of wool
and such other domestic duties as belong to women.
Laws were also established by her, by virtue of which she
led forth the women to the contests of war, but upon
the men she fastened humiliation and slavery. And as
for their children, they mutilated both the legs and the
arms of the males, incapacitating them in this way for
the demands of war, and in the case of the females they
seared the right breast that it might not project when
their bodies matured and be in the way; and it is for
this reason that the nation of the Amazons received the
appellation it bears.[1]

Diodorus' account is amplified by his near contemporary the
geographer Strabo, who situates the Amazons further east towards
the Caspian Sea and includes more information about their lifestyle.[2] He emphasizes the importance they gave to raising horses
and to archery, and confirms the detail about the cauterizing of
the right breast to facilitate javelin throwing. This detail is evidently linked to an etymological perspective (Greek *a-*, a prefix
meaning 'not', + *mazos*, a dialectal variant of *mastos*, or 'breast'); it
recurs throughout the ancient tradition, and still persists as a key
part of contemporary conceptions of the Amazon. Some modern
scholars have taken the ancients to task for misusing etymology
so as to generate the 'factoid' of the single breast.[3] It is true that
the ancient artistic tradition fails to corroborate the image of
the single-breasted Amazon, and even in antiquity alternative
etymologies were floated, such as 'not bread' (i.e. the Amazons
were meat-eaters), or 'living together', or 'with girdles'.[4] It is also
true that modern etymologists have suggested a whole range of
possible derivations, from words meaning 'husbandless' or 'warriors' or 'wearing belts'.[5] Nevertheless, it is vital to realize that
ancient etymologies were designed to do a quite different job from

modern ones.[6] Whereas modern etymology deploys the findings of historical linguistics to trace developments in the meanings of words over time, ancient etymology uses language to speculate about multiple aspects of the world. In repeatedly coming back to the idea of a breast that had been deliberately maimed or in some other way minimized,[7] ancient writers (who were, with few exceptions, men) were making an ideological point, by implying that there was something partly un-maternal or even unfeminine about the idea of a woman dedicated to ultra-militarism. To be credited with only a single breast put the Amazons into a category common in Greek myth, that of a character who combined a special power with a counterbalancing defect. For women to be the equals of men in martial prowess meant – according to Greek assumptions – that they were *more* than women. To possess that kind of extraordinary power and yet still remain human demanded, according to the logic of Greek myth, that their power be limited by a corresponding flaw. Just as the superhuman insight of the seer Teiresias was counterpoised by his physical blindness, so the Amazons' supra-female fighting capacity was counterbalanced by something that rendered them less than complete women. They were not *always* depicted thus: the logic of Greek myth is not rigid. But when they *were* so imagined, they were exemplifying the mythical logic of power-with-defect.

If focusing on the Amazons' breast(s) illustrates one kind of fascination with these women, another relates to their sexual practices. For a two-month period every spring, reports Strabo, the women climbed up to a nearby mountainous area to copulate promiscuously ('anyone with anyone') with males from a neighbouring tribe (the Gargarians).[8] The female babies born after these interludes were raised by the Amazons themselves; the males were looked after by the Gargarians. What is clear from this account is that the Amazons were organized – a trait that Strabo, revealingly, confesses that he finds astonishing. The

women founded cities and conducted long-range military expedi-
tions, activities that demonstrated a sense of common purpose
and depended on a high degree of discipline. Their arrangements
for childbearing and child-rearing were systematic too, geared
as they were to promote and continue the Amazons' preferred,
largely male-free lifestyle.

The descriptions of the Amazons by Diodorus and Strabo
belonged to an imaginative tradition going back hundreds of
years. Already for Herodotus (5th century BCE), the Amazons
were an independent-minded group of women who gave as good
as they got in their dealings with men. The historian portrays
them as the ancestors of the Sarmatians, dwellers in the steppes
of Scythia.[9] Some Amazons, relates Herodotus, had once been
seized by Greeks from their homeland near the river Thermodon
and abducted on board ship. Although they escaped by murdering their captors, the Amazons' ignorance of sailing left them at
the mercy of wind and wave. They drifted northwards across the
Black Sea, eventually ending up in the territory of the Scythians.
True to type, these Amazons were organized and aggressive: they
stole horses from a grazing herd, and soon came into violent conflict with the local Scythian males. But most tales about Amazons
concern sex as well as violence; after all, the very fact that the
Amazons constituted an ongoing ethnographic group entailed
that they reproduced. Herodotus describes how the Amazons
suggested to the young Scythian men that the two communities
should marry, pool their resources and head north-east beyond the
river Tanais (present-day Don). Typically, it was the Amazons who
made the running in the prenuptial negotiations; as Herodotus
puts it, 'the men were unable to learn the women's language, but
the women succeeded in picking up the men's'.[10] Marriage did
nothing to erode the Amazons' independence, a characteristic
that persisted in their alleged descendants the Sarmatians, whose
women hunted on horseback, sometimes went to war dressed in

male clothing, and were forbidden from marrying till they had killed an enemy in battle.

The ethnographic perspective on the Amazons is not restricted to historians and geographers. In his epic poem about Jason and the Golden Fleece, Apollonius of Rhodes provides his own vignette of Amazonian society, as the Argonauts sail past the mouth of the river Thermodon on their voyage along the Black Sea coast. Apollonius derives Amazonian militarism from their ultimate ancestor, the war god Ares.[11] But Ares' bedmate on the relevant occasion was the nymph Harmonia, a detail that might hint at another familiar aspect of Amazonian society: its orderliness ('harmony').[12]

The literary sources are complemented by hundreds of representations by artists. Such images regularly demonstrate the women's involvement in battle, often on horseback (see opposite, above), armed with spear, battle-axe or bow. What impresses is not only

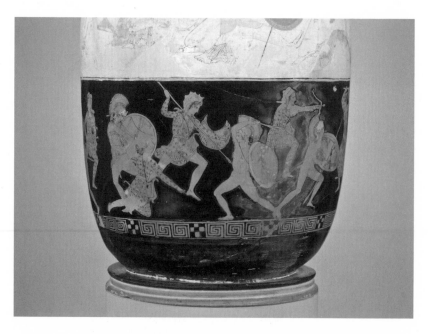

Attributed to the Eretria Painter, Amazonomachy, terracotta *lekythos*, c. 420 BCE.

Sarcophagus with
Amazons, from Cyprus,
second half of the
4th century BCE.

Naked Amazon
in combat,
Corinthian *lekythos*,
c. 575–550 BCE.

the Amazons' capacity to match their Greek opponents in aggressiveness, but also their visible difference, especially as expressed through their distinctive costume of soft cap, belted, patterned tunic and decorated leggings (see p. 102). Occasionally, though, their separateness is marked by the total or partial absence of clothing (see p. 103, below). Prominence is often given to Amazonian breasts, even if, as we have noticed already, the women are not depicted as single-breasted (see opposite). Martial prowess mixed with eroticism: the classic Amazonian cocktail.

Turning from the Amazons imagined as a collective to myths about individual, named warrior women, we begin with the most famous of them all: Penthesilea. Texts that mention her range from the few surviving fragments of an early epic poem called the *Aithiopis* (perhaps 7th century BCE) to the thousand-line-long first book of the *Posthomerica* by the epic poet Quintus of Smyrna (perhaps 4th century CE), which took up the narrative of the Trojan War where the *Iliad* had left off. Penthesilea was the daughter of Ares and an Amazon queen called Otrere. From Quintus we learn that, having accidentally killed her sister Hippolyte (Penthesilea hurled her spear at a stag but missed),[13] Penthesilea had to leave her homeland to seek ritual purification. This she received from Priam at Troy, a debt she repaid by helping him, at the head of a troop of her fellow Amazons, during the siege of the city by the Greeks. When at last she succumbed to a spear thrust from Achilles (see p. 106), the peerless hero fell in love with her, either when their eyes met just before she died, or when he stripped the armour from her corpse to reveal the beautiful woman beneath. Instead of slaying her, observes Quintus, Achilles might have borne her to his home to be his bride – another variant on the familiar double-edged Amazonian theme that combined prowess on the battlefield with sexual attractiveness. Not surprisingly, this duality, expressed through the exchange of gazes, proved irresistible to visual artists. One of the most famous of all Greek vases, Exekias' black-figure

Statue of a wounded Amazon, 1st–2nd century CE.

Attributed to Exekias, Attic amphora with
Achilles and Penthesilea, c. 530–525 BCE.

amphora now housed in the British Museum, unforgettably cap-
tures the crucial moment. Shifting the balance away from violence
and towards the erotic – and from armour towards nudity – is the
scene on a 2nd-century CE sarcophagus from Thessaloniki in which
Achilles tenderly supports the dying Amazon (see opposite); in so
doing he conveniently displays to the viewer not only his own
heroically naked body, but hers too.

Another Amazon who became embroiled with one of the
mightiest Greek heroes was Queen Hippolyte (to the Romans,
Hippolyta). The hero was Heracles, whose ninth Labour involved
leading an expeditionary force into Amazonian territory and
obtaining Hippolyte's belt. Sometimes unhelpfully called a 'girdle',
this was no humble item of intimate clothing, but rather a talisman of sovereignty conferred by Ares.[14] The fact that this time,

Achilles holding Penthesilea, sarcophagus from Thessaloniki, *c.* 180 CE.

in contrast with most of his other Labours, Heracles did not act alone showed just how formidable the Amazons were. One version of what happened was that Hippolyte handed over the belt without bloodshed (see p. 202), perhaps as a ransom for her sister Melanippe, whom Heracles had seized; but that scenario does not credit Heracles with much effort.[15] More dramatic, and certainly more violent, was an account reported by Apollodorus. In this version the goddess Hera, Heracles' inveterate opponent, disguised herself as an Amazon and convinced the real Amazons that Heracles was abducting their queen. In the battle that followed, Heracles slew Hippolyte and captured the belt.[16]

Many of the greatest Greek heroes included encounters with the Amazons in their list of accomplishments. To Achilles and Heracles we can add Bellerophon, whose slaughter of these 'women the equal of men' is mentioned already in the *Iliad*.[17] Theseus was another; his Amazon was Antiope.[18] Their relationship illustrates an important truth: that one of the most variable features of Greek mythical narratives consists of the psychological motivations of the characters. In his mytho-biography of Theseus, a work situated on the fuzzy boundary between legend and history, the essayist Plutarch (*c.* 45–*c.* 120 CE) records a series of variants of the Theseus–Antiope encounter.[19] One scenario was that Theseus accompanied Heracles on his visit to the Amazons and was rewarded with Antiope as his trophy for services rendered on the battlefield. Alternatively, Theseus captured Antiope when he made his own independent expedition against the Amazons. Alternatively again, he did not capture her but tricked her: when she was sent to offer Theseus gifts from the initially well-disposed Amazons, Theseus invited her on board his ship – and promptly sailed off. But others told a quite different tale. On this view, Antiope (sometimes named as Hippolyte) fell in love with Theseus and became his wife.[20] Their son would be the ill-starred Hippolytus.

The fact that Antiope married was an untypical lifestyle change for an Amazon. The normal pattern was that the warrior women lived apart from men except in the mating season. Interestingly, in the case of non-Amazon women who in some way resembled the Amazons, the idea of independence from men could be projected into its most extreme form: virginity. The classic case is Camilla, the warrior *virgo* who led her all-female troop of cavalry into battle against Aeneas, as described in Virgil's *Aeneid*.[21] She was not an Amazon by birth or residence, since her tribe were the Volsci of central Italy. But she was *like* an Amazon, as were her female comrades in battle Larina, Tulla and the axe-wielding Tarpeia.[22] Like the authentic Amazons, Camilla was a magnificent horsewoman; like them, she brandished bow, javelin and axe with equal lethalness. Also typically Amazonian were her breasts, one of which she exposed as she rode; it was below that very breast that she was speared to death by Arruns, Aeneas' Etruscan ally. Appropriately enough, it was the divinity who had most in common with the Amazons, the virgin archeress Diana (to the Greeks, Artemis), who avenged Camilla when she sent one of her faithful nymphs to shoot Arruns dead. Though Camilla's lifestyle excluded sexual relations with men, men did not find her unattractive; far from it. When she passed by, says Virgil, young men streamed from house and field to marvel at her smooth shoulders, her flowing hair, her quiver and her lance.[23]

In many myths about Amazonian military action, the warrior women were represented as repelling an external threat, or (as at the siege of Troy) as helping their allies to do so. Camilla likewise aided native Italians to resist incomers. But Amazonian militarism did not restrict itself to homeland defence. As Diodorus put it, 'the nation of the Amazons, after it was once organized, was so distinguished for its manly prowess that it not only overran much of the neighbouring territory but even subdued a large part of Europe and Asia'.[24] One foreign campaign in particular made an indelible mark on Greek myth: the Amazons' legendary invasion of Greece.

There are few clearer cases than this of the ideological purpose that Greek mythology could be made to serve. We spoke of an invasion of Greece; but what was actually alleged to have taken place was an invasion of *Athens*, which the Athenians heroically repelled. From the beginning of the 5th century BCE onwards, this imagined event held a place of honour in the patriotic Athenian self-image. Numerous myth-tellers shared in lauding this example of military prowess, a glorious antecedent of the Athenians' starring role in a subsequent and undeniably historical event: the defeat of the Persian expedition to Greece in the early 5th century BCE.[25] Already the poet Pindar and the dramatist Aeschylus knew of the incursion of the Amazons, but for a detailed account we need to return to Plutarch's *Life of Theseus*.[26] The motivation for the invasion, Plutarch tells us, was to avenge Theseus' abduction of

Antiope (or Hippolyte). Different sources gave different accounts of the Amazons' route into Greece, but the upshot was that they made their way to Athens and seized two topographically modest hills there, the Areopagus and the Pnyx, from which to threaten the Athenians' loftier citadel, the Acropolis. The conflict was protracted, fierce and balanced on a knife edge. Some said that, after three months of war, a treaty was negotiated; what every source agreed on was that the Amazons were eventually driven off. In many visual 'Amazonomachies' there is an evident equivalence between Greek and Amazonian combatants, in terms of who has the upper hand. However, certain patriotically pro-Athenian written sources were less even-handed. In his *Funeral Oration*, composed to praise Athenians who died in a recent war, the orator Lysias (c. 445–c. 380 BCE) unequivocally states that the women got what they deserved:

> [The Amazons] were accounted as men for their high courage, rather than as women for their sex ... Ruling over many nations, they had in fact achieved the enslavement of those around them; yet, hearing by report concerning this our country how great was its renown, they were moved by increase of glory and high ambition to muster the most warlike of the nations and march with them against this city. But having met with valiant men they found their spirit now was like to their sex; the repute that they got was the reverse of the former, and by their perils rather than by their bodies they were deemed to be women. ... They perished on the spot, and were punished for their folly, thus making our city's memory imperishable for its valour; while owing to their disaster in this region they rendered their own country nameless. And so those women, by their unjust greed for others' land, justly lost their own.[27]

Like every Greek myth, that of the Amazons could be shaped and exploited. It suits Lysias to ignore the motif of justified Amazonian retaliation for a wrong done to them, and to stress instead that they were bent on a land grab. But whatever the nuances in motivation, the Amazon invasion achieved iconic status. If one serviceable definition of myth is 'a socially powerful traditional story', then the Amazon invasion of Athens was a myth par excellence.

From late antiquity to modernity

When it comes to the post-classical re-imagining of tales about the Amazons, all three of our strands achieved prominence at various times. For successive generations of ancient Athenians, the mythical defeat of the Amazon invasion was a marker of their ancestors' valour and a source of reflected glory for themselves. However, when the Athenian city-state declined in importance and eventually became no more than a distant memory, myth-tellers no longer derived the same kind of ideological benefit from recalling that episode as a specifically Athenian achievement. But the generalized theme of the Amazonomachy – a battle between Amazons and *Greeks* – retained its impact, especially in the visual arts. As for our two other thematic strands – the gender-focused ethnographic perspective, and the exploits of individual, strong and fascinating warrior women – these never ceased to mesmerize readers of texts and viewers of art, long after the demise of the civilizations that had originally told the stories.

It is difficult to conceive of a human society whose members' lives are not decisively shaped by considerations of sex and gender; the ethnographic model of the Amazons offers one way of thinking about these issues. However, the question of how to evaluate that model has been answered in very different ways. About Amazonian procreative practices, as we have seen, Greek and Roman writers were not univocal. On the one hand, the Amazons were said to have led an exclusively female existence for most of the time; to that extent they could be praised as paradigms of chastity. On the other hand, the propagation of their group inevitably entailed sexual intercourse with men at certain times; those couplings, represented sometimes as promiscuous and usually as untrammelled by the normal prescriptions of marriage, could be condemned as morally reprehensible. This double perspective opened the way for opposed perceptions of Amazonian sexual morality, either as virtuous or scandalous.

In the European Christian worlds of late antiquity and the Middle Ages, both perceptions are found.[28] Condemnation of Amazonian wickedness goes back at least as far as the North African Christian apologist Tertullian (c. 160–240 CE), who used the myth to vilify his inveterate opponent, the 'heretic' Marcion. Marcion came from the Euxine (Black Sea) region, which gave Tertullian useful ammunition for a no-holds-barred assault:

The sea called Euxine, or 'hospitable', is belied by
its nature and put to ridicule by its name. Even its
situation would prevent you from reckoning Pontus
hospitable: as though ashamed of its own barbarism
it has set itself at a distance from our more civilized
waters. Strange tribes inhabit it – if indeed living in a
wagon can be called inhabiting. These have no certain
dwelling-place: their life is uncouth: their sexual
activity is promiscuous, and for the most part unhidden
even when they hide it: they advertise it by hanging
a quiver on the yoke of the wagon, so that none may
inadvertently break in. So little respect have they for
their weapons of war. They carve up their fathers'
corpses along with mutton, to gulp down at banquets.
If any die in a condition not good for eating, their
death is a disgrace. Women also have lost the gentleness,
along with the modesty, of their sex. They display their

breasts, they do their house-work with battle-axes, they prefer fighting to matrimonial duty.[29]

Naked and libidinous, with a touch of cannibalism thrown in: not much to be said for *that* bunch of women. Tertullian's negative take on the Amazons persisted into the Middle Ages, so that, in his lengthy *Song of Troy* (12th–13th century), the poet Herbort von Fritslar could envisage them as savage, mannish creatures possessed by the Devil.[30]

However, the positive evaluation was commoner in the Middle Ages than the negative. In the 13th-century *Alexander Romance* by the Austrian poet Rudolph of Ems, what comes across is the Amazons' courtliness, their belonging to a world of chivalry and gallantry. An Amazon thus became the prototype of the Christian ideal of the *virgo militans*.[31] Nowhere is respect for the Amazons more evident than in the writings of Christine de Pizan, whom we discussed in relation to the myth of Medea. Christine's pioneering *Book of the City of Ladies* describes the creation of a sacred city by the Ladies Reason, Rectitude and Justice. At the head of the city was the Virgin Mary, but another powerful role model was Athena/Minerva, regarded by Christine as a brilliantly gifted and inventive young woman whom her contemporaries foolishly declared to be a goddess (see pl. VIII).[32] Also exemplary, for their courage and ingenuity, were the Amazons, whose realm, according to Christine, lasted for over 800 years.[33] A detail worth mentioning is that Christine makes a rather unusual differentiation in respect of the motif of the maimed breast: Amazons of noble birth supposedly had the left breast cauterized to facilitate the bearing of a shield, whereas non-nobles lost the right breast in the interests of archery.

Early modern travellers' tales from across Europe repeatedly depict the Amazons in terms of gender-dominated ethnography. In the immensely popular 14th-century work known as *The Travels of*

Sir John Mandeville, they appear as noble and wise warriors, whose queen was elected on the basis of her fighting ability.[34] They did have male lovers but lived apart from them, visiting them for eight or nine days at a time in order to conceive. As for their children, Mandeville refers to them via a variation on the familiar theme of Amazonian breasts:

> If any of them bears a child and it is a son, they keep it until it can speak and walk and eat by itself and then they send it to the father – or they kill it. If they have a girl child, they cut off one of her breasts and cauterize it; in the case of a woman of great estate, the left one, so that she can carry her shield better, and, in one of low degree, they cut off the right, so that it will not hinder them shooting.

There were varying opinions about the Amazons' location. Mandeville placed them near Chaldea (southern Iraq). According to the chronicle by Gaspar de Carvajal (*c.* 1500–1584), by contrast, the mid-16th-century Spanish *conquistador* Francisco de Orellana famously encountered a tribe of Amazon equivalents in South America:

> These women are very white and tall, and have hair very long and braided and wound about the head, and they are very robust and go about naked, [but] with their privy parts covered, with their bows and arrows in their hands, doing as much fighting as ten Indian men, and indeed there was one woman among these who shot an arrow a span deep into one of the brigantines, and others less deep, so that our brigantines looked like porcupines.[35]

Many of the stock motifs recur in Carvajal's account: the women consorted with males from a neighbouring territory at certain times when the desire came upon them; they killed male children and sent the bodies to their fathers, but female children they raised themselves and instructed them in the arts of war; they were ruled by a woman; and so on. The mighty river Amazon was named in their honour. Another writer and explorer who located them in South America (this time Guyana) was Sir Walter Raleigh. According to his narrative (1596), they mated with neighbouring males annually in April. He mentions a story that each woman cut off her right breast but says that he does not believe it.[36] As late as the 18th century, ethnographers still included the Amazons in their purview. In writing about the customs of the Iroquois and the Huron, for

After Guilio Romano, *Marfisa*, mid-17th century.

example, the Jesuit missionary Joseph-François Lafitau suggested in 1724 that the gynaecocratic political arrangements among those peoples might have originated among the ancient Amazons, from whom they might (he thought) have been descended.[37]

When it comes to the exploits of individual Amazon-like women, the Renaissance offers some striking representations. Particularly impressive are two contrasting female warriors in Ludovico Ariosto's sophisticated tale of chivalric derring-do *Orlando Furioso* (1532). The female knight Bradamante falls in love with the Saracen warrior Ruggiero, whom she eventually marries in the poem's final Canto (after his conversion to Christianity), when he has defeated her in combat (which was the condition she stipulated). Ruggiero's sister, the headstrong, lioness-suckled Marfisa,[38] goes much further in battle-hardened ferocity: '[She] welcomed the clash of arms and chargers, the flight of spears and arrows, the shedding of blood, the commerce of death.'[39] She dresses like a male knight, remains undefeated, never marries, and eventually enlists in Charlemagne's army (see p. 115). Although the narrator likens her to Penthesilea,[40] she never succumbs to an 'Achilles moment'. For all her golden curls and delicately beautiful face, she is a free spirit unconstrained by ties to men or women: 'I belong to nobody, only to myself.'[41]

Among the spiritual descendants of these great-hearted women is Marianne (the embodiment of the French Republic) as evoked in Delacroix's iconic portrayal of *Liberty Leading the People* (1830; see opposite, above). Like so many Amazonian characters, Marianne expresses the essence of her physicality through her breasts: their exposure signifies freedom from constraint. As Marina Warner has argued, what counts especially is the asymmetry of the posture, recalling the 'slipped tunic' often worn by ancient Amazons (see opposite, below left): '[It] suggests both the breast's function as nourishment (one at a time is revealed to feed) and the ardent hoyden, so caught up in the action of the moment that she has no

Eugène Delacroix, *Liberty Leading the People*, 1830.

Wounded Amazon, from the altar
of the Artemision, Ephesos, second
half of the 4th century BCE.

Honoré Daumier,
The Amazons, 1842.

thought for her person.'[42] More discreet, but still partially visible, are the breasts of the two principals in Honoré Daumier's delicious lithograph *The Amazons* (1842; see p. 117, below right), a cross between a military parade and a schoolgirl gymkhana. Ever since classical antiquity, retellings of Greek myths have made room for the ridiculous as well as the sublime.

Our final mythological strand concerns the Amazons' invasion of Greece. As we said a moment ago, the specifically Athenian dimension of this event diminished in importance in post-classical myth-telling, in proportion to the decline of the Athenian city-state whose ideological purpose it previously served. However, when reconceived – and sometimes relocated away from Athens – as the basis for a generalized 'Greeks against (wild) non-Greeks' / 'civilized versus barbarian' / 'self versus other' opposition, the image of the Amazonomachy continued to flourish. Few versions of this theme can rival the tremendous panache of Rubens's

Peter Paul Rubens, *The Battle of the Amazons*, c. 1615.

action-packed oil on wood *The Battle of the Amazons* (c. 1615).[43] The focal point is the bridge; the location is presumably the river Thermodon, in the Amazons' Anatolian homeland. The brutality of the scene, exemplified by the headless corpse dripping blood from the edge of the bridge into the body-strewn river below, exceeds anything in the ancient artistic tradition of Amazonomachies.

Recent and contemporary Amazons

Perhaps the single most influential name in the modern interpretation of the Amazons is that of J. J. Bachofen, philologist, anthropologist and sometime professor of Roman law at the University of Basel (1815–1887).[44] In Bachofen's view, the evolution of human culture can be seen as a progression from a gynaecocratic (female-powered) to a patriarchal social order. The gynaecocratic stage can be subdivided into (1) an 'Aphroditean' phase, when procreation took place on the basis of women's promiscuous sexual relations as they had been forced upon them by men; and (2) a 'Demetrian' phase, characterized by orderly, marriage-based social arrangements and matrilinear succession. Between those two phases there was, according to Bachofen, an intermediate stage corresponding to the lifestyle of the Amazons, when women asserted a temporary claim to independence. Only after the completion of all three of these female-oriented phases did social arrangements develop to the stage of 'father-right', the condition of society in which males held the upper hand.

Bachofen's schematic and speculative idea that a gynaecocratic phase preceded the advent of patriarchy has proved enormously influential, and not just within academia. It has been taken up, for example, by a number of scholars working on Mediterranean prehistory and by some feminist thinkers[45] (not to mention by Friedrich Engels, who put Bachofen on a par with Darwin and Marx). However, the problem with Bachofen's central thesis is that it relies on a highly simplistic view of myth. 'All the myths relating to our subject,' he wrote, 'embody a memory of real events experienced by the human race. They represent not fictions but historical realities. The stories of the Amazons ... are real and not poetic.'[46] But the truth is that myths are imaginative creations rather than mere 'reflections' of historical or other real-world events and circumstances. In spite of the enthusiastic reception of Bachofen's ideas in certain quarters, it remains true that 'Matriarchy in the true sense has not been shown to have existed anywhere in Aegean or Near Eastern prehistory, and to this extent ... it plays no role in the history of Greek religion.'[47] It follows from this that an 'Amazonian' phase of human development is equally impossible to verify.

Another attempt to interpret Amazonian myths as reflections of social reality has been put forward by the historian and folklorist Adrienne Mayor.[48] In her view, ancient stories about the Amazons, far from being a purely fictional part of the Greco-Roman *imaginaire*, are in fact reflections of real-world communities of female, horse-riding, bow-wielding, nomadic warriors in regions from the northern Black Sea area to the steppes of Central Asia. Mayor's approach has attracted many supporters, but also many detractors.[49] On the plus side, there is the verve of the writing and the impressive breadth of data invoked; a serious weakness, though, is a tendency to lump together ancient and modern, mythical and historical evidence in a haphazard way. But maybe we can reach a compromise between the convincing and unconvincing features of Mayor's thesis by replacing the metaphor of *reflection* (an idea that underlies Bachofen's argument too) with that of *refraction*. We can then acknowledge both certain partial correspondences between the lifestyle of the mythical Amazons and that of women in certain ancient and more modern warrior communities, and the 'refractive' function – the exaggeration and the selective highlighting of certain features at the expense of others – that is the stock-in-trade of myth, as experiences and memories of real-world phenomena become adapted, moulded and reworked into a tool for thinking and feeling about the world.

Throughout the 20th century and into the 21st, the Amazon myth has continued to weave its spell. One emphasis has been on the notion of the Amazon as horse-rider. The association between Amazons and equestrianism can sometimes be just a fact of language: for example, *amazona* in, among other languages, Spanish and Modern Greek means simply 'female rider' (unlike the English word 'Amazon', which typically designates a woman who is tough and muscular). But sometimes the imagery of Amazons-as-riders has been taken much further. The impact of the athletic female body beautiful, combined with horse-riding expertise and the symbolism of armour and weapons, was exploited by the propagandists of Nazi Germany. Between 1936 and 1939, at the climax of an equestrian event in Munich in which SS riders had previously played a significant part, naked 'Amazons' – evidently the future mothers of the Aryan master race – rode in a spectacular cavalcade at the Nymphenburg Palace. Such displays were presumably aimed primarily at satisfying the voyeuristic fantasies of males, not least because Nazi ideologues targeted any aspect of homosexuality, female as well as male, for vicious eradication.

Night of the Amazons, Nazi propaganda poster, 1937.

Vastly different from such fantasies in its imaginative scope is the science fiction novella *Consider her Ways*, written by John Wyndham as long ago as 1956 but still riveting today.[50] Wyndham articulates a dystopian (or could it be utopian?) vision of a society from which all males are absent, having died out as a result of a virus that accidentally got out of control (the virus proved lethal to males but not to females). In the new, post-viral world, society is divided into various castes, each displaying physical characteristics appropriate to its social function. The model deliberately adopted by the ruling caste (the 'Doctorate') is that of ants. The worker females, for example, known as 'Amazons', are tough and muscular, and wear a distinctive uniform of sleeveless vest, denim trousers and workers' boots. (The child-bearing 'Mothers', by contrast, have grotesquely inflated bodies and wear clothes of pastel pink.) Wyndham's vision provokes reflections about what it is to envision a world whose assumptions about gender differ *toto caelo* from our own. In a world – our real, contemporary world – in which the presence of a quite different sort of virus overturned assumptions that were hitherto felt to be impregnable, Wyndham's vision has taken on an even more powerful resonance.

The Amazon myth has, it goes without saying, been taken up by women to express their individual aspirations, their collective endeavours and sometimes their sexual orientation. In the early part of the 20th century, the American expatriate writer Natalie Clifford Barney (known as 'the Amazon') founded a lesbian circle in Paris, whose members included leading artistic and intellectual figures of the day. Ever since then, the concept of the Amazon *qua* inhabitant of an imagined utopia has received star billing in numerous lesbian-oriented writings, especially from the 1960s to the 1980s.[51] Given the overlap between utopian fiction and science fiction, it is no surprise that the latter genre too has showcased the possibility of a society of Amazon-like women, as in Joanna Russ's novel *The Female Man* (1975), whose protagonist would make any self-respecting mythical Amazon proud to call her a sister: 'My mother's name was Eva, my other mother's name Alicia; I am Janet Evason. When I was thirteen I stalked and killed a wolf, alone, on North Continent above the forty-eighth parallel, using only a rifle.'[52] The female solidarity that finds its symbol in the Amazons expresses itself here through the disciplined aggression of hunting.

The image of an independent, tough, glamorous, weapon-toting female has reached its apogee in contemporary popular culture, in which Amazonian symbolism often plays a part. In the cult fantasy TV series *Xena: Warrior Princess*, the central character starts out on, morally speaking, 'the dark side', but eventually, after an encounter with Heracles, takes the path of redemption. Thanks to her relationship with her friend and possible lover Gabrielle, Xena has been embraced by some fans as a lesbian icon. Although her arms and legs are partly bare, Xena also wears armour – especially (of course) a breastplate (see overleaf, left). In a sense, this aggressive bodily display signals empowerment. As Marina Warner puts it, 'Within the phallic dialectic of conquest and battle, the Amazon, with her masculinized female appearance, effectively provides women today with freedom of speech.'[53] Yet this same imagery has its uncomfortable side, even its dangers, by bringing its images close to the region of pornography. Warner again: 'Pornography arms women and sheathes them too; implacable expressions and cruel gestures are its stock-in-trade.'[54] Rivalling Xena for iconic status is Wonder Woman, the superhero originally created for DC Comics in 1941. Officially known as Princess Diana of Themyscira (*sic*; she is also referred to as Diana – of course – Prince), she is, according to one version of her origin, the daughter of Zeus and the Amazon queen Hippolyta, and spends her time fighting for justice. As important as her genealogy is her clothing: breastplate (again: of course) and pelvic girdle serve ostensibly to sheath and shield, but in fact to emphasize the physical characteristics of her sexuality (see overleaf, right).

The continuing durability of the mythical Amazon-as-icon is clear. What is, or ought to be, also clear is that this durability is completely unaffected by the answer to the question, 'Do the Amazons reflect a real-world society that might once have existed?' The ambiguous symbolism of the female breast, the literally and metaphorically double-edged quality of armed aggression by women, the fascination of imagining a society in which permanent, institutionalized relationships between the sexes play no part – here are just a few of the issues raised by this myth. Myths are first and foremost thought experiments. The myth of the Amazons is one of the most productive and enduring experiments of all.

Xena, 1996.   *Wonder Woman* poster, 2017.

CHAPTER 5

Oedipus

Of all mythological characters, perhaps none exemplifies more clearly than Oedipus the continuing vitality of ancient Greek stories in the modern world. Freud has played a major part in this prominence, but the myth of Oedipus has far more to it than can be summed up under the heading of a Complex. In this chapter we shall be paying most of our attention to this 'other story'. It is true that, as a mythical figure, Oedipus is complex – but that is quite a different thing from 'having a Complex'. In what does this complexity consist? A major aspect of Oedipus' persona is that he is a thinker, a man beset by mysteries and puzzles that he strives obsessively to resolve. But he is also committed to the world of action, sometimes aggressively so; though never warlike or serially combative on the pattern of an Achilles or a Perseus or a Heracles, his mythical profile is that of a man easily provoked and capable of lethal violence. What completes this profile, and further enriches its complexity, is something else again: Oedipus is the unwitting perpetrator of the most horrific moral transgressions imaginable. In short, his actions and sufferings are a unique amalgam of the cerebral and the visceral.

In the Introduction we looked at a number of themes that pervade Greek mythology. Four of these dominate the story of Oedipus: family, politics, choice, and human interaction with the gods. Family: the myth explores the contorted relationships between Oedipus and his parents, his wife and his children. Politics: Oedipus is the ruler of a *polis* (a city-state), and his personal actions and sufferings have a fundamental impact on the lives of its citizens. Choice: the myth narrates the devastating emotional cost incurred by a man who chooses, come what may, to uncover the truth about his own identity. Humans and gods: one of the engines that drives events is an oracle from the god Apollo; another is the role of Apollo's seer Teiresias. What binds these themes together is an additional motif: the inevitable limitations of human understanding. At the heart of the myth are two transgressions committed by Oedipus in total ignorance of the true nature of his actions: he kills a man who, it subsequently emerges, was his father, and he marries a woman who, it is later revealed, is his mother. It is Oedipus' lack of awareness that rescues the myth from being merely a sequence of phenomenally improbable coincidences and transforms it into a story whose implications are representative of the human condition. We all act in a state of incomplete knowledge about our origins and our relationships. Oedipus' situation is, it is true, an exaggeration of that general condition of partial unawareness. This is what myths do: they exaggerate, sharpen and heighten issues taken from everyday life. Yet about Oedipus' fate each one of us might say: there but for the twists of fortune go I. This suits the myth perfectly to tragedy, the genre in which the exaggerations and sharpenings and heightenings characteristic of myth appear in their most potent form. And it is to tragedy that the most blisteringly powerful version of the Oedipus myth belongs: Sophocles' *Oedipus Rex* (in Greek, *Oedipus Tyrannos*, usually Latinized as *Tyrannus*). In that work, the pervasive imagery of blindness, both literal and metaphorical, expresses a sense of the inevitable boundaries that confine the physical and mental capacities of human beings, however insightful and privileged those human beings may seem to be.

Before getting to Sophocles, though, we need to take a step back. Already in the *Odyssey* some broad outlines of the Oedipus myth are sketched out. In Book 11 Odysseus is narrating the eerie events that befell him during his visit to the Underworld. Among the souls of the dead whom he encountered was that of Oedipus' mother, here named as Epikaste:

> [She] in the ignorance of her mind had
>   done a monstrous
> thing when she married her own son.
>   He killed his father
> and married her, but the gods soon
>   made it all known to mortals.
> But he, for all his sorrows, in beloved
>   Thebes continued
> to be lord over the Kadmeians, all
>   through the bitter designing
> of the gods; while she went down to
>   Hades of the gates, the strong one,
> knotting a noose and hanging sheer
>   from the high ceiling,
> in the constraint of her sorrow, but left
>   to him who survived her
> all the sorrows that are brought to pass
>   by a mother's Furies.[1]

The fact that Oedipus' mother/wife is Epikaste rather than Iokaste (Jocasta), as she is usually called in later tradition, illustrates the variability of names that we often find in Greek myths; this applies especially to women, perhaps a reflection of their status as 'adjuncts' to the main story, a role in which the predominantly male myth-tellers frequently cast them. A different sort of variability is exemplified by Odysseus' assertion that Oedipus continued to rule in Thebes even after the revelation about his family relationships; other mythical accounts had him go into exile immediately after the truth came out. Yet another and more significant variant relates to the detail that 'the gods soon made it all known to mortals'. Such active and explicit divine involvement is more at home in epic than in tragedy, where the purposes of the gods are often hidden from mortal gaze – something emphatically true of Sophocles' play.

Before leaving Homer's brief narrative, we need to register two gaps, which the later tradition will amply fill. The first is Oedipus' self-blinding, the hideous punishment that he inflicts on himself when the truth about his identity is revealed. The second is the overcoming of the monstrous Sphinx, a triumph that earns Oedipus the hand of the newly widowed queen and the right to occupy the vacant throne. We know of this episode especially from visual sources; in fact, it is the most commonly depicted scene in the whole of the myth – and some artists, such as the Achilles Painter, were drawn back to it repeatedly (see opposite). The story went that the goddess Hera sent the Sphinx as retribution upon the city of Thebes for a sexual crime committed by its king, Laius. (Laius had been the guest of King Pelops on a visit to the Peloponnese, and had desired and abducted Pelops' young son.) The Sphinx was a monstrous hybrid, with a woman's head, a lion's body and the wings of a bird. Its behaviour was as monstrous as its shape: it ate people, selecting its victims by asking each passer-by a riddle. The puzzle it posed was as follows: What has a single voice, and goes on four legs, then on two, then on three?[2] (The answer was man – a creature that crawls as a child, stands erect as an adult and uses a stick in old age.) If the passing traveller got the answer wrong, he or she ended up as the Sphinx's next meal. Only someone clever enough to solve the riddle could outwit the Sphinx, a defeat that would cause her to throw herself from a high rock to her death. That clever person was Oedipus – his shrewdness marking

Attributed to the Achilles Painter, Oedipus and the
Sphinx, Attic red-figure amphora, 450–440 BCE.

him out as a rather untypical breed of hero. (One would not describe Achilles or Agamemnon or Orestes or Helen or Electra or Heracles or Hecuba or Jason as especially *intelligent*; Odysseus and Medea, on the other hand, yes.) Through his confrontation with the Sphinx, Oedipus solved a general enigma about human identity. But could he solve the particular problem of his own identity? Which brings us to *Oedipus Tyrannus*.

The Greek tragedy par excellence

So as not to misunderstand Sophocles' play, we have to allow the plot to unfold in exactly the order that he designed it. That way we avoid attributing the characters with more complete knowledge of earlier events than they actually have; in other words, we let them retain their lack of knowledge until what is, for each character, their climactic moment of realization – the completion of their 'jigsaw'.

When the play opens, the city of Thebes is suffering from a plague. Conscientious ruler that he is, Oedipus is moved by the sufferings of his people. We should not be misled by the word *tyrannus* (more exactly transliterated from Greek as *turannos*) in the play's title; although it can mean 'despot', it can also simply denote a monarchical ruler, without negative overtones. Faced with the present crisis, Oedipus has sent his wife's brother Creon to seek guidance from Apollo's oracle at Delphi. When Creon returns, he reports the oracle's response: that the cause of the plague is a crime that has brought *miasma* (religious pollution) upon the city. The crime was the killing of Oedipus' predecessor, Laius; find and punish those responsible, and the plague will be lifted. So at one level the play is a murder mystery – which is unusual for Greek myth, since normally there is no doubt about the identity of a killer. Indeed, in many cases those who kill (Medea, Clytemnestra, Heracles, Theseus, Orestes, Odysseus ...) make no attempt to hide what they have done; rather, they boast of it.

But Oedipus is different. The reason he does not conceal anything is that he is unaware of having anything to conceal.

About the death of Laius Oedipus knows nothing (he believes), so he questions Creon about it. Creon relates that the killing was perpetrated by brigands – that is to say, by more than one brigand: such at least was the account given by the sole surviving eyewitness, one of Laius' servants. Oedipus resolves to find this band of murderers – a process that will take place in the full glare of public scrutiny, for present on stage throughout Oedipus' investigations, and hearing every word that is said, is the chorus of Theban elders. Oedipus will need all the help he can get, for he is (he believes) an outsider, 'a stranger to the story and a stranger to the deed'.[3] Yet, outsider though he may (seem to) be, he will fight to avenge Laius 'as though he had been my father'.[4] Not for nothing has Sophoclean irony become proverbial.

Always ready to seek external counsel, Oedipus asks the opinion of the chorus, who advise him to consult Apollo's blind seer Teiresias. But Oedipus, ahead of the game, has already summoned him. Why has he still not arrived? When he does eventually enter, accompanied by the boy who guides his faltering steps, the reason for the delay becomes clear: Teiresias is deeply reluctant to reveal what he knows (for *his* jigsaw has long been complete). Only under dire threats from Oedipus does Teiresias speak out:

> I say that you are the murderer of the man whose murderer you seek! ...
>
> I say that you are living unawares in a shameful relationship with those closest to you, and you cannot see the plight you are in.[5]

To Oedipus – on the basis of what he (thinks he) knows – these are meaningless insults. The same incomprehension greets Teiresias' riddling allusions to Oedipus' origins:

TEIRESIAS. I would never have come if you had not sent
    for me.

OEDIPUS. I did not know that your words would be
    foolish,
    or else I would hardly have summoned you to my
    house.

TEIR. I am foolish, as it seems to you; but wise to the
    parents who gave you birth.

OED. What parents? Wait! Who among mortals gave me
    birth?

TEIR. This day shall be your parent and your destroyer.

OED. What you say is too riddling and obscure.

TEIR. Aren't you the supreme solver of riddles?

OED. You taunt me about a skill in which you'll find that
    I excel.[6]

Shrewd politician that he is, Oedipus makes a perfectly reasonable inference: that Teiresias could have uttered his scurrilous nonsense only if he had been suborned by a possible rival to Oedipus' throne – the obvious candidate being Jocasta's brother Creon. A furious argument ensues between Oedipus and Creon, which is only partly calmed by Jocasta. On learning that the quarrel sprang from the words of a seer, Jocasta tries to reassure Oedipus by mocking the unreliability of prophecy. In so doing, she takes the plot forward in a crucial but not yet conclusive direction. She recalls that an oracle came once to Laius from Apollo's shrine at Delphi, predicting that he was destined to die at the hands of his son by Jocasta. Yet that son did not kill Laius, since Laius was killed by brigands at a place where three roads meet. So Jocasta soothes Oedipus, telling him to pay no heed to prophecy, for in this case prophecy was worthless.

A place where three roads meet … In the Greek symbolic imagination there is something ominous about such a place; crossroads are associated, for example, with the worship of Hecate, goddess of magic and witchcraft.[7] But for Oedipus such a location is ominous for a different reason. Jocasta's words plunge him into turmoil, since they remind him of an incident that immediately preceded his coming to Thebes: he killed a man fitting Laius' description, together with his entourage of servants, at a place where three roads meet. (It was a case of ancient road rage: neither man would lose face by giving way on a track too narrow to accommodate both.) Could *I*, Oedipus fearfully wonders, have been Laius' murderer – the very murderer I am pursuing? Nevertheless, one shred of hope remains: the man who reported the crime spoke of *brigands*, in the plural. If he sticks to his testimony, Oedipus is in the clear, since Oedipus was travelling alone. This lone eyewitness must be found, since he holds the key to the investigation.

The dialogue between Oedipus and Jocasta is central to the play's development, and it has more to tell us. Before describing the confrontation at the place where three roads meet, Oedipus explains how he came to be there in the first place. He was desperately trying to get away from home, since an oracle had come from Delphi predicting that he would lie with his mother and kill his father. To avert those ghastly, taboo-breaking possibilities, he had to put as much distance as possible between himself and his home city of ... Corinth; for his father and mother were (he had always believed) Polybos and Merope, king and queen of that city, where he had been raised. As long as Oedipus remains convinced of this genealogy, vital pieces of his jigsaw are bound to elude him.[8]

Those pieces will soon be assembled. The first is supplied by a messenger from Corinth, who announces that Oedipus' 'father', Polybos, is dead, and that Oedipus will succeed him. This report brings Oedipus sorrow but also relief, since the fear that had driven him from Corinth – the prediction that he would kill his father and lie with his mother – has, at least in so far as concerns his father, proved groundless: the old man died a natural death. Yet there

Attributed to the Capodarso Painter, Oedipus discovering
the truth, red-figure *calyx krater* from Sicily, 330–320 BCE.

remains the other half of the prediction, so Oedipus still has to
keep away from Corinth. At this point the messenger intervenes,
in order (he thinks) to calm Oedipus' anxieties:

> CORINTHIAN MESSENGER. Don't you know you have no
> reason to fear?
> OEDIPUS. Why not, if these people are my parents?
> COR. MESS. Because Polybos was no relation to you![9]

The messenger, a shepherd, reveals that, long ago, baby Oedipus
was handed to him by another shepherd, a local Theban, while the
pair of them were jointly tending their herds on Mount Cithaeron.

The infant was a foundling, with its ankles pierced and pinned together. For Oedipus, one course of action remains in order to discover his ultimate origins: to find this other, Theban shepherd. The chorus intervenes:

> I think he is no other than the man from the fields that
> you were eager to see before; but Jocasta here could tell
> that best.[10]

That simple utterance completes Jocasta's jigsaw. She rushes from the scene, desperately imploring Oedipus to cease his investigation. But he refuses, since *his* jigsaw still has one vital piece missing. But not for long: for the Theban shepherd is, as the chorus said, none other than the servant who has already been summoned – the sole surviving eyewitness of Laius' murder. Oedipus' twin questions – 'Who murdered Laius?' and 'What is my origin?' – are about to be answered.

When the Theban herdsman (and eyewitness) arrives on stage, he is recognized by his fellow shepherd. Four lines suffice for the hapless Theban to complete *his* jigsaw:

> CORINTHIAN MESSENGER. Tell me now, do you
>   remember giving me a child, to bring up as my own?
> THEBAN SHEPHERD: What? Why are you asking me that?
> COR. MESS. This man, my friend, was once that baby.[11]

Oedipus' questioning becomes even more urgent, but the Theban shepherd – not surprisingly, knowing what he now knows – is even more reluctant to speak out than Teiresias had been. Only when threatened with torture and death does he reveal that the foundling came from the house of Laius and was said to be his child. 'But your wife inside the house,' the wretched shepherd adds, 'could best tell you about that.'[12] This is the final piece of the final puzzle. Oedipus' last words before he dashes from the stage summarize his individual reaction to his fate, in language as contorted as the relationships they describe:

Alas! Alas! All comes out clear.
Light, may I now look upon you for the last time,
I who am revealed as born from those I should not have
    been born from;
As living beside those I should not have consorted with;
As killing those I should not have killed.[13]

The chorus's inference is more universal:

Ah, the generations of mortals,
I count your existence as equal to zero.
For what man, what man wins more of happiness
Than a seeming, and after seeming, a decline?
Taking your fate as an example,
Your fate, unhappy Oedipus,
I consider nothing pertaining to mortals as blessed.[14]

The dénouement gives free rein to anguish. A second messenger
appears, bringing news from within the house. Jocasta has hanged
herself in a frenzy of shame, in the bedroom she shared with
her husband/son; when he burst in upon her corpse, Oedipus
tore the golden pins from her robe and stabbed them repeatedly into his eyeballs. 'You would have been better dead than
alive but blind,' observes the horrified chorus.[15] However, given
Greek beliefs about the passing of the souls of the dead to the
Underworld, suicide would have left Oedipus with a post-mortem
confrontation with both Laius and Jocasta – something he would
have found unbearable.[16] Better to see nothing at all, ever again.
The final acts in the drama are orchestrated by Creon, now in
charge of the city. To Oedipus' plea that he be cast out onto the
mountain (Cithaeron) that fostered him, Creon replies that such
a possibility depends on the advice of Apollo. One thing that *is*
in Creon's gift is to let Oedipus briefly embrace his daughters/sis-
ters – until Creon orders him to let go of them again; for Oedipus

has conceded all control over his life to others. The inference the chorus draws from what they and the audience have witnessed is not a moral about the fantastic improbability of life's fortunes, but something far more representative and general: 'Call no mortal happy, until he has passed the ultimate limit of his life without suffering grief.'[17]

There's more to it than *Oedipus Tyrannus*

In his treatise on *Poetics*, Aristotle observes that the finest sort of 'recognition' (*anagnorisis*) is one accompanied by a 'reversal' (*peripeteia*) – like (Aristotle adds) that in Sophocles' *Oedipus*.[18] This comment has a lot to recommend it, in view of the importance given by Sophocles to Oedipus' transition from blind unawareness to self-recognition, which accompanies his change in status from (apparently) Corinthian outsider to (actually) native-born Theban. But for all its paradigmatic status as *the* Greek tragedy, *Oedipus Tyrannus* was far from being the only ancient theatrical version of the myth – not surprisingly, since the plot's intricate development and explosive finale made it eminently stage-worthy. But there were non-dramatic retellings too; and, as usual, there were significant variations. Some myth-tellers reported that, following the oracle's prediction of the dire crimes that Laius' child was destined to commit, baby Oedipus was put into a little chest and thrown into the sea, only to be rescued by Polybos and his wife (here named as Periboea) when he floated ashore at Sicyon, near Corinth.[19] (In myth, the sea can function as the equivalent of a mountain, since both are imagined as areas of strangeness and wildness where astonishing reversals can take place.) Another variant had Oedipus blinded by Laius' servants instead of by his own hand.[20] Yet another variation kept Jocasta alive after the revelation of the truth, only for her to commit suicide when her two sons by Oedipus had killed each other in single combat.[21] It was even said, in mitigation of the horror of incest, that Oedipus' children were not by Jocasta at all, but by a woman named Euryganeia.[22]

Ostensibly closer to Sophocles, but still very different in detail and especially in mood, is *Oedipus*, the dramatization by the Roman tragedian Seneca (*c.* 4 BCE–65 CE). In this oppressively gloomy vision, the central character anticipates his own doom right from the outset:

> I fear things unspeakable – that my father shall be slain
> by my own hand. Of this the Delphic oracle warns me,
> and assigns to me another and still greater crime ...
> Phoebus threatens the son with his father's bedroom,
> with its infamous bed, defiled by wicked passion ...
> I dread everything, and do not trust myself to myself.[23]

Another difference from Sophocles involves the creepy necromantic invocation of the shade of Laius – gore-bespattered, filthy and raving – who proclaims Oedipus' deeds of parricide and incest in all their impious monstrosity. As in Sophocles, Oedipus suspects Creon of underhand dealing, but Seneca, as so often, ups the ante: Oedipus has his brother-in-law thrown into a rocky dungeon, on the principle that a proper ruler should instil fear and not care overmuch about being hated.[24] This Oedipus would be at home in Tacitus' account of the dynastic intrigues of the Julio-Claudian emperors.

Seneca follows Sophoclean precedent with the dialogue between the two shepherds, but the theatre that Seneca really ought to have composed for was Grand Guignol: it was not just that the baby Oedipus' legs were pierced with an iron rod, but (recalls the Theban herdsman) the wound swelled up with a hideous and festering infection.[25] As in Sophocles, the Senecan Oedipus robs himself of eyesight, but with the Senecan Jocasta things take a new direction. Instead of hanging herself, she stabs herself with a sword – through the womb. The symbolism is evident: it was the part of her anatomy that welcomed the son who was her husband and produced the children born from that incestuous union. But there may be more going on. In Tacitus' riveting account of the murder of Nero's mother, Agrippina cries out to the soldier who is about to stab her, 'Strike my womb!' As there were persistent rumours about Nero's incestuous relationship with his mother, there may be an implied assimilation between Jocasta and Agrippina, though which direction the influence travelled in is uncertain.[26] If Agrippina's death were to have been modelled on Senecan dramatic precedent, that would be a remarkable example of life imitating myth.

Seneca's tragedy is one kind of 'sequel' to *Oedipus Tyrannus*. For a different kind we need to go back to Sophocles. The tragedy he wrote at the end of his life, *Oedipus at Colonus*, carries Oedipus' story forward to the mysterious and (to invoke that concept once again) enigmatic end of the hero's troubles. Having wandered for years as a blind and reviled outcast, sustained only by his loving daughter Antigone, Oedipus arrives at last at the grove of the Eumenides (Furies) at Colonus, in the territory of Athens, a city governed by its benevolent yet forceful ruler Theseus. On learning the identity of the location, Oedipus recognizes the ultimate divine context of his fate, for yet another Apolline oracle has predicted that this would be the very spot in which he would reach the terminus of his wretched existence, bringing good fortune to those who granted him sanctuary and offered him a final resting place. True to Athens' self-proclaimed standing as a haven for those in need, Theseus welcomes the strange would-be immigrant, even after learning the terrible truth of his identity. Oedipus retains his ferocious resentment towards those Thebans who once cast him out (Creon and his own sons, Polynices and Eteocles) and who now want to reap the benefits that, after his death, he can bestow. But his final passing will take place on a note not of ferocity, but of calmness. A note of mystery, too, as is reported by an amazed messenger – a mystery of which only one living man has some inkling:

> But by what death that man perished, no mortal could tell but Theseus. For no fiery thunderbolt from a god did away with him, nor a sea storm arising at that time, but either there was some messenger from the gods, or the unlit foundation of the earth that belongs to those below opened in kindliness. For the man was taken away with no lamentations, nor suffering with disease, but – if such a thing can be said of any mortal – he died in a way that was astonishing.[27]

The strange aura surrounding Oedipus' passing extends also to his place of burial, which not even his daughters are allowed to see (Antigone has been joined at Colonus by her sister, Ismene). But if Antigone's first wish cannot be granted ('Let us see our father's tomb'), Theseus willingly accedes to her second ('Send us back to Thebes, in the hope that we can prevent our brothers from slaughtering each other')[28] – a detail that hints at the memorable and tragic events recorded in another great Sophoclean tragedy, *Antigone*.

Before leaving the Greco-Roman tellings of the Oedipus myth, a couple more observations are in order. One concerns Oedipus' name, which means, on the commonest and most plausible interpretation, 'Swollen Foot' – an allusion to the deformity he suffered as an infant after the piercing and pinning together of his ankles.[29] As the outstanding Dutch scholar of myth and religion Jan Bremmer has pointed out, the role of this mutilation is of secondary importance in the ancient myth.[30] It is simply an intensification of the plight of the exposed baby, who, after all, could not have walked anyway. Modern interpreters who locate Oedipus' lameness at the heart of their reading of the myth are thus focusing on an element that in antiquity was peripheral.

The other general observation concerns 'fate'. Just as Laurence Olivier famously (and misleadingly) encapsulated the plot of *Hamlet* as 'the tragedy of a man who could not make up his mind', so *Oedipus Tyrannus* has often been seen as conveying a message about the inexorability of fate and, as a necessary corollary of that, the absence of human free will. It is worth stressing, therefore, that, in spite of the importance of the predictions of the Delphic oracle in Oedipus' story, at least two crucial features of the drama are entirely independent of such predictions. When Oedipus determines to pursue the truth at any cost, and when he subsequently resolves to blind himself, these two decisions are presented by Sophocles not as behaviour over which Oedipus had no control, but as conscious human choices that stem from his personality. He had the freedom to behave differently, but he did not do so.

Oedipus' afterlife
Since classical antiquity, countless writers and artists have returned to the Oedipus theme.[31] Two contrasting but inextricable images have predominated: that of an individual whose consummate knowledge brings him triumphant success, and that of the same individual's catastrophic downfall, precipitated either by an excessive desire to know or by the machinations of 'fate' (whatever that might be), or by a combination of those factors. The permutations have been endless; we have space to pick out just a few striking examples.

One of the most unusual readings of Oedipus' story is that of the philosopher, scientist and polymath Francis Bacon. In 'Sphinx, or science', the twenty-eighth essay from *The Wisdom of the Ancients* (1609), the emphasis is all on Oedipus' positive achievements. In Bacon's view, the Sphinx stood allegorically for science, '[which] may, without absurdity, be called a monster, being strangely gazed at and admired by the ignorant and unskilful'.[32] The Sphinx (= science), suggested Bacon, put various difficult questions to

Oedipus puts out his eyes, Jocasta commits suicide,
Eteocles and Polynices kill each other; the Talbot Master, miniature
from Boccaccio's *De claris mulieribus, c.* 1440.

men, and the attempted answering of them involved alternative and radically different consequences: 'dilaceration' (i.e. being 'torn apart' mentally) to those who fail to resolve them, and 'empire' to those who succeed. According to Bacon, the Sphinx posed two sorts of riddle, concerning the nature of things and the nature of man; the riddle posed to Oedipus was of the latter sort. The successful solution brought power: 'for he who has thoroughly looked into and examined human nature may in a way command his own fortune, and seems born to acquire dominion and rule'. The prospect of 'dilaceration' was rather disconcerting for anyone thinking of embarking on scientific research, but Bacon drew a further, mitigating moral from the myth. 'We must not omit that the Sphinx was conquered by a lame man, and impotent in his feet; for men usually make too much haste to the solution of the Sphinx's riddles.' In other words, the way forward for the would-be scientist is research that is careful and painstaking – and thus less likely to lead to 'dilaceration'.

What a contrast there is between Bacon's meditative allegory and Percy Bysshe Shelley's gross and bawdy parody *Oedipus Tyrannus; or, Swellfoot the Tyrant* (1820). More Aristophanic than Sophoclean, the play is a rollicking satire on the regime of the dissolute and dysfunctional George IV, in the context of the trial for adultery of his estranged wife Caroline.[33] The closest the play comes to (distantly) mirroring Sophocles is in its opening, where Tyrant Swellfoot of Thebes presides over a scene at the Temple of Famine, where a troop of starving, supplicant pigs are roundly abused by their despotic ruler, who for his part fondly and vacuously contemplates the fat rotundities of his own body:

> this kingly paunch
> Swells like a sail before a favouring breeze,
> And these most sacred nether promontories
> Lie satisfied with layers of fat; and these

Boeotian cheeks, like Egypt's pyramid ...
Sustain the cone of my untroubled brain,
That point, the emblem of a pointless nothing![34]

Swellfoot gets his comeuppance when his estranged queen, Iona Taurina, transforms her royal consort and his court into a variety of filthy and ugly animals – probably the first and last time in the history of the reception of classical mythology that Jocasta and Circe have been distilled into a single individual. The farce ends when Iona, nattily got up in hunting gear, riotously pursues the metamorphosed courtiers at the head of a pack of pigs, with a Minotaur (a.k.a. John Bull) as her sturdy mount.

Usually less idiosyncratic than Bacon, and never as riotous as Shelley, are literally hundreds of other adaptations of the Oedipus story, whether inspired by Sophocles (most often *Oedipus Tyrannus*; more rarely *Oedipus at Colonus*) or by Seneca (whose *Oedipus* appeared in its first modern edition in *c.* 1474–84), or by a mixture of the two. Numerous major authors have successively rethought the myth. In France, Pierre Corneille, Voltaire and André Gide each wrote an *Oedipe* for the stage (in 1659, 1718 and 1931 respectively); Jean Cocteau's play *La Machine infernale* (premiered in 1934) and Alain Robbe-Grillet's novel *Les Gommes* ('The Erasers'; 1953) are contrastingly thought-provoking explorations of the same myth. In English, writers as diverse as John Dryden (*Oedipus: A Tragedy*, 1679), T. S. Eliot (*The Elder Statesman*, 1959) and Ola Rotimi (*The Gods Are Not To Blame*, 1968) have conducted their own theatrical explorations; the last-mentioned playwright adapts the tale to a Yoruban context. Hugo von Hofmannsthal (*Oedipus and the Sphinx*, 1906) and Friedrich Dürrenmatt (with the comic and profound story *The Dying of the Pythia*, 1976) in German, and Tawfiq al-Hakim (*King Oedipus*, 1949) in Arabic, are others who have stamped their authority on the story. Into the bargain, ever since a musical performance of Sophocles' *Oedipus Tyrannus*

Jean-Auguste-Dominique Ingres, *Oedipus and the Sphinx*, 1808.

Gustave Moreau, *Oedipus and the Sphinx*, 1864.

inaugurated the stupendous Palladio-designed Teatro Olimpico at Vicenza in 1585 (with choral music by Andrea Gabrieli), adaptations of the myth in opera, oratorio, ballet and other musical forms have proliferated. Few versions, though, have equalled Igor Stravinsky's tremendous oratorio *Oedipus Rex* (1927), in which the limpid libretto is delivered in Latin, interspersed by the words of a Narrator speaking in whatever may be the vernacular language of the audience. The moment of revelation is shattering:

THE SHEPHERD AND THE MESSENGER.
> He was found on the mountain, abandoned by his mother;
> We found him in the mountains.
> He is the son of Laius and Jocasta!
> He is the slayer of Laius, his father!
> The son of Laius and Jocasta!
> Husband of Jocasta his mother!
> You should never have spoken.
> Silence would have been better, never to have spoken that word:
> That he was abandoned by Jocasta and found on the mountain.

OEDIPUS.
> Wicked in my birth; wicked in my marriage; wicked in my murdering. All now is light.[35]

Compared to the multitude of theatrical and musical versions, visual re-imaginings have been far fewer. In modern as in ancient art, the main focus has been on the confrontation with the Sphinx. Iconic paintings by Jean-Auguste-Dominique Ingres (1808) and Gustave Moreau (1864) each portray the attempt of one individual to face down, to penetrate the defences of, another (see p. 145 and opposite). Both images also explore new affective territory, in that they carry a powerful erotic charge. Ingres aligns the forehead of a near-naked Oedipus with the Sphinx's breasts; in Moreau's even more extraordinary vision, the bold exchange of gazes between handsome youth and female hybrid, not to mention the Sphinx's physical adhesion to Oedipus, quite obviously suggest (reciprocal?) lust. But the confrontation could also be represented quite differently. The French caricaturist Honoré Daumier gives a characteristically ironical twist to the subject (1842; see opposite, above), while the Greek-born Italian artist Giorgio de Chirico, whose Oedipus poses quizzically in a manner resembling that of Rodin's *Thinker*, has a take on the scene that is suitably enigmatic (1968). Much rarer than images featuring the Sphinx are those that draw on the stage action of *Tyrannus* or *Colonus*. Renoir's painting (1895), based on a stage performance of a French adaptation of Sophocles' tragedy, depicts the emergence of the self-blinded Oedipus from his palace (see opposite, below). Yet, for all its painterly skill, this is hardly one of the artist's most memorable works. There is something about this moment in the myth that cries out for realization on stage; a canvas, even one painted by Renoir, somehow lacks the necessary punch.

So far, the elephant in our room has been Sigmund Freud, according to whose world-shaking theory, set out first in 1899 in his *Traumdeutung* (Interpretation of Dreams), Oedipus' relationship with his parents constitutes the key to an understanding of the human psyche (a Greek-derived word meaning 'soul'). In their examination of the extent to which Oedipal themes are in fact universally pervasive, Allen Johnson and Douglass Price-Williams summarize the theory like this:

> Freud regarded the Oedipus complex as the centerpiece of psychoanalytic theory ... Based upon analysis of his own dreams, and his study of Sophocles' *Oedipus Rex* and Shakespeare's *Hamlet*, he concluded that every boy passes through a phase in which he wishes to kill his father in order to marry his mother.

Honoré
Daumier,
*Oedipus with
the Sphinx,*
1842.

Pierre-Auguste
Renoir, *Oedipus
Rex*, 1895.

In learning to control and reject these unacceptable wishes, Freud argued, the growing boy acquires morality and discipline, enabling him to achieve maturity and to find satisfaction in socially approved forms of work and love. The old wishes, however, are not abolished but repressed; they live on in the unconscious. Oedipal stories are evidence that residues of the Oedipus complex, resolved though it may be, continue to inform human activity throughout life.[36]

Not for nothing did a reproduction of Ingres's painting of Oedipus with the Sphinx hang on the wall of Freud's consulting room. Within the psychoanalytical movement, Freud would himself be cast in the role of the ultimate problem-solver, and the logo of the International Psychoanalytical Press featured the Oedipus/Sphinx confrontation.[37] But the more fundamental question is not whether Freud himself could be viewed as an Oedipus-equivalent, but whether *everyone* can be so viewed. The theory does indeed claim universality, by virtue of every boy's alleged unconscious wish to kill his father and marry his mother: 'His destiny moves us only because it might have been ours.'[38] The theory had an anthropological as well as a psychological dimension, since it cohered with Freud's (wholly speculative) idea that the development of primitive society from Nature to Culture took place at a pivotal moment when a group of brothers, who had killed their father and taken his women, experienced guilt for so doing and thenceforward agreed to prohibit incest and parricide. The advent of the human family was adaptive in an evolutionary sense, but this came at a price: impulses of aggression towards the father, and attraction towards the mother, did not disappear but became repressed. It was in myth, as well as in dreams, that they sometimes found expression.

To describe Freud's theory as controversial would be a massive understatement. Both within and outside psychoanalysis there has been fervent disagreement about virtually every aspect of the Oedipus complex, but especially its alleged innateness and universality. Major post-Freudian thinkers about the psyche have been split: opinions have ranged from the endorsement (qualified by numerous refinements) of Jacques Lacan, to the militant opposition of Gilles Deleuze and Félix Guattari (the title of their book *L'Anti-Oedipe* says it all) and Michel Foucault, who regarded the complex as a tool of oppressive medical control.[39] Feminists have castigated Freud's masculinism, which cast riddle-solving as a characteristically male activity and assumed that the male body, male drives and male impulses were normative reference points.[40] One feminist-oriented critic reaches the trenchant conclusion that 'it is hard not to think of the Oedipus complex as an error of massive and devastating proportions'.[41] Many of those who stress the positive validity of non-traditional gender roles within the family (e.g. the raising of children by two parents of the same sex) have been particularly sceptical about the conceptual utility of the complex. As the author of the present book is not a psychoanalyst nor a psychologist nor a neurologist, it would be absurd for him to adjudicate on such fundamental and still contentious questions. What seems more sensible is to highlight some ways in which Freud's ideas about Oedipus have shaped the wider, especially artistic, imagination. After all, works of art conceived in the light of Freudian theory have every right to be judged on their own merits, regardless of how that theory is scientifically evaluated.

A classic example of such a work is Max Ernst's surreal *Oedipus Rex* (oil on canvas, 1922), one of the most unsettling visions in the entire history of European art.[42] A preternatural sense of clinical calmness contrasts with pain implied by the horrific – but weirdly bloodless – penetration of the thumb and forefinger by a metal spike. Another image of penetration is that of a partly open walnut, which is shot through with an arrow. Why a walnut?

Critics have suggested a possible physical analogy with the brain (the overall shape) or the vulva (the crack), penetrated (albeit off-centre – an *ineffective* penetration?) by a traditional symbol of the phallus. Equally and additionally possible is an allusion to Hamlet's statement 'O God, I could be bounded in a nut-shell, and count myself a king of infinite space, were it not that I have bad dreams' (*Hamlet*, II. ii); after all, Hamlet himself was notoriously susceptible to analysis in terms of the Oedipus complex.[43] The imagery of control pervades the painting: a hand grasps the nut; a female bird is literally 'fenced in', while a male bird is tethered. But hinted at too is the possibility of escape – there is a mini-balloon in the background. The whole image is – appropriately enough – an enigma, incapable of definitive solution. Ernst has created a 'designer dream', whose ideal viewer is a Freudian-interpreter-cum-Oedipal-riddle-solver.

In spite of exceptions like Max Ernst, it is characteristic of this intensely plot-sensitive myth that it is in the theatre and the cinema, rather than in the visual arts, that the greatest impact as been achieved. Occasionally the tone has been comic, as in the Woody Allen short film *Oedipus Wrecks* (1989), about a New

Film still from Woody Allen's *Oedipus Wrecks*, from *New York Stories*, 1989.

York lawyer called Sheldon (played by Allen) who is constantly embarrassed by his oppressive mother (see opposite). When she disappears after being called on stage to participate in a magician's act, her son's psychological torments diminish – until a gigantic image of his mother starts appearing in the sky over the city, from which vantage-point she continues to heap embarrassment on him, with the whole city as her audience. The crisis is alleviated when Sheldon consults and falls for a psychic called Treva. When Treva meets his mother, she approves of her son's choice and comes back down to earth. Even if the closest we get to Sophocles is the film's punning title, the idea that the very mention of Oedipus entails a psychoanalytical dimension confirms the all-embracing influence that Freud has had on the myth's contemporary reception.

Comic treatments such as that by Allen (and we recall also those by Shelley and Daumier) have been the exception; the prevalent tone has been one of grim seriousness. Rita Dove's powerful verse drama *The Darker Face of the Earth* (1994) relocates the story to the antebellum South of the United States. Amalia, the married white mistress of a plantation owner, takes a black slave (Hector) as her lover. When in due course she bears him a child, she and her husband have the baby put into a sewing basket and sent secretly away into slavery (the husband places a pair of spurs – the equivalent of the Sophoclean metal pins – into the basket, hoping the baby will thereby be killed). On reaching adulthood, he is bought (under the name of Augustus Newcastle) by Amalia; subsequently, oblivious of his origins and true identity, she takes him as her lover. Augustus attains heroic status as the supporter of a revolt against the slave-owners and kills Hector in a violent confrontation. When the old injury that Augustus suffered from the spurs prompts him to confront Amalia, she reveals that she is his mother and that Hector was his father. While Amalia stabs herself from shame, Augustus is lauded by his freedom-chanting fellow slaves, who know nothing of his personal tragedy. What is powerfully new in Dove's vision is the all-dominating institutional framework of slavery, but many of the plot details, as well as the overall atmosphere, deliberately recall the Greek original. Especially notable is the presence of a voodoo prophet called Scylla, whose ominous, trance-induced predictions fulfil the same framing and proleptic function as those of Teiresias.

Wholly different in tone, but no less explicit in its debt to Sophocles, is Steven Berkoff's outspoken play *Greek* (1980), set in the working-class East End of London. In a competition for the work of literature with the most extensive repertoire of anatomically explicit swearwords, *Greek* would have few rivals; Berkoff does not do understatement. The filthy-mouthed anti-hero is Eddy, whose (alleged) parents take him one day to a carnival, where 'a gypsy, a fortune teller' predicts 'a violent death for this son's father /... [then] something worse than death / and that's a bunk-up with his mum'.[44] The plague-equivalent in the play is poverty; to escape it, Eddy leaves home. One day he quarrels with the manager of a restaurant, kills him by verbally insulting him to death (!), and goes off with and marries the man's wife. It is a love match that leads Eddy on to better things. For him, the plague is almost over, but to ensure its end he must solve the Sphinx's riddle; this is one moment where a Greek mythological character makes a direct and startling appearance. Eddy's successful solution fits the play's pervasive sexual imagery:

> SPHINX. So here goes: what walks on four legs in the
> morning, two legs in the afternoon and three legs in
> the evening?
> EDDY. Man! In the morning of his life he is on all fours,
> in the afternoon when he is young he is on two legs
> and in the evenings when he is erect for his woman he
> sprouts the third leg.

SPHINX. You bastard, you've used trickery to find out the
riddle.[45]

Eventually, though, the truth of Eddy's origins comes out. His real
parents had taken him on a boat trip down the Thames: a stray
German mine blew the vessel up (truly a 'fateful' coincidence),
but the toddler survived and was picked up by a couple – Eddy's
future 'parents'. When Eddy learns all this, the revelation leads
him to no culminating act of self-harm. As Berkoff says in his
preface to the play:

> In writing my 'modern' Oedipus it wasn't too difficult
> to find contemporary parallels, but when I came to the
> 'blinding' I paused, since in my version it wouldn't have
> made sense, given Eddy's non-fatalistic disposition, to
> have him embark on such an act of self-hatred – unless I
> slavishly aped the original.

In fact, in his concluding speech (not without memories of Molly's
monologue at the end of James Joyce's *Ulysses*), Eddy joyfully celebrates the ecstasy of sex with his mother, whose body he has
experienced from two quite different perspectives.

We have repeatedly stressed the cerebral, problem-solving
aspects of the Oedipus myth. One feature of this problem-
solving – a feature that will bring our discussion to its conclusion – is particularly noteworthy: the connection with arithmetic.
Oedipus cracks the Sphinx's code by realizing that one and the
same individual can walk on four legs, or two legs, or three.
At the culmination of the drama, the Sophoclean chorus discovers
that the multiple generations of mortals are equal to zero.[46] The
riddle of Oedipus' identity comes down to the 'equation' of one
man with a plurality of brigands. It is a nice touch, then, that at
one point in the reception of Oedipus' myth we find an intriguing new twist on this association with numbers. A memorable

song about Oedipus by the prodigiously talented 20th-century American satirist Tom Lehrer ends like this:

> So be sweet and kind to mother now and then have a chat,
> Buy her candy or some flowers or a brand new hat,
> But maybe you had better let it go at that,
> Or you may find yourself with a quite complex complex
> And you may end up like Oedipus.
> I'd rather marry a duck-billed platypus
> Than end up like old Oedipus Rex.

It may not be entirely coincidental that among Lehrer's other accomplishments was his consummate numerical skill: he lectured on mathematics at some of the most prestigious universities in the United States.

CHAPTER 6

The Judgment of Paris

In Agatha Christie's novel *Lord Edgware Dies*, Jane Wilkinson, the estranged wife of the eponymous and odious baron, seems to have a watertight alibi for the time of his stabbing: all her fellow guests confirm her attendance at a dinner party that exactly coincided with the time of the murder. But a chance occurrence calls her alibi into doubt. One of the other dinner guests, Donald Ross, happens to be at a lunch with Jane some time afterwards. When the conversation turns to Paris, the prince of Troy, Jane misunderstands 'Paris' to mean the French capital, the centre of fashion and frivolity – whereas at the dinner party she had talked knowledgeably about Homer and Greek mythology. Puzzled by the inconsistency, Ross tries to communicate his suspicions to Hercule Poirot but is murdered before he can do so. Nevertheless, Poirot's remorseless little grey cells soon discover the truth: the woman who attended the original dinner party was not Jane but Carlotta Adams, an impressionist paid by Jane to impersonate her. Unfortunately for Jane's alibi, and fatally for the intelligent and cultured Carlotta (Jane murders her too), Carlotta was better informed about the Greek myths than Jane was.

This tiny but pivotal detail of Christie's plot depends on the assumption that a reference to 'the Judgment of Paris' could plausibly be misunderstood at the date (1933) when the novel was first published. Such a lack of automatic intelligibility is surely even truer today. Yet the Judgment still remains a potent icon, even if some of its meanings within its ancient contexts have been forgotten. The episode describes the dilemma of the Trojan prince Paris, who has to decide which of three goddesses – Hera (Juno), Athena (Minerva) or Aphrodite (Venus) – is the most beautiful. This fleeting mythological moment raises a number of issues fundamental not only to Greek and Roman hearers and readers of myths, but to everyone who reflects on human life.

Discord on Mount Pelion

It all began at the wedding of the mortal hero Peleus to his immortal bride, the sea nymph Thetis. Previously Zeus himself had been courting Thetis, but thought better of it after learning of a prophecy that the son to whom Thetis would give birth was destined to be more powerful than his father. To avert the risk of overthrow by his own offspring, Zeus prudently married Thetis off to a mortal instead. For all Peleus' heroic qualifications – *inter alia* he was an Argonaut and participated in the Calydonian boar hunt – his union with Thetis was never going to be idyllic, in view of the gap in status between the two (not to mention that she tried to elude Peleus' clutches by metamorphosing herself into various scary shapes, from fire and water to a snake and a lion). Eventually the gulf between them would lead to their separation. Thetis longed to make their child, Achilles, immortal, and attempted to do so by burning away his mortality in a fire, but a horrified and uncomprehending Peleus caught her in the act, thus preventing Achilles' immortalization. Thetis abandoned her husband and rejoined her fellow Nereids at the bottom of the sea, leaving her baby son to grow up to young manhood and die gloriously and tragically at Troy. Of course, in Greek myth one should never underestimate the extent of the variants. At the end of Euripides' play *Andromache*, Thetis makes Peleus immortal and predicts that they will live happily together ever after in her father's palace under the sea. But it is the inauguration of the marriage, not its sequel, that concerns us here.

The wedding was celebrated on Mount Pelion in Thessaly, the region where Peleus had become king. (The tale of the Judgment spans two mountains: Mount Pelion, in the heart of Greece, and Mount Ida, near Troy. Mountains were key sites of convergence between the mortal and immortal worlds, and events on Pelion and Ida involved exactly this kind of convergence.) The predominant mood on Pelion was joyful; with the Muses doing the vocals, it could hardly have been otherwise. But not everything was harmonious, because not everyone was invited. The Roman mythographer Hyginus (2nd century CE) puts it like this:

> Jupiter is said to have invited to the wedding of Peleus and Thetis all the gods except Eris, or Discordia [as she was known by the Romans]. When she came later and was not admitted to the banquet, she threw an apple through the door, saying that the fairest should take it. Juno, Venus and Minerva claimed the beauty prize for themselves. A huge argument broke out among them.[1]

Eris ('Strife' or 'Discord') was a minor deity, but a fascinating and unsettling one. In his poem *Works and Days*, the poet Hesiod gave her a double personality. One aspect embodies the spirit of constructive emulation that spurs neighbours and co-workers – ploughmen, craftsmen, beggars, bards – to try to outperform their fellows. But her other aspect is harsh and cruel, since she promotes 'evil war and battle'.[2] It is this disruptive Eris who predominates in the mythological tradition. In another Hesiodic passage she is the mother of Toil, Forgetfulness, Starvation, Pain, Battles, Combats, Bloodshed, Slaughter, Quarrels, Lies, Pretences, Arguments, Disorder and Disaster; in the *Iliad* she strides through the throng of battle creating havoc and sorrow.[3] In thinking about Greek gods and goddesses, we have to forget about any necessary connection with 'the good'. These divinities are powerful rather than virtuous; they stand for life in all its rough-edged and sometimes unpleasant complexity. What the discordant face of Eris represents may not be nice, but it is part of human experience. Disrespect her at your peril. It was precisely her sense of being disrespected that prompted her to throw the provocative apple.

Why an apple? Some sources specify that it was not just any old piece of fruit, but that it was made of gold, and that it came from the legendary orchard of the Hesperides, the nymphs who guarded the apples with the help of a terrible, hundred-headed serpent.[4] (It took a Heracles to steal these apples, and their theft was the peerless hero's eleventh Labour.) Since these golden apples had allegedly been presented by Gaia as gifts at the wedding of Zeus and Hera, they already carried nuptial symbolism.[5] More generally, ordinary apples figured in wedding ceremonies in many parts of Greece. Sometimes, indeed, they are specifically said to have been *thrown*, an act that could be accompanied by aphrodisiac incantations.[6] What Eris did at the wedding of Peleus and Thetis was to invert this symbolism by turning harmony into dissonance. But whatever the provenance and symbolism of the apple she threw, what mattered was that, at least according to some ancient accounts, it bore an inscription. The version that seems today to be universally assumed to be the 'authentic' wording – and which can be found on thousands of internet sites about mythology – is: 'For the most beautiful' or, in Greek, *tēi kallistēi*. But in antiquity there was no agreement about what inscription the apple bore – if it bore one at all. (To take just one example, in a dialogue by Lucian the inscription runs: 'Let the beautiful one take it.')[7] What *was* agreed was that the apple was designed to be presented to the winner of a beauty contest between goddesses, a challenge that no self-respecting deity could resist. After all, there was a pervasive assumption in Greek and Roman culture that beauty was an integral quality of a divinity – male and female alike (exceptions, such as Hephaestus, prove the rule). It follows that to be thought less beautiful than one's fellow divinities was an insult not to be borne lightly.[8]

So far, our account has cast Eris as the prime mover in the affair. But the cataclysmic conflict eventually precipitated by the Judgment is the mightiest military confrontation in the whole of classical mythology: the Trojan War. Somehow (many myth-tellers felt) such a clash of civilizations should have been motivated by something more serious than a momentary loss of face to a minor deity. Hyginus, we recall, related that it was Zeus who missed Eris off the guest list. Was this just a memory lapse on Zeus' part or was there more to it? In ancient myth, few things happen by chance, and myth-tellers were quick to ascribe deliberate intent to Zeus' act of omission. It was, they said, nothing less than Zeus' plan to kick-start the Trojan War, an explanation whose origins went back at least as far as the Archaic epic known as the *Cypria*, dating back perhaps to the 7th century BCE and known to us today only in fragments. Various reasons were given for Zeus' ploy. Some said he wanted to ensure that his daughter Helen would become famous for having unleashed war between Europe and Asia. Others maintained that his aim was more general: to enable either the demigods in general (the heroic offspring of divine and mortal parents), or Achilles in particular, to achieve fame in that conflict. According to yet another variant, the gods wanted to relieve Gaia (the Earth) of the burden of human overpopulation; a major war would be the drastic but effective solution.[9] On all those readings of events, it was the Olympian gods – usually Zeus in particular – who lay behind the action. Eris was just the catalyst.

Choice on Mount Ida

The discord created by events on Mount Pelion brought about an extraordinary situation: in spite of their usually effortless superiority over human beings, on this occasion the gods needed to call on the help of a mortal. Answering the question 'Which of the three deities is the most beautiful?' required an external arbiter disengaged from reputational quarrels between the gods. For Zeus himself to adjudicate would have been unthinkable: it would have involved him in endless recriminations from the two losers. So the scene shifts north-eastwards, to another mountain top. Hyginus resumes his narrative:

> Jupiter ordered Mercury to take [the three goddesses]
> to Mount Ida to Paris Alexander and order him to judge.
> Juno promised him, if he judged in her favour, that
> he would rule in every land and surpass everyone in
> wealth; Minerva, if she left the winner, that he would
> be the strongest among mortals and know every skill;
> Venus, however, promised that he would marry Helen,
> daughter of Tyndareus, the most beautiful woman
> in the world. Paris preferred this last gift to the previous
> ones and adjudged Venus to be the most beautiful.
> Because of this, Juno and Minerva were hostile to the
> Trojans. Alexander, at the prompting of Venus, took
> Helen from his host Menelaus from Lacedaemon to
> Troy, and married her.[10]

This summary raises numerous issues, some straightforward, some more intricate. What is the role of Mercury (Hermes)? Who is 'Paris Alexander'? What makes him a suitable judge? What do the goddesses look like? How do they try to influence Paris' choice? And finally: what are the consequences of the Judgment?

HERMES/MERCURY

Hermes is the god who mediates between opposites. He links
the above and the below: for instance, he guides the souls of
the dead down into the Underworld. He links the inside and
the outside: for instance, he is the god of keyholes. He presides
over trade and barter, linking buyer with seller. He is the god of
travellers, heralds and messengers – the ultimate go-between. In
short, he is the boundary-crosser par excellence.[11] The ultimate
boundary is that which differentiates immortals from mortals,
and Hermes mediates that opposition too. In the specific case we
are thinking about, he reprises some of his classic roles. As the
god of travellers, he accompanies the three female divinities on
their journey from Pelion to Ida. As the divinity who mediates
between above and below, and between mortal and immortal, he
facilitates the goddesses' transition from the world of the gods to
that of mortals, as they literally 'condescend' to seek the opinion
of a mere man.

PARIS ALEXANDER

Paris' back-story is intriguing and ominous, with a hint of the
Oedipal about it. His ancestry was royal: he was the son of King
Priam and Queen Hecabe (Hecuba) of Troy. But just before he
was born, his mother dreamed that she gave birth to a fiery torch
that brought destruction on the city. Alarmed at the omen, Priam
consulted a dream-interpreter, on whose advice the king decided
to get rid of the infant, handing it to a slave with instructions to
expose it on nearby Mount Ida. However – and here is the similarity with Oedipus (and with Romulus and Remus, and Moses,
and many another legendary foundling) – the baby miraculously
survived, was suckled by a she-bear, and was eventually found and
brought up by a shepherd. The mythographer Apollodorus sums
up his early life like this: 'Paris grew to be a young man who was
both more beautiful and stronger than most, and he received the

second name Alexandros ['Defender of Men'] because he repelled robbers and defended [*alexēsas*] the flocks.'[12]

A SUITABLE JUDGE

Paris' life as a herdsman brought him into contact with all kinds of powers of nature, including the local nymphs; it was one of these, Oenone, whom he married (see below). So at the time of the Judgment Paris was no inexperienced virgin but a man who already knew about sex – indeed, sex with a divinity (they had a child). Another characteristic that fitted him for his role as arbiter of beauty was that he was himself extraordinarily good-looking. As the satirist Lucian expressed it in his dialogue *Judgment of the Goddesses* (the speaker is Zeus): 'You are handsome yourself, and knowledgeable about erotic matters.'[13] The Trojan royal family was famous for its incredibly good-looking males: the youthful Ganymede aroused the lust of Zeus himself, while Tithonus, another Trojan prince, became the lover of Eos (Aurora), goddess of the dawn.

Athena, Hermes, Aphrodite, Oenone, Paris and Eros, on a fragmentary Roman sarcophagus, 2nd century CE.

As well as his good looks, there was one other characteristic of Paris that involved the aesthetics of desire: his clothes. Image after image and text after text portray him as splendidly clad. Nowhere is this clearer than on a fine vase in Karlsruhe (see below), where he upstages all the deities present thanks to his gorgeously embroidered raiment. This is not your average shepherd: Paris' finery marks him out as 'other' – a royal Trojan with more than a hint of the 'oriental', rather than the Hellenic, about him. The same emphasis on adornment comes across in a description of a pantomime on the theme of the Judgment, as described in the *Metamorphoses* by Apuleius (2nd century CE): '[The performer] was handsomely dressed to represent the Phrygian shepherd Paris, with

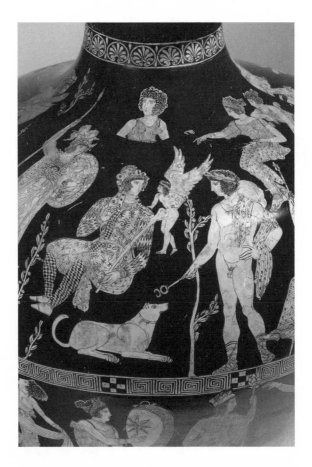

Paris with Hermes,
detail of Attic *hydria*,
c. 440 BCE.

exotic garments flowing from his shoulders, and his head crowned with a tiara of gold.'[14] Paris had been associated with finery since the start of his mythological career: it was one of the things that Helen would find irresistible about him – especially, according to one source, his embroidered trousers and gold necklace.[15]

THE GODDESSES' APPEARANCE

The Judgment is quintessentially visual: everything depends on what the goddesses look like. But their appearance varies a great deal. On an amphora in New York (see below, left), there is virtually nothing to distinguish the three deities, all of whom are fully and modestly clothed; Paris retreats towards the right, presumably over-awed by his unexpected visitors. On another amphora of similar date in Basel, there is again little to differentiate them, except for the helmet held by Athena.[16] But elsewhere in the artistic tradition

Attributed to the Swing Painter, Judgment of Paris, terracotta neck-amphora, c. 540–530 BCE.

Attributed to the Penthesilea Painter, The Judgment of Paris, terracotta *pyxis*, c. 465–460 BCE.

the differentiations are more strongly marked. On a beautifully painted cylindrical box (*pyxis*; see opposite, right), Aphrodite is readily identifiable, her identity being symbolized by the winged figure of Eros looking up at her. She is even more clearly demarcated in a painting from the House of Jupiter at Pompeii (see below), where she reveals almost all. The same is true on a mosaic from Jaén in Spain, which is also notable for the elaborate clothes

The Judgment of Paris, fresco from the
House of Jupiter in Pompeii, 1st century CE.

The Judgment of Paris, detail of Roman mosaic from
Cástulo, near Jaén, Spain, 1st–2nd century CE.

worn by Paris; he has not, however, lost his identity as shepherd,
as witnessed by the presence of his flock and sheepdog (see above).

To authors of texts, no less than to visual artists, the scene
offered plenty of scope, with the emphasis usually falling on
Aphrodite. Sometimes her robes are described as supremely deli-
cate, as in this lovely fragment from the *Cypria*:

> She put on garments that the Graces and Seasons had
> made for her and dyed in spring flowers – such flowers
> as the Seasons wear – in crocus and hyacinth and
> flourishing violet and the lovely bloom of the rose, sweet
> and delicious, and heavenly buds, the flowers of the

fragrant narcissus. In such perfumed garments Aphrodite clothed herself at all seasons.[17]

But sometimes the tone is more risqué. Lucian's Paris decides that, in order to conduct a thorough inspection, he really needs the goddesses to strip.[18] In the theatrical show described by Apuleius, the performer playing Venus (Aphrodite) leaves little to the imagination:

> She vaunted her unblemished beauty by appearing naked and unclothed except for a thin silken garment veiling her entrancing lower parts. An inquisitive gust of air would at one moment with quite lubricious affection blow this garment aside, so that when wafted away it revealed her virgin bloom; at another moment it would wantonly breathe directly upon it, clinging tightly and vividly outlining the pleasurable prospect of her lower limbs.[19]

The voyeuristic reader enjoys the luxury of being able to savour the performance from behind an extra layer of concealment: the internal narrator at this point in the story is the sex-obsessed ass into which the novel's central character has been transformed.

THE BRIBES

Paris' choice was, it goes without saying, impossible, since each of the goddesses was in her own way perfect. What made his decision feasible was that he was actually choosing not between goddesses, but between bribes, each of which derived from the area within which the goddess in question was pre-eminent. Hera was associated with marriage and the family, and also, as Zeus' consort, with the exercise of power and authority. Athena, alongside her patronage of craftsmanship, was the invincible warrior goddess who embodied the organized use of martial force. Aphrodite's province was more restricted, but within it she was supreme: sexual desire, whether inside or outside marriage, and whether homosexual or heterosexual. The terms of the bribes are described differently in different sources, but the common denominators are clear: Hera promised Paris royal power and domination; Athena, victory in war; Aphrodite, the prospect of marriage to Helen, the most beautiful woman in the world.[20] What every source agrees on is the outcome: Aphrodite got the apple, and Paris got Helen.

THE SEQUEL

The most straightforward case is that of Hermes: post-Judgment, he continued in his usual role as mediator between opposites. The three goddesses merit a little more attention. True, their spheres of activity remained the same, but the Judgment did affect their attitudes and behaviour. The resentment felt by the two losers towards Paris expanded to include the city he belonged to: throughout the ten-year siege of Troy, Hera and Athena sided with the Greeks, whereas Aphrodite naturally favoured the opposite camp, aiding the Trojans in general and Paris in particular. (All this is wonderfully described in Homer's *Iliad*.) Later on, when her son Aeneas escaped from the destruction of Troy, Aphrodite/Venus would lovingly lend her support to him, as Virgil memorably narrated in the *Aeneid*.

In contrast to the subsequent careers of the four divinities present at the Judgment, the experiences of Paris were complicated and troubled. After all, he was a mere mortal, and (as the Greeks saw it) the lives of mortals tend to lack the behavioural predictability and immunity to passing events that goes with being divine. While Paris was still a herdsman, funeral games were celebrated at Troy to honour the (so it was believed) long-dead son of Priam – none other than Paris himself. A bull from Paris' herd was selected as the prize for the games, and Paris determined to enter the competition himself to win it back. As the logic of the story demanded, he was victorious; recognized as the son of Priam, he was welcomed back into the royal family.[21] At first sight his progression from city to mountain pasture and back to the city corresponds to an initiatory schema familiar from anthropology and folklore, according to which the adolescents of certain societies leave home, go out into wilds for an intermediate, probationary period and then return as fully-fledged adult males.[22] But there was something anomalous about Paris. Even while he was a herdsman, he already had traits that linked him with the sophisticated world of the aesthetic and the beautiful, and this connection never left him. And when he returned to the city and regained his royal identity, he was no military leader on the pattern of an Achilles, an Ajax or a Hector (you cannot imagine any of *them* being chosen to arbitrate in a dispute about female loveliness). It was as if he were always marginal, never fully integrated into the world of warfare.

The next and, in terms of its consequences, disastrous stage of Paris' career took him to Sparta. Ignoring the advice of Trojan seers (including Cassandra) who had predicted the horrific consequences of his action, Paris journeyed to the home of Menelaus and his wife, Helen. Breaking the sacred bond of hospitality, Paris not only went to bed with Helen but carried her off with him to Troy. Although some said she had no choice – wasn't the power of love irresistible? – Helen's elopement earned her a predominantly bad press throughout the ancient mythological tradition (although the account of her in the *Iliad* is marvellously nuanced and largely sympathetic).

The Homeric account of Paris reinforces his connection with beauty and sexuality, even amid the carnage at Troy. In a duel with Menelaus, Paris manages to escape with his life only thanks to Aphrodite, who conceals him in a mist and whisks him off to his sweetly scented bedroom. The goddess then disguises herself as an elderly servant and gives Helen a beguiling message:

Come this way: Alexandros is calling you back to the house. He is there in the bedroom, on the carved bed, shining in his beauty and his clothing. You would not say he had come from fighting against a man – you would think he was going to the dance, or had just left dancing and was taking his rest.[23]

When she reaches the bedroom, Helen begins by mocking Paris' skill as a warrior and comparing his valour unfavourably with that of Menelaus. But the conversation can end in only one way: the two of them go to bed to enjoy each other. There is no shortage of passages in the *Iliad* that show Paris in the thick of the fighting, but he has so much 'history' that he remains a man apart.

Two more episodes round off Paris' career. The first enhances his reputation as a fighter: he was said to have killed Achilles with an arrow, although it needed Apollo to direct it to Achilles' only vulnerable spot: the heel.[24] The second takes us back to the centre of Paris' emotional life: his relationship with women. His marriage to Oenone ended tragically. After he had deserted her to pursue Helen, the nymph's jealousy never slept. It lay within her power to heal Paris if ever he were hurt, but when he was critically wounded by an arrow fired by the Greek hero Philoctetes Oenone refused to cure him. Eventually she relented, but it was too late. Though nymphs were sometimes said to live for ever, they might also be thought of as merely long-lived and still subject to death. So it was with Oenone. She threw herself onto Paris' funeral pyre and died at his side.[25]

After antiquity

When the myth of the Judgment was received by subsequent cultures, some original meanings were downplayed or ignored, while others developed new energies in the light of fresh cultural

172

circumstances. Two aspects of these developments are worth looking out for. First, the choice between goals: what should human beings be striving for? Second, the beauty pageant featuring a man gazing at and evaluating half- or completely naked females: what are the implications of this (arousing? nauseating?) scenario?

A significant figure in relation to later tradition was the (possibly North African) writer Fabius Planciades Fulgentius (late 5th century CE), who compiled an elaborate set of allegories under the title *Mythologies*. His differentiation between the three goddesses took preceding tradition in a new direction, which would enable the moral implications of Paris' choice to retain their validity even when Greco-Roman polytheism had given way to Christian beliefs. For Fulgentius, Minerva/Athena stands for the contemplative or meditative life, dominated by virtuous dedication to the pursuit of knowledge. The active life, symbolized by Juno/Hera, seems at first sight worthy, but for Fulgentius it entails the covetous pursuit of possessions and a disreputable desire to cling on to them. As for Venus/Aphrodite, her embodiment of lustful pleasure-seeking puts her firmly at the bottom of Fulgentius' (though not Paris') priorities. One respect in which Fulgentius echoes earlier tradition is that he homes in on the idea of clothes. His approach is characteristically allegorical. Minerva wears a cloak with three folds, 'either because all wisdom is many-sided or because it is kept hidden'. Juno 'has her head veiled, because all riches are always hidden'. Venus is, of course, naked, 'either because she sends out her devotees naked or because the sin of lust is never cloaked or because it suits only the naked'.[26]

Hardly less influential than Fulgentius' moralizing was a shift in the narrative context of the Judgment. Numerous writers and artists, going back at least as far as the *History of the Fall of Troy* attributed to Dares Phrygius (perhaps 5th century CE), imagined that Paris saw the goddesses in a dream.[27] This motif would prove popular and long-lived. In John Gower's poem *Confessio Amantis* (The Lover's Confession, *c.* 1390), Paris recalls how he once got lost while hunting:

> and on the gras
> Beside a welle I lay me doun
> To slepe, and in a visioun
> To me the god Mercurie cam;
> Goddesses thre with him he nam,
> Minerve, Venus, and Juno,
> And in his hond an appel tho
> He hield of gold with lettres write.
> And this he dede me to wite,
> Hou that thei putt hem upon me,
> That to the faireste of hem thre
> Of gold that appel scholde I give.[28]

A similar scene is depicted in an illuminated manuscript of a work by Christine de Pizan, in which the hunter has presumably nodded off after stopping to quench his thirst (see opposite). Everything about the scene is decorous and courtly, but that certainly was not the atmosphere surrounding every male's fantasy about the three goddesses. Lucas Cranach the Elder, for one, turned Paris' vision into something far more titillating. As court painter to the electors (princes) of Saxony in Wittenberg, Cranach kept coming back to the theme of the Judgment, and in a work dating to 1528 gave a particularly suggestive account of it (see pl. IX). Mercury, with the air of a benevolent great-uncle, cradles an up-to-date variant of the apple: a crystal orb. In the figure of Paris, who looks upwards in vacant rapture, the herdsman has clearly given way to the knight errant; the heavy armour he is wearing must be keeping him as warm as toast. By contrast, the three easy-going women he is fantasizing about are wearing next to nothing, but it does not seem to be worrying them. Who is who? It's hard to be sure, though the

Attributed to the Master of the Cité des Dames and workshop, miniature of the Judgment of Paris, in Christine de Pizan's *L'Épître Othéa, c.* 1410–14.

Antoine Watteau, *The Judgment of Paris*, c. 1718–21.

awkward posture of the one in the middle – contrived so that she can gaze seductively at the viewing electors while simultaneously showing them her naked behind – looks likely to leave her with a nasty crick in the neck.

The Judgment offered a (literally) golden opportunity to explore the relationship between viewer/voyeur and more or less unadorned femininity, in both painting and the decorative arts.[29] Rubens, like Cranach, went for out-and-out sensuality, though some thought he went too far: the Cardinal-Infante Ferdinand, writing in 1639 to his brother Philip IV of Spain, observed that the goddesses in one of the painter's renderings of the myth were 'too naked'.[30] But there was scope for variation. A canvas by the French painter Antoine Watteau (see opposite) gives us a boyishly bashful Paris, in whom any sense of power conferred by his status as prize-giver is overshadowed by the embarrassment that accompanies his near nakedness.

Even more innovative was the line taken by Hans Eworth, a Flemish artist who worked in Tudor England. His oil painting *Elizabeth I and the Three Goddesses* (1569) reworks the ancient myth into a celebration of the cool authority of the English queen (see overleaf). Eworth's 'Paris' is none other than Elizabeth I herself, who keeps the orb in her own possession while magnificently dismissing the three pretenders – Juno irate, Minerva distressed, Venus sedate and rather insipid. The work – which we know belonged to Elizabeth – bore a contemporary Latin inscription in elegiac couplets, which may be translated as:

> Juno was powerful in royal might, Pallas's mind was sharp,
> Venus's beauty shone in her rosy face.
> Elizabeth then came and, overwhelmed, Juno fled,
> Pallas was silenced, and Venus blushed.[31]

In classical antiquity and ever since, myths have spoken just as effectively about politics as they have about morality.

It has to be admitted, though, that in the case of the Judgment

Hans Eworth, *Elizabeth I and the Three Goddesses*, 1569.

of Paris politics comes well down the list of topics that the myth has most often been used to explore. Morality, especially sexual morality, figures far more prominently. But not everyone has taken the same view about what the moral of the story actually is. The Renaissance humanist Marsilio Ficino (1433–1499) took a typically reflective approach. In a letter to the Florentine statesman Lorenzo de' Medici, Ficino meditated on the contrasting characteristics of three types of life: the active (symbolized by Juno), the contemplative (symbolized by Minerva) and the voluptuary (symbolized by Venus).[32] What makes Ficino's view unusual is that he regards Venus as standing not just for the pleasures of the flesh, but for music and poetry too. This takes the debate about life choices in a new direction. True enough, Paris went for the wrong option: to choose Venus to the exclusion of Juno and Minerva was bound to cause problems. But to opt exclusively for the provinces of either of the other two goddesses – even that of contemplative

Minerva – was not the right solution either. Hercules, for example, had once been obliged to choose between an agreeably easy life and a glorious but tough one (this was when he symbolically came to a crossroads presided over by Virtue and Vice, and had to decide between them); he ended up with a (literally) laborious life of struggle. Socrates, on the other hand, put all his eggs into the basket of knowledge, and suffered for his rejection of both the active life and the life of pleasure. The only solution, in Ficino's opinion, lay in a *combination* of the provinces of the three goddesses: power, wisdom and (aesthetic) pleasure.

One of three

One intriguing feature of the Judgment is less often discussed than its intrinsic interest merits: the number three. The three Gorgons, the three Moirae (Fates), the three Graces, the three Graiae (grey-haired crones with one eye and one tooth between them), as well as the Capitoline Triad of great Roman divinities (Jupiter, Juno and Minerva) – groups of three are a recurring feature of Greek and Roman myth and religion. But the idea of the triad extends far beyond the culture of classical antiquity. In religious belief across the millennia and across the world, the symbolism of three crops up repeatedly. The Christian Trinity of Father, Son and Holy Spirit, and the three Christian virtues of Faith, Hope and Charity (or love); the Hindu Trimūrti (Brahma, Vishnu, Shiva); the Threefold Path of Good Thoughts, Good Words and Good Deeds in Zoroastrianism; the three Norns of Norse mythology; the Wiccan Rule of Three – these are just a handful out of countless examples. We find the same prominence in folklore: the Three Little Pigs, Goldilocks and the Three Bears, The Three Wishes, The Three Billygoats Gruff, Cinderella ... Philosophers, too, from the Pythagoreans to Hegel, have found the number three to be richly significant.

Within this vast range of phenomena there is a subset that involves a choice between three options. To this group the

Judgment of Paris evidently belongs. So also do two other memorable examples, found in plays by Shakespeare. Although neither storyline is exactly parallel to the Judgment, a comparison will help us to identify what they have in common and what sets each apart from the others. That will, in turn, offer another interpretative perspective on the myth of the Judgment.

In *The Merchant of Venice*, such are the attractions of the play's heroine, Portia, that she is pursued by many suitors. But she herself is powerless to decide which one to accept since, according to the terms of her father's will, she is obliged to marry the man who 'correctly' chooses between three caskets: gold, silver and lead. Each casket bears an inscription. Gold: 'Who chooseth me shall gain what many men desire.' Silver: 'Who chooseth me shall get as much as he deserves.' Lead: 'Who chooseth me must give and hazard all he hath.'[33] The three caskets are not the only example in the play of a significant trio. Now that several potential suitors have pulled out because of the quixotic nature of the riddle of the caskets, the field is reduced to three. The first of these, the Prince of Morocco, makes the mistake of going for gold. 'All that glisters is not gold', reads the scroll inside the casket; in other words: 'Don't be misled by appearances.' The second suitor, the Prince of Aragon, opts for silver. Wrong again: anyone who arrogantly assumes that he deserves nothing but the best is a fool, and within the silver casket there appropriately lies the portrait of a fool. The last of the three suitors is Bassanio, a Venetian gentleman who truly loves and is truly loved by Portia. Realizing that the outward allure of gold and silver may be mere empty show, Bassanio opts for the casket made of humble lead ('Thy paleness moves me more than eloquence').[34] He opens it, and joyfully discovers Portia's portrait within. As so often in folk tales, it is the third, last and seemingly unprepossessing option that is the one to go for. The only suitor who knew how to discriminate between substance and appearance has gained his just reward.

A second Shakespearean judgment-of-three constitutes the premise of an even greater drama. As *King Lear* opens, the ageing king proclaims his intention to transfer his regal power to his three daughters. He asks the same question of each daughter in turn, and will distribute their inheritances according to his evaluation of their answers. The question is: 'Which of you shall we say doth love us most?'[35] The first and second sisters to reply, Goneril and Regan, outdo each other in the hypocritical lavishness of their rhetoric, earning equally munificent rewards from their father. To Cordelia, the youngest of the three, such sham praise is anathema. Reticent in her speech, she undertakes simply to love her father 'according to my bond', that is, just as much as a daughter should love her father – and no more than that.[36] Crassly misunderstanding the temperaments and merits of his children, Lear casts Cordelia out with nothing. Thus are the seeds sown of the heart-wrenching tragedy that lies in store.

What differences and similarities are there between the plots of these plays and the myth of the Judgment? In *Lear*, the adjudicator is not, like Paris, a neutral outsider. On the contrary, he is a uniquely interested party: the preposterously self-centred idea of 'Who loves me most?' is enough to demonstrate the extent of his involvement. However, in another way Lear does play the role of Paris, since it is he who assesses the relative qualities of the three 'contenders', even if his original intention is not to prefer one to the others, but to make an apportionment from which all three will benefit according to their worth. A more interesting similarity with Paris lies in the fact that Lear makes his decision on the basis of the contenders' rhetorical persuasiveness (or, in Cordelia's case, the lack of it), persuasiveness that amounts, in effect, to bribery (or, in Cordelia's case, a refusal to bribe). In *The Merchant*, the case is rather different. Portia, who presides over the process of selection, plays a role that is analogous not to that of Paris, but to that of Helen: she herself is the ultimate prize.

Although later in the play, in the court case between Antonio and Shylock, Portia will indeed guilefully assume the role of judge, in the episode of the caskets she has no adjudicatory role. Unlike the patterns in *Lear* and the Judgment of Paris, in *The Merchant* there is no single selector but a sequence of three. And none of them is a neutral outsider: the personal happiness of each depends on the decision. Perhaps the most important contrast between, on the one hand, the myth of the Judgment and, on the other hand, *Lear* and *The Merchant* is that in the Judgment there is no sense of a disjunction between gaudy, outward show and inner moral value. In the Judgment, what you see is what you get: Paris simply has to decide what it is, from among the different attractions on offer, that he truly wants.

Perhaps the most important common factor in the three story patterns is that they all pose the fundamental question of how we rank the importance of love. In the Judgment, the kind of love at issue is sexual passion, the province represented by Aphrodite and embodied in Helen. Paris evidently rates that sort of love as the highest good. In *The Merchant*, love involves more than just sexual passion, although between Portia and Bassanio it is certainly part of the mix. At all events, Bassanio's choice, unlike that of his two predecessors, will be guided by love alone ('If you do love me, you will find me out,' Portia assures him before the choice.[37]) In *Lear*, the sorts of love implied by the king's interrogation of his daughters are the bonds between parent and child and between husband and wife; to selfish Lear's annoyance, Cordelia states that her future husband will receive half her love.

Closely related to love in our three examples is the topic of (often, but not always, dysfunctional) marriage. In the Judgment, the scene of the original discord is a wedding, and the union of Paris and Helen, foreshadowed in Paris' choice, will sow the seeds of yet greater discord by shattering another marriage, that between Helen and Menelaus. In *The Merchant*, the question of whom Portia will marry is a central pillar of the drama. In *Lear*, although Goneril and Regan are already married, Lear's division of his property will in effect bestow dowries upon them. The dowry of the honourable and loving but, for now, despised Cordelia will be literally nothing, but the King of France values her at her true worth and takes her as his bride. His affection cannot halt the ultimate tragedy, however, which brings about, among other deaths, those of Lear and Cordelia, after their sublime but agonizingly brief reconciliation.

What all three story patterns have in common is an exploration of the goals of human aspiration. What ends are really important in human life? What should we value most? Each example creates a different kind of thought experiment through which to seek an answer.

The Judgment in modern times

Recent and contemporary re-imaginings of the Judgment have tended to be the sphere of artists rather than writers. (Gore Vidal's 1952 novel *The Judgment of Paris*, about a man tempted by three women of contrasting temperament, is an exception, but opinions differ about its merits.) What is different about the majority of modern artistic representations is their tone. The closer we come to today, the more often do we find artists responding to the myth in a mood of parody or satire. This reflects how increasingly difficult it has become to take at face value a scenario that locates power in the eyes of a man, while consigning women to the role of willing recipients of male appreciation (see p. 184). A notable feminist turning of the tables can be seen in a work by the Chicago-born artist Mary Ellen Croteau (see p. 185, above). The only genitals in question – even if they are implied rather than explicitly depicted – belong not to the female divinities but to a naked and shame-faced Paris. All the power resides in the unimpressed gazes and no-nonsense postures of the trio of women who are sizing him up – ethnically diverse, obviously intelligent,

and fully and elegantly clothed. Another way of deflating Paris'
pretensions is to see him as nothing better than a prospective
client trying to decide between the relative charms of three pros-
titutes; a painting by George Grosz and a drawing by Picasso are
variations on this theme.[38] More basically even than that, Paris
has been envisaged as a cockerel; the symbolism in a painting by
Federico Jiménez Fernández is hardly accidental (see opposite,
below).[39] But the prize for humour goes to the American artist
Eleanor Antin (see pl. x). Warlike Minerva totes a rifle; Juno, the
apron-clad home-maker, has brought her vacuum cleaner to the
forest (all those untidy leaves); Venus looks a million dollars in her
glamorous evening dress, with sweet little Cupid in tow; Mercury

Donald Trump,
former President
of the United States,
with three beauty
contestants, 2005.
As so often, the
concept of the beauty
contest depends on
the idea of the gaze,
and on contrasts
in clothing.

Mary Ellen Croteau, *The Judgment of Paris*, 1997.

Federico Jiménez Fernández, *The Judgment of Paris*, c. 1882.

and Paris are like a pair of outrageously camp beach boys. The only one who looks semi-detached is Helen, sitting lost in thought at the far left. It's not surprising that she is preoccupied, as her fate lies in the hands of this wildly improbable sextet.

This chapter took as its point of departure an Agatha Christie novel in which the misunderstood phrase 'the Judgment of Paris' provided Hercule Poirot with a vital clue. But there was another myth – or sequence of twelve myths – that Christie also exploited to show off the talents of the same great Belgian detective. In the collection of short stories entitled *The Labours of Hercules*, Poirot walks in the footsteps of his mighty mythical predecessor, achieving a dozen cerebral successes to match the physical triumphs of his namesake.[40] It is to this sequence of Greek myths that we now turn.

CHAPTER 7

The Labours
of Heracles

Heracles (in more exact transliteration from Greek, Herakles;
to the Romans, Hercules) is the hero par excellence: Odysseus,
Jason, Perseus, Aeneas, even Achilles pale beside him.[1] True, he
sometimes receives help from his nephew and sidekick Iolaus,
from his trusty comrade Theseus or from the goddess Athena. Yet
he usually relies on his own individualistic resources, and above
all on his super-heroic physique. But his mythical persona is much
more complicated than the description 'superhero' might imply,
since his weaknesses are as remarkable as his strengths. His capacity
for strong-arm tactics shows a disturbing tendency to turn into
something profoundly ambivalent, and the superiority conferred
on him by his muscle power can sometimes be reversed. At various points in his career he goes mad, slaughters his wife (Megara)
and their children, obediently performs services for a feeble
coward (Eurystheus), becomes the slave of one woman (Omphale),
and perishes in agony at the hands of another (his second wife,
Deianira), even if this 'death' is merely the prelude to an eternal
existence among the Olympian gods. Of any hero(ine) from any
culture – Robin Hood, Sindbad, Lancelot, Wonder Woman, Flash
Gordon, Xena the Warrior Princess – one may trivially say: 'S/he
is larger than life.' But of Heracles one may truly say: 'He exceeds

the limits of life itself', since eventually he transcends the ultimate boundary, that between life and death. To be sure, a sceptical ancient myth-teller such as the satirist Lucian could report the mischievous allegation that, even when Heracles became a god, he was only a marginal divinity, an 'illegal resident' among the gods.[2] But the evidence for the defence was stronger. Not only did Heracles overcome both Geras (Old Age) and Thanatos (Death) in single combat, but he also fought alongside the Olympians in their cosmic battle against the Giants. As a result, in the words of Hesiod's epic poem *Theogony*, 'having performed a great deed among the immortals, he dwells free from trouble and free from old age for all time'.[3]

In antiquity, texts and images representing Heracles were everywhere. As well as starring in countless mythological narratives, he figured regularly as an exemplar in philosophical discussions about 'the good life'. Politics was another area in which his precedent was repeatedly invoked, when, from Archaic Greece to the Roman Empire, individuals and groups staked claims to authority and legitimacy.[4] Additionally, there is a wealth of archaeological and literary evidence from across the Greco-Roman world for cults to Heracles as a hero who became a god. Even the roughest sketch of this vast body of material would burst the bounds of the present chapter. By confining ourselves to just one group of his exploits – the so-called 'Labours' – we give ourselves at least a chance (given that we are talking about Heracles, we had better call it a *fighting* chance) of covering a decent portion of the ground.

Retelling the Labours in classical antiquity

The word 'labour' – more usually 'Labour', with upper-case 'L', investing this group of exploits with a higher profile and a separate identity – is the conventional rendering in English of the Greek noun *athlon*. But a more accurate translation would be 'competition' or 'contest'. The fact that *athlon* is the etymological root of modern

English words such as 'triathlon', 'pentathlon', heptathlon' and 'decathlon' confirms a sporting connection that existed already in antiquity (the pentathlon featured in the ancient Olympic Games). According to the poet Pindar, for example, the ancient Olympics had been founded by none other than Heracles, and the twelve Labours could be thought of, at least from one perspective, as an exercise in extreme sport.[5] But attempting the Labours was no game: many of Heracles' adversaries were wild beasts or monsters. Nevertheless, success demanded the same combination of skills that were needed in the real-world Olympics: tremendous strength, formidable endurance and (from time to time) considerable ingenuity.

Heracles' *athla* (the plural form) were sometimes distinguished from both his *parerga* ('side actions') – exploits carried out as incidental accompaniments to the Labours – and his *praxeis* ('deeds').[6] But equally often ancient writers about myth made no such distinction. Another question on which opinions differed was how many Labours there were. By far the commonest answer was twelve: this was the number of exploits sculpted on the metopes of the Temple of Zeus at Olympia (c. 460 BCE), and the same figure is given by, among others, the Hellenistic poets Theocritus and Apollonius of Rhodes.[7] But twelve was not the only option: some myth-tellers mention ten or, more hyperbolically, a thousand or ten thousand.[8] There were other variables, too, the most significant of which concern the motivation for the Labours, and, closely related to that, the question of where the Labours fitted into the overall trajectory of the hero's career.

The general motivational framework for the Labours is implied already in the *Iliad*, in the story of Heracles' birth from the union between Zeus and a mortal woman, Alcmene.[9] Hera was furious at this latest in the catalogue of Zeus' infidelities and decided to get her own back with a trick. When Alcmene was on the point of giving birth, Zeus boasted that the child who was about to see the light of day, 'of the race of men who come from my own blood', would rule over those around him.[10] Having goaded Zeus into ratifying this with a binding oath, Hera persuaded the goddess of childbirth Eileithyia to delay Alcmene's parturition while simultaneously bringing prematurely to term that of another mother-to-be, Nicippe. The child that Nicippe bore was Eurystheus, a great-grandson of Zeus – and thus also one of the race of men who came from Zeus' 'own blood'. Constrained by his oath, Zeus was forced to look on while the son whom Alcmene would eventually bear – named, ironically enough, 'Heracles' ('Hera's Glory') – was obliged to obey the orders of Eurystheus, who would, indeed, in spite of the feebleness of his character, 'rule over those around him' in his role as king of all the Argolid, including Mycenae and Tiryns.

As far as the specific occasion for the Labours is concerned, some myth-tellers presented their successful completion as the necessary precondition for the hero's promotion to the status of a god, in recognition of the benefits he conferred on humanity by slaying monsters and performing other civilizing deeds.[11] According to a less positive slant, the Labours were an act of religious expiation for Heracles' murder of his wife, Megara, and their children.[12] More idiosyncratic was the version dramatized by Euripides in his magnificent but sometimes underestimated tragedy *The Madness of Heracles*. As the play opens, Megara, her three little sons and Heracles' father, Amphitryon, sit huddled in supplication at Zeus' altar in Thebes. They fear for their lives, terrorized as they are by the city's tyrant Lykos ('Wolf Man'). Heracles is absent, for he is carrying out the Labours as an act of filial piety (this is the idiosyncratic motivation). Having accidentally caused the death of his uncle Electryon, Amphitryon had been forced to flee from his home in Argos; Eurystheus would allow him to come back from exile only once Heracles had successfully completed the Labours. As the drama unfolds, Heracles returns in triumph from his final Labour and rescues his family. But then, in a catastrophic reversal of fortune, he is plunged into madness by the goddess Lyssa, whom the vindictive Hera has driven into unwilling action. Deluded into imagining that the children he sees before him belong not to himself but to Eurystheus, Heracles slaughters them along with their mother, and is prevented from killing his own father only when Athena hurls a rock at him.

By placing the Labours not as the culmination of Heracles' career but as the prelude to an episode of the grimmest pathos, Euripides implies a dramatic message that is the opposite of 'Services rendered deserve a glorious reward'. The actual message is (to put it crudely, but not inaccurately): 'Even at the zenith of human achievement, good fortune is wafer-thin.' There is, however, a glimmer of hope. As the tragedy draws to a close, Heracles' comrade Theseus persuades him to abandon thoughts of suicide, and instead to endure his fate and soldier on into the future. This compellingly moving scene demonstrates the power of friendship in the face of every disaster that the gods can throw at humanity.

One point that every myth-teller agreed on was the fact that it was weak Eurystheus who sent Heracles out on this series of seemingly impossible tasks. A similar pattern is echoed in a number of other myths in which a hero is sent out to perform an exploit from which – or so the sender fervently hopes – the hero will not return alive. Classic examples are Bellerophon (commissioned by King Iobates to slay the fearsome Chimaera) and Jason (ordered by Aietes to plough a field with fire-breathing oxen). There are similarities too with the tales of Perseus and Medusa, and Theseus and the Minotaur, though in those cases the heroes' exploits are self-chosen rather than imposed by another. More so than any of these partially comparable stories, the tale of mighty Heracles at the beck and call of feeble Eurystheus illustrates one of the key elements of Heraclean mythology: its embodiment of paradox.

The Dodecathlon

Even when our sources list the number of Labours as the canonical dozen, not all agree about the order. The sequence followed here is that recorded by, for instance, the mythographer Apollodorus (other myth-tellers, such as Diodorus Siculus, order them slightly differently).

1. THE NEMEAN LION

Traditionally regarded as the first Labour, the hero's encounter with the lion took place close to home: the small community of Nemea was located in the Argolid. In addition to the conventional leonine attributes of formidable strength and ravenous jaws, the beast possessed the superadded distinction of being invulnerable. Since it was impervious to arrows, Heracles had to strangle it with his bare hands (see pl. XI).[13] When he brought the pelt back to Mycenae as proof of success, Eurystheus was so frightened that he hid in a large *pithos* (storage jar). Throughout the rest of his career, Heracles would literally inhabit the evidence of this first victory: as countless artistic representations confirm, the lion's invulnerable skin, with the paws tied round the wearer's neck, would serve as a combination of clothing and armour. Together with his trademark club, the lion skin constituted the hero's instantly recognizable badge of identity.

2. THE LERNAEAN HYDRA

The only feature of the Nemean lion that could be described as monstrous was its invulnerability – provided, that is, we assume that part of what it is to be a monster is that it involves transgressing or superseding a 'natural' boundary. About the creature that was the target of the second Labour, however, there can be no doubt: the multi-headed water snake known as the Hydra was certainly 'monstrous', on virtually any definition of the word. Like the lion, it was local: the swamp at Lerna was just south of Argos. But the beast

IX

Lucas Cranach the Elder, *The Judgment of Paris*, 1528.

x

Eleanor Antin, *Judgment of Paris (after Rubens)*, from *Helen's Odyssey*, 2007.

XI
Kleophrades Painter,
Nemean lion, Attic
*stamnos, c.*490–480 BCE.

XII
Attributed to the Eagle
Painter, Lernaean
Hydra, Caeretan
hydria, 520–510 BCE.

HERAKLES WRITES HOME

XIII
Marian Maguire, *The Labours of Herakles:
Plate VIII: Herakles Writes Home*, 2007–8.

XIV Jan Brueghel the Elder, *Orpheus in the Underworld*, 1594.

XV
Odilon Redon, *Orpheus*, c.1903–10.

did not stay put in its marshy home; according to Apollodorus, it made forays onto dry land and wrought havoc on the surrounding livestock. Apollodorus' account is, in fact, particularly graphic:

> The Hydra had an enormous body with nine heads, eight of them mortal and the one in the middle immortal. Heracles mounted a chariot driven by Iolaus and travelled to Lerna. He brought his horses to a halt and found the Hydra on a hill by the Springs of Amymone, where she had her lair. He shot flaming arrows at her and forced her to come out. As she did so, he seized her and put her in a hold, but she wrapped herself round one of his legs and held on tight. Heracles got nowhere by smashing her heads with his club, for when one was smashed, two heads grew back. An enormous crab came to assist the Hydra and pinched Heracles' foot. Because of this, after he killed the crab, he, for his part, called for Iolaus to help. Iolaus set fire to a portion of the nearby forest and with the burning pieces of wood he scorched the stumps of the heads, preventing them from coming back. Having overcome the regenerating heads in this way, Heracles then cut off the immortal one, buried it, and placed a heavy rock over it by the road ... As for the Hydra's body, he cut it open and dipped his arrows in her bile.[14]

The intriguing detail about the single immortal head is unique to Apollodorus – just one more illustration of the teeming variability of Greek myth. Variable, too, is the number of heads. Diodorus put the figure at a hundred; visual artists inevitably opted for a lower total, suiting the number to the space available (see pl. XII).[15] As to how Heracles proved to Eurystheus that he had completed the Labour, we are not told. (Did he drag the nasty corpse up the road from Lerna to Mycenae?) One detail that permeates the tradition is the notion that Heracles collected the Hydra's venomous bile (*cholē*) in order to dip his arrows into it. Thus, as with the Nemean lion, the Hydra provided the hero with a powerful keepsake to be used in combat. The lion skin became his defensive armour; the Hydra's bile gave him a lethal weapon of attack.

3. THE KERYNEIAN (OR KERYNITIAN) HIND

Catching a female deer was, on the face of it, child's play compared with the first two Labours. True, the hunt involved Heracles in a slightly longer trek, since the animal's habitat was around 80 km (50 miles) north-west of Argos. But the deer was in no sense a vicious killer; the worst that could be said of it – it was Euripides who mentioned this – was that it was a menace to farmers.[16] However, even if it was not a monster, the deer was certainly special: it had horns (unlike real female deer); not only that, it had *golden* horns; and it was sacred to Artemis. The quality Heracles needed in order to capture it was stamina: according to different myth-tellers, he had to pursue it for a year, maybe even journeying as far north as the Danube.[17] Apollodorus relates that he had to travel no further than Arcadia but, having done so, he met with a major problem, in the shape of Artemis.[18] Even for a hero of the stature of Heracles, the wrath of this goddess, in the heart of her own sphere of influence in the wilds of nature, was something to be avoided. He managed it by using a tactic for which he was rarely noted: skilful negotiation. The fault for the deer's capture was not his own, he argued; rather, the blame lay with the man who had given the order. Apparently convinced, Artemis let him go on his way. He shouldered the deer and carried it back to Eurystheus as proof of his third achievement.

4. THE ERYMANTHIAN BOAR

Mount Erymanthos is in the northern Peloponnese, a little to the south-west of the habitat of the Keryneian deer. The boar that lived there was, in contrast to some of Heracles' explicitly monstrous adversaries, biologically conventional: for all its ferocity, it belonged

Heracles bringing the Erymanthian boar
to Eurystheus, Attic amphora, 540–530 BCE.

to a natural species. Mythical boar hunts were occasions for the display of aristocratic prowess: the two most famous examples were the Calydonian hunt, involving many of the greatest heroes from the generation before the Trojan War, and the hunt in the forests near Mount Parnassos described in *Odyssey* Book 19, in which the boar gored Odysseus in the leg before he speared it to death. Both of these hunts were collective undertakings. For a single individual to catch a boar was a much taller order, but that was the task that Eurystheus set Heracles. Myth-tellers paid little attention to the capture itself, although Apollodorus specifies that Heracles drove the creature up into the snow to slow it down, enabling him to put a lasso round it.[19] What most narrators found more interesting was the sequel. Much trickier than killing the boar in its habitat was the prospect of conveying it back to Mycenae alive: a symbolic act of domestication. Heracles managed it, then rounded off the exploit by brandishing the beast above Eurystheus, who had once more taken refuge in a storage jar (see p. 195). Greek vase painters never tired of representing this comic scene.

5. CLEANSING THE AUGEAN STABLES

The fifth Labour kept Heracles in the Peloponnese. This time he had to journey to Elis, the territory ruled over by King Augeas. For once, the exploit involved neither beast-slaying nor personal combat: it was a matter of hygiene. Eurystheus ordered him to clean out, within the space of a single day, the vast quantities of dung from the stables where he kept his many herds of cattle. Rather than using brute strength, Heracles relied on ingenuity: he diverted the waters of a nearby river (according to some sources, two rivers) to wash away the muck. Although the episode was already depicted around 460 BCE on a metope of Zeus' temple at Olympia (the great sanctuary was itself in Elis, so the myth was a local one), this Labour offered little scope to visual artists, but it did give more opportunity to writers. Diodorus interpreted the exploit simplistically:

Surely, then, we may well marvel at the inventiveness
of Heracles; for he completed the extraordinary
task he had been set without incurring any disgrace
or submitting to something that would render him
unworthy of immortality.[20]

But other myth-tellers read more into the story, playing off the
different demands of Augeas and Eurystheus. In Apollodorus' version, for example, when Heracles first came to Augeas, the hero
made no mention of Eurystheus' command; instead he simply
promised to clear out the stables in return for a wage of one tenth
of the cattle.[21] Augeas agreed, believing the task to be impossible.
When Heracles fulfilled his side of the bargain, Augeas reneged,
alleging, rather implausibly, that because (as he had by now found
out) Heracles had been *ordered* to do the task, no payment was due.
Further complication ensued when (still according to Apollodorus)
Eurystheus disqualified the Labour because Heracles had been paid
to do it (even though in fact he had not). The motif of the unful-
filled bargain occurs elsewhere in Heracles' career, notably when
he rescued Hesione from a sea monster on the understanding that
her father, the Trojan king Laomedon, would give him as payment
some divine horses (which had been Zeus' gift as compensation
for abducting Ganymede). Heracles' characteristic reaction was
to return with an army to sack Troy and kill Laomedon. But the
Augeas episode offered no such possibility of payback. Heracles
was locked into the sequence of Labours; he had no choice but to
carry on to the bitter end.

6. THE STYMPHALIAN BIRDS

If any single Labour best illustrates the truth that Greek myths are
inherently pluralistic, it is the one involving the birds that infested
the mountain-girt marsh of Stymphalos in Arcadia (see overleaf).
Opinions differed about the nature of the nuisance they created.

Hercules and the Stymphalian birds, detail of Roman mosaic
from Llíria, near Valencia, first half of the 3rd century CE.

One suggestion was that they were simply incredibly numerous and were damaging the surrounding crops; according to another view, they fired off their feathers like arrows; an even more startling variant held that they were man-eaters.[22] Equally variable is the way in which Heracles was said to have tackled them. The most imaginative version was that he scared them off by standing on a mountain top and making an almighty din with a rattle or with bronze castanets, made by Hephaestus and supplied by Athena. More conventional was the idea that he picked them off with arrows or shot them down with a catapult.

The detail about the divinely provided castanets is worth reflecting on. For every hero, life consisted of walking a tightrope: the conflicting claims of this deity or that had somehow to be reconciled. Today your progress might be destabilized by Hera's wrath or Artemis' resentment; tomorrow the help of Athena or Hephaestus might help you achieve success. It was, on the face of it, a similar story for ordinary human beings in the everyday world of the myth-tellers and their audiences: if you failed to perform a ritual sacrifice for one or other of the gods, repercussions were sure to follow for you and your community. However, a crucial difference between the world of mythology and the world of the everyday is that myths crystallize and dramatize and highlight and sharpen the concerns of ordinary life, making the tensions more extreme, the disasters more catastrophic, the achievements more glorious – and *everything* more memorable. In no set of myths are the tensions more extreme, the disasters more catastrophic and the achievements more glorious than in those that feature Heracles.

7. THE CRETAN BULL

Coming in (usually) at number 7 was the first Labour to take Heracles beyond the Peloponnese: Eurystheus ordered him to capture a wild bull from Crete and bring it back to Mycenae. Between Crete and bulls there were multiple mythical links, which built on real-world connections going back at least as early as the Minoan palaces, famed for their wonderful artistic displays of taurine imagery.[23] Heracles' combat appears repeatedly in art, especially in Attic vase painting, where his virtuosity at wrestling and lassoing are powerfully in evidence. The literary references are less striking and somewhat conflicting. The sources agree that it was a special bull; but which special bull? Some said it was the very animal that had carried Europa across the sea to Crete so that Zeus could enjoy her. However, according to most myth-tellers, that bull was not just sent by Zeus: it was actually Zeus himself in a state of temporary metamorphosis – and therefore certainly unavailable for Heracles or anyone else to capture. A variant story identified the bull seized by Heracles with the magnificent white specimen that featured in the myth of King Minos. During a dynastic dispute, Minos had once prayed to Poseidon to send a bull from the sea to prove his claim to sovereignty. The god complied, but Minos refused to reciprocate by sacrificing the animal to him. Poseidon's cruel and unusual punishment was that Minos' wife, Pasiphae, should become infatuated with the bull, mate with it and father the Minotaur. If *that* was the bull that Heracles seized, its destructive connection with Crete was to continue. Once Heracles had brought it to the Argolid to show to Eurystheus, he released the animal. Roaming free as far as Attica – and transforming its identity to 'the Marathonian bull' – it gored to death Minos' son Androgeos, only to be subsequently killed by Theseus. Paradoxically, then, perhaps the most significant consequence of Heracles' capture of the bull was to move it from Cretan to Athenian territory, thus adding one more to the numerous links between those two major loci of mythological action.

8. THE MARES OF DIOMEDES

After Crete, Heracles was sent northwards to Thrace. (Eurystheus' orders were becoming ever more geographically demanding.) This time the Labour involved creatures that were behaviourally rather than anatomically monstrous: mares that ripped people apart with their jaws and ate them.[24] They belonged to the Thracian king Diomedes, son of the war god Ares. (Several other Greek myths, such as those about the rapist Tereus and the murderer Lycurgus, depicted Thrace as a place of barbarous cruelty.[25]) According to Diodorus, Heracles sated the animals' hunger by feeding their master to them; when their full stomachs rendered them more docile, he drove them south to Mycenae.[26] What happened then? Myth-tellers disagreed about whether Eurystheus dedicated the animals to his patron deity, Hera, or whether he let them go.[27] One variant of what happened up in Thrace had the effect of integrating Heraclean mythology into local political culture. Apollodorus preserves the story that Heracles had the help of a young man called Abderos (Hermes' son and Heracles' lover). At one point Heracles entrusted the mares to Abderos to look after, but they tore the boy apart. Next to Abderos' tomb Heracles founded a city, Abdera – just one of the countless places in the Greek world that liked to claim a connection with the exploits of the peerless legendary hero.[28]

9. THE AMAZON'S BELT

The next trophy Heracles had to fetch took him north-east, to the southern shore of the Black Sea. His objective was the war belt (sometimes, less impressively, called a 'girdle') belonging to an Amazon queen, who is named in different sources as Andromeda or Hippolyte or Melanippe.[29] The episode is variously depicted as peaceable or violent, the latter being the strong preference, especially among visual artists, for whom the episode was a hugely popular one. Among the writers, Diodorus gives an elaborate account of Heracles' expedition at the head of an army of followers, which ends with the killing of many Amazons after a fierce and bloody battle.[30] Instead of slaughtering her too, Heracles

Heracles and the belt ('girdle') of Hippolyte, Campanian bell *krater*, 325–310 BCE.

releases the Amazon commander Melanippe from incarceration on condition that she pay a ransom – the war belt. More rarely, the handover is depicted as amicable (see above).

A common thread running through most of the Labours is that the opponents whom Heracles encounters are *different*; defeating a run-of-the-mill army of male warriors would be no kind of achievement for Heracles, and it certainly would not qualify as a Labour. But these several opponents are each *differently* different. One recurrent feature, however, is some kind of anomaly, whether anatomical or behavioural. What marks the Amazons out as worthy adversaries for a Labour is not only their fighting prowess but, in their case too, their embodiment of anomaly – certainly a behavioural anomaly, in view of their all-female lifestyle, and possibly an anatomical anomaly too (those single breasts).

10. THE CATTLE OF GERYON(EUS)

Labour number 10 sounds, at first blush, pretty routine in comparison with some of the other tasks imposed by Eurystheus: Heracles just had to rustle some herds of entirely non-monstrous cattle and drive them to Mycenae. But in fact it was anything but routine, because of two factors: the owner of the cattle, and their location.

The herds belonged to Geryon, son of Chrysaor, who was himself the offspring of Poseidon and the Gorgon Medusa (Chrysaor had been born from Medusa's neck after she had been decapitated by Perseus).[31] The monstrosity in Geryon's ancestry on his grandmother's side came through in his anatomy: numerous sources portray him as a three-in-one freak. Opinions differed about whether he was merely three-headed or actually three-torsoed, as well as about what he looked like below the waist (two legs or six?). Geryon's own plurality was matched by that of his two-headed hound, Orth(r)os; it was hardly surprising the dog's anatomy was unusual, since his parents were Typhon and Echidna, making him the brother of the Hydra and Cerberus.[32] The difficulty of dealing with Geryon's multiplicity was compounded by his location. He lived at the world's western limit, an island named Erytheia ('the red land'): the place of the setting sun. After journeying to the far south-west of Spain and performing numerous 'side exploits' en route, Heracles crossed the river of Oceanos in the huge golden bowl in which Helios used to sail eastwards every night from the site of sunset, to be ready to rise again each dawn. That Helios lent him his super-bowl was not exactly altruism: Heracles aimed his bow at the god, who generously let him use the transportation in recognition of his audacity.

Numerous ancient images illustrate Heracles' combat with Geryon (see overleaf). For accounts of his elaborate return journey to Mycenae – cattle and all – we rely on written sources. According to one version, he had to load the cattle into Helios' bowl, sail across

Attributed to a painter of Group E, Heracles and Geryon,
Attic amphora, *c.* 550–540 BCE.

Oceanos as far as Tartessos in Spain, and then drive the herds over-
land across a good part of the European mainland before handing
them over to Eurystheus in Mycenae. What was Eurystheus to
do with them? Greek ritual practice almost invariably involved
sacrificing domesticated animals; sacrificing a wild animal was
not usually an option. The animals Heracles had brought back
were indeed domesticated, so Eurystheus' course was obvious. In
acknowledgment of the patronage of his long-standing supporter,
Hera, he sacrificed the beasts to her.[33]

11. THE APPLES OF THE HESPERIDES

Most ancient narratives about Heracles' gathering of these marvel-
lous fruits agree on a number of points.[34] The apples were golden;
the tree they grew on was tended by the Hesperides, nymphs

who dwelt at a far-off place usually thought of as located in the far west; although no ancient Greco-Roman source says that the apples conferred immortality or eternal youth (in contrast to a superficially comparable theme in Norse mythology), they were special enough to have been presented as a wedding gift by Gaia to Zeus and Hera; their guardian was a terrifying snake called Ladon, the monstrous – some said, hundred-headed – offspring of Typhon and Echidna. But on one central feature of the story opinions diverged. According to some myth-tellers, the credit for slaying Ladon and picking the apples belonged to Heracles alone.[35] But an alternative tradition linked the Labour to an intriguing encounter between Heracles and Atlas, the Titan who had been condemned, as punishment for his opposition to Zeus, to bear the world on his shoulders for all eternity. According to that alternative version, Heracles had received some shrewd advice from Prometheus, whom the hero had just liberated by shooting the eagle that was everlastingly gnawing him. Apollodorus takes up the story:

> Prometheus told Heracles not to go after the apples himself, but to take over holding up the sky from Atlas and send him instead ... Heracles followed this advice and took over holding up the sky. After picking three apples from the Hesperides, Atlas came back to Heracles. Atlas, not wanting to hold up the sky, said that he would himself carry the apples to Eurystheus and bade Heracles to hold up the sky in his stead. Heracles promised to do so but succeeded by craft in putting it on Atlas instead. For at the advice of Prometheus he told Atlas to hold up the sky because he wanted to put a pad on his head [to soften the crushing weight]. When he heard this, Atlas put the apples down on the ground and took over holding up the sky, so Heracles picked them up and left.[36]

Atlas holds out the apples of the Hesperides to Heracles, who, backed
by Athena, and with a cushion on his shoulders, supports the world.
Metope from the temple of Zeus at Olympia, *c.* 470–457 BCE.

In this version, there is, for once, more to Heracles than brute strength: although the ruse had been Prometheus' idea, Heracles has enough nous to carry it out successfully. As for the fate of the apples, all myth-tellers agreed that Heracles took them back to Eurystheus, after which they were eventually given to Athena, who in turn restored them to the Hesperides. As was invariably the case, Heracles' Labours did not in the end affect the status quo.

Yet another take on events – and a rather poignant one – can be found in Apollonius' epic about the voyage of the *Argo*, narrated from the rare perspective of a victim of the Labours. One of the Hesperides sorrowfully complained to the Argonauts about a heinous act committed the previous day:

> Bitter is the grief he left behind for us. Yesterday some
> man came, most foul in his violence and his appearance,
> his eyes blazing under his fierce brow, quite pitiless! He
> wore the skin of a giant lion, untreated and untanned;
> he carried a thick olive branch and a bow, with which he
> shot and killed this creature here.[37]

The Argonauts were overjoyed to learn that their former comrade Heracles had been so recently in the area, for he had dropped out of their expedition soon after its inception when he had stayed behind to search, frantically but in vain, for his young lover Hylas. But the Hesperides, robbed of their precious fruit, were far from happy. Some of those adversely affected by Heracles' Labours deserved what they got: no one would shed many tears for Diomedes. But Ladon, who was only doing his proper job as a guard-snake, now lies a rotting corpse; and the nymphs have lost their precious treasure. Heroism can have its dark side, and not all of Heracles' exploits were achieved without causing pain and grief.

12. CERBERUS

Only the greatest of heroes – such as Odysseus, Theseus, Aeneas and Heracles – managed to penetrate 'the undiscovered country from whose bourn no traveller returns' and come back alive. To do that, they had to get past Cerberus, guardian of the boundary between the world of the living and the world of the dead. With two, three, fifty or a hundred dog-heads, with a snake for a tail and more serpents growing from his back, Cerberus looked like a cross between the Hydra and Geryon's hound, with a touch of the Chimaera thrown in. It was reported that a poisonous plant sprang up where his vomit or saliva dribbled onto the ground.[38] Hesiod relates that he ate raw flesh, had a voice of bronze, and was shameless and strong.[39] But he was not all violence: he also had a cunning trick:

> On those who enter [Hades] he fawns with his tail and
> both his ears, but he does not let them leave again, but
> keeps watch, and eats whoever he catches going out of
> the gates.[40]

Heracles' twelfth and last task was to fetch Cerberus from Hades' realm and show him to Eurystheus. The spatial location of the Land of the Dead was ambiguous: in the *Odyssey*, Odysseus simply sailed to it; Aeneas, on the other hand, went down to it ('the descent to Avernus is easy' – 'facilis descensus Averno' – as Virgil unforgettably put it).[41] Heracles' route also entailed a going down. It took him, according to most reports, through a cave at Tainaron, the southernmost point of the Greek mainland at the end of the central prong of the Peloponnese – not quite a world's end location on the pattern of the homelands of Geryon or the Hesperides, but a significant boundary-cum-portal none the less. (Ovid mentions a differently remote access point: a cave in Scythia).[42] Already in the *Odyssey* Heracles tells Odysseus how he seized the hellhound thanks to the help of Hermes and Athena; Athena was his usual helper, while Hermes was the habitual mediator between life and death, between above and below.[43] Apollodorus provides a little more detail: Heracles throttles the hound until it submits – the ultimate act of domestication.[44] The amusing sequel is depicted in many a visual image: Eurystheus hides as usual in his storage jar, waving his arms in abject terror at the sight of the beast from hell (see below).

For all their prodigiousness, Heracles' Labours did not alter the fundamental parameters of the cosmos or humanity's place within it. His final Labour was no exception: it was rounded off when Heracles returned Cerberus to his infernal kennel. Any other outcome would have threatened the integrity of the normal boundaries between the above and the below, between life and death. Such an eventuality was inconceivable.

Attributed to the Eagle Painter, Eurystheus, Heracles and Cerberus, Caeretan *hydria*, 6th century BCE.

Thinking with Heracles

Narrating the Labours in their mythological sequence or, in the case of artists, capturing moments from that sequence in visual representations, were not the only ways of approaching them. Another strategy, often described as 'rationalization', consisted in asking the question 'What ordinary truths underlie these myths?' A typical practitioner of this strategy is the 4th-century BCE author known as Palaephatus (perhaps a pseudonym: the name means 'teller of old tales').[45] His approach is relentlessly consistent and essentially reductivist. The Hesperides were, in his view, two ordinary women whose father owned sheep (in Greek, *mēla*) that had beautiful (hence, metaphorically, 'golden') fleeces; the theft of beautiful *sheep* was misremembered as the taking of golden *apples* (in Greek, also *mēla*).[46] In a similar vein, Hydra was the name of a fort controlled by King Lernus; Eurystheus sent Heracles to sack the fort, but whenever one of the bowmen defending the fort fell, two others took his place; eventually Iolaus helped Heracles to take the fort by setting fire to it ...[47] This perspective can display a good deal of ingenuity and remains incredibly popular today (a centaur is just a confused memory of a man on a horse; the idea of a Cyclops must – surely? – have developed when someone found the skull of a dwarf elephant, with a big central cavity resembling a single eye-socket, etc.).[48] But such an approach involves one fatal drawback: to regard myths as stories that simply reflect the ordinary world is to bleach out the very quality of imaginative daring – the departure from the everyday – that makes a myth a myth.

More suggestive than Palaephatan rationalizations are various philosophical debates in which Heracles was invoked, either as a positive role model or as an example to be pooh-poohed.[49] For the Cynics, Heracles was a model of patient endurance, carrying out his Labours without being sidetracked by the temptations of pleasure or deterred by the struggles of hard work. The Stoics, too, not least their emblematic representative Epictetus, admired Heracles' selfless devotion to the cause of confronting lawlessness and bringing civilization to the world.[50] Such an approach found expression in the work of Heraclitus (perhaps 1st century CE), whose *Homeric Problems* includes a defiantly untraditional view of what constituted Heracles' real qualities:

> We must not suppose that he attained such power in
> those days as a result of his physical strength. Rather,
> he was a man of intellect, an initiate in heavenly wisdom,
> who, as it were, shed light on philosophy, which had been
> hidden in deep darkness ... The boar which he overcame
> is the common incontinence of men; the lion is the
> indiscriminate rush towards improper goals; in the same
> way, by fettering irrational passions he gave rise to the
> belief that he had fettered the violent bull. He banished
> cowardice also from the world, in the shape of the hind
> of Ceryneia. There was another 'labour' too ... in which
> he cleared out the mass of dung ... in other words, the
> foulness that disfigures humanity. The birds he scattered
> are the windy hopes that feed our lives; the many-headed
> hydra that he burned, as it were, with the fires of
> exhortation, is pleasure, which begins to grow again
> as soon as it is cut out.[51]

Yet Cynicism and Stoicism were not the only philosophical shows in town. As championed by the great Roman poet Lucretius, Epicurean doctrine had no time for routine monster-slaying: 'The gaping jaws of that Nemean lion, or the bristly Arcadian [i.e. Erymanthian] boar – what harm could they do us now?' For Lucretius, the man who truly deserved a place among the gods was not a tough guy who did no more than get rid of a few wild beasts, but a genuinely inspired individual – none other than Epicurus – who defeated and banished from his mind, 'by words not by weapons', such moral enemies as pride, meanness and self-indulgence.[52] Freeing humanity from fear – which is what Epicureans claimed their master had done – was worth infinitely more than anything achieved through the use of huge biceps and a massive club.

After antiquity

Like all Greco-Roman myths, that of the Labours was enmeshed in an intricate narrative network of schemes and intrigues, loves and hatreds, involving the gods and their relationships with human beings. That network, generated and sustained by the myth-tellers and their audiences, was integrated into a complex system of religious beliefs and ritual practices, a system that the myths supported, commented upon and sometimes called into question. Long after these beliefs and practices had ceased to be a dominant mode of engaging with the world, the myths still evinced extraordinary staying power – but they did so in altered forms.

To explore this in more detail, we begin with the period from late antiquity to the Renaissance. Two aspects stand out. First there was the ethical dimension: should Heracles' deeds be seen in a positive or a negative light – or a combination of the two? Second, Heracles' travels took him through vast swathes of territory, extending across the whole of the Mediterranean region and sometimes far beyond. Remembered or invented traces of his presence played a notable part in the mental lives of many peoples living in such places; this applies in particular to matters concerned with leadership politics.

ETHICS

As regards Heracles' moral standing, we find a vast amount of material in the literature and iconography of Christian Europe. The early Fathers of the Christian church disagreed about his merits.

Tertullian ridiculed the hero's right to deserve divine honours:

> If it was for his valour in intrepidly killing wild beasts,
> what was there so very memorable in that? Do not
> criminals condemned to the games, even though they are
> consigned to compete in the vile arena, dispatch several
> of these animals at one time, and that with greater zeal?[53]

Lactantius took a similar line, even if his tone is less dismissive:

> Is it so magnificent if he overcame a lion and a boar; if
> he shot down birds with arrows; if he cleansed a royal
> stable; if he conquered a virago, and deprived her of her
> belt; if he slew savage horses together with their master?
> These are the deeds of a brave and heroic man, but still
> a man; for those things that he overcame were frail and
> mortal ... But to conquer the mind, and to restrain anger,
> is the part of the bravest man; and these things he never
> did or could do.[54]

But an alternative and increasingly popular gambit was to stress not
only Heracles' virtues, but even an analogy between the greatest
pagan hero and Christ, especially regarding the ability to confront
and overcome death itself (a point made in the *First Apology* of
Justin Martyr, c. 155 CE).[55] Visual proof that Heracles could take
his place in an early Christian *imaginaire* is provided by a set of
wall paintings in Chamber N of one of the 4th-century catacombs
in the Via Latina at Rome. Although the imagery is dominated
by scenes from the Old and New Testaments, Heracles is given
his share of the limelight too, in contrastingly heroic postures.
These evoke his ability to confront a monstrous adversary (the
Hydra; the snake guarding the golden apples; Cerberus) and – most
relevantly to the physical and spiritual location of the images in
a catacomb – even to overcome death itself. One painting (see
overleaf) shows him restoring the dead Alcestis to her husband,

Alcestis, Heracles, Cerberus and Admetus. Wall painting,
Via Latina catacomb, Rome, 4th century CE.

Admetus, having outwrestled Thanatos, god of death; as confirma-
tion of his ability to bestride the life–death boundary, he holds
the three-headed Cerberus firmly by the collar(s).[56]

Few post-classical visions of the antagonists faced by Heracles
during the Labours can match those imagined by Dante in *Inferno*.[57]
Dante's Cerberus, repulsive gaoler of the third circle of hell, torments the souls of the Gluttonous, steeped as they are in mire
and drenched in everlasting rain: 'His eyeballs glare a bloodshot
crimson, and his bearded jowls are greasy and black; pot-bellied,
talon-heeled, he clutches and flays and rips and rends the souls'.[58]
Deeper in hell, Geryon, who airlifts Virgil and Dante down from
the seventh to the eighth circles, is equally repellent, but differently so.[59] As befits his role as an 'unclean image of Fraud', he is
multiple in form, but the nature of his multiplicity extends far
beyond the triple shape attributed to him in classical mythology.

His smooth face is that of a just man, but he has hairy paws and a gaudily iridescent reptilian body culminating in a venomous sting like that of a scorpion (see overleaf). The obverse of Heracles' opponents is of course the figure of Heracles himself – not, for Dante, a Christ-equivalent, but emphatically, as the glorious performer of mighty deeds, an embodiment of good against evil.[60]

An ultra-positive evaluation of Heracles, representing a figure who incarnates God on Earth, can be found in the early 14th-century *Ovide moralisé*.[61] Indeed, throughout the Middle Ages and into the Renaissance Heracles was widely represented as an admirable embodiment of the 'active life' and a symbol of the defeat of vice by virtue, especially the 'virtue of strength'.[62] In 'The Monk's Tale' from Chaucer's *The Canterbury Tales*, the narrator adds to the litany of Heracles' praises:

> For Hercules, victor of sovereign power,
> His labours sing his praise and lasting fame,
> Who in his time was human strength in flower ...
> Was never hero since the world began
> That slew so many monsters as did he.

Even so, Heracles was subject to Fortune's destructive throw of the dice, and owed his downfall to Deianira and the deadly robe that, all unknowing, she sent to him:

> Wise is the man that well has learnt to know
> Himself; beware! When Fortune would elect
> To trick a man, she plots his overthrow
> By such a means as he would least expect.[63]

But usually it was the positive that was accentuated. In his allegorical treatise *De laboribus Herculis* (1406), the chancellor of Florence Coluccio Salutati gave a densely allegorical reading of the hero's exploits, characterizing them as the deeds of a *vir perfectus* ('perfect man').[64] In similar vein, dating from the mid-16th century,

William Blake, *Geryon conveying Dante and Virgil down towards Malebolge*,
illustration for *The Divine Comedy* by Dante Alighieri, 1824–27.

are the parallels between Christ and Heracles adumbrated in
Pierre de Ronsard's *L'hymne de l'Hercule chrestien*.[65] Differently
laudatory is the repeated invocation of Heracles as the heroic-
chivalric model to whom Arthur and his knights are compared
in Spenser's *Faerie Queene* (1590–96). One instance among many
comes in Book 5, where Arthur's confrontation with the tyrannous
Souldan (= Philip II of Spain) is likened to Heracles' triumphant
destruction of the bloodthirsty Thracian king Diomedes. Later in
the poem we meet another despotic opponent trounced by Arthur,
three-bodied Geryoneo, the son of the ancient monster Geryon.[66]
Geryoneo is another Philip II equivalent, for Philip ruled three
kingdoms: Spain, Portugal and the Low Countries.

POLITICS

These passages from Spenser shift the focus from ethics to politics, an aspect of Heracles that came to the fore in the Renaissance.[67] In thinking about this development, it would be a mistake to isolate the twelve Labours as if they constituted a separate ideological package – not least because there was no exact correspondence between ancient and later versions of what the Labours actually were. Many medieval and Renaissance writers and artists followed the precedent of Boethius' massively influential *Consolation of Philosophy* (523 CE), which omitted five Labours that most ancient authors included in their lists (hind, Augean stables, bull, Amazon's belt and Geryon), replacing them with the hero's fights against the river god Achelous, the Centaurs and the giants Antaeus and Cacus, as well as his Atlas-related feat of supporting the sky on his shoulders.[68] However, that there is flexibility about what counted as a Labour and what did not is of little consequence beside the main point: that Heracles exercised a dominant role in the political ideologies of many European countries in virtue of his prowess at defeating dangerous and often monstrous opponents. This emphasis is what governed the privileging of certain exploits and the minimizing of certain others (such as the hind, the Amazon's belt and the Augean stables).

As regards Heracles in the Renaissance, Italy is the obvious starting point. An image of Heracles had appeared on the seal of Florence since 1281, to symbolize the heroic track record on which the city liked to pride itself: that of trouncing tyrannies and other wicked adversaries.[69] Baccio Bandinelli's *Hercules and Cacus*, the sculptor's signature work, was placed at the entrance to the Palazzo Vecchio next to Michelangelo's *David*. In Ferrara, imagery relating to Heracles was dominant at the Este court, especially in sculptures, paintings, tapestries and fountains. The Este family claimed Heracles as its ancestor, a boast expressed in the name of Ercole d'Este, who ruled from 1471–1505. Federico II Gonzaga, a

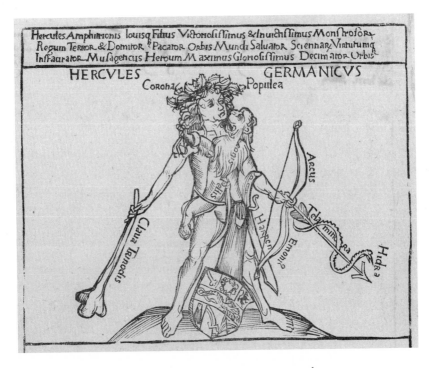

Emperor Maximilian I as Hercules Germanicus, woodcut, 1495–1500.

son of the incomparable Isabella d'Este, was portrayed as Heracles on the ceiling of the Camera dello Zodiaco in the Ducal Palace at Mantua: he holds a club with a gold ribbon round it inscribed 'UBIQUE FORTIS' ('Strong everywhere').[70] Offering spurious support for all these Italianate Herculeses were the writings of Annius of Viterbo, a 15th-century Dominican friar who concocted a rigmarole of pseudo-history that, among other things, purported to document details of the hero's travels from Spain to Italy and his alleged civic foundations there.[71]

The connection between Heracles and the Germans rested on the authority of Tacitus, according to whom 'They say that Hercules, too, once visited them, and they sing of him as the first of all brave men when they are about to go into battle.'[72] It was an association that was actively exploited in the 15th and 16th centuries. The Holy

Hans Holbein the Younger, *Luther as Hercules Germanicus*, 1519.

Roman Emperor Maximilian I was depicted as a rather improbable 'Hercules Germanicus' (see opposite). Charles V, Maximilian's grand-son and successor, was repeatedly linked with Heracles: a painting of the emperor by Parmigianino (c. 1530) portrayed the hero as a toddler, handing Charles a big globe of the world. More striking (literally) than these images of Maximilian and Charles is Holbein's portrait of Martin Luther in the guise of a distinctly super-heroic kind of Hercules Germanicus (see above). Among the worthies he has bludgeoned into oblivion with his wickedly spiked club are Aristotle and Thomas Aquinas; a diminutive Pope Leo X (with three tiaras – Geryon?) hangs from a ring through Luther's nose.

The Heracles connection repeats itself, to a greater or lesser extent, in a dozen other European countries, including England, where the French poet and historian Bernard Andreas (*fl.* 1500) celebrated the exploits of the first Tudor king in *Les douze triomphes de Henry VII* (the key word being 'douze').[73] But it was above all in France that the Herculean connection was promoted, to bolster the prestige of successive monarchs. As with Germany, there was classical precedent: Diodorus had reported, in the context of Heracles' travels to and from Geryon country in Spain, that the hero founded the city of Alesia (in present-day Burgundy). On that occasion he was invited into the bed of a beautiful Celtic maiden who bore him a son named Galates, ancestor of the Gallic people.[74] From François I (r. 1515–47) until well into the 18th century, French kings presented themselves, and were depicted by others, as 'Hercules Gallicus'.[75] Pride of place went to Henri IV, whose marriage to his second wife, Marie de Medici, was celebrated with a processional entry into Avignon in 1600 – an event recorded in André Valladier's *Labyrinthe royal de l'Hercule gaulois triomphant* (1601), which included engravings of seven triumphal arches, each linking a Herculean Labour with a comparable feat by Henri.

From the Renaissance till today

In comparison with such symbolically potent figures as Oedipus, Medea and Prometheus, Heracles cannot be said to occupy a distinctive social-psychological niche in today's perceptions of the human condition. Even if we take a longer view, looking back over the whole of post-Renaissance culture, a similar conclusion suggests itself. This comparatively limited presence applies more conspicuously to the Labours, but less so to other, darker dimensions of his mythical profile – the paradoxical combination of weakness with the capacity for explosive violence, both outwardly directed and self-destructive.

Representative in this respect are some re-performances or re-imaginings – by comparison with those based on other Greek tragedies, relatively few in number – of Euripides' *The Madness of Heracles* and Sophocles' *Women of Trachis*, works that depict, respectively, the hero's crazed obliteration of his family and his agonizing death at the hands of his second wife, Deianira. Frank Wedekind's play *Herakles* (written 1917, first performed 1919) is not so much a translation as a grim exploration of failure: it dramatizes a depressing story – in (of course) twelve scenes – of psychological deterioration, the Labours being so many stages in a downward path of humiliation, even if this leads ultimately to deification. More imaginatively innovative is British dramatist Martin Crimp's *Cruel and Tender* (2004), a relocation of the *Women of Trachis* into the world of global insecurity. The general who sets out to eradicate the Hydra of terrorism by means of bloody campaigns in Africa finishes up as an unrepentant war criminal; the wife who takes deadly revenge on him does so using a biochemical weapon wrapped in a pillow.

In contrast to such ultra-serious treatments are those that see the funny side of the man with the massive biceps. Here the Labours return to the limelight. Inevitably, the feat that most readily lends itself to comic treatment is that of the Augean stables. Honoré Daumier was on typically glorious form when, in a lithograph made in 1842, he portrayed Heracles in the middle of this menial task (see overleaf). Bull-necked, running seriously to fat, and stark naked apart from a pair of waders, the mighty man has met his match in the shape of a cow's bottom. Nor was Daumier the only person to have found humour in the relationship between Heracles and heaps of dung. The Swiss dramatist Friedrich Dürrenmatt wrote his memorable satire *Hercules and the Augean Stables* (1954) as a send-up of a peculiarly modern (and stereotypically Swiss) dilemma: what does a hero do when his cunning plan to cleanse the ordure problem in Elis is blocked by endless rounds of bureaucracy? Clearing out masses of muck is nothing compared to the task of obtaining the right permits and permissions from a series of Boards and Ministries. At another level, though, the play is more than just

Honoré Daumier, *The Augean Stables*, 1842.

tremendously funny: it dramatizes the incompetent inability of a government to deal with an environmental catastrophe.

When it comes to modern re-imaginings of the Labours as a full set of twelve, Agatha Christie's set of short stories *The Labours of Hercules* (1947) – as we mentioned at the end of the last chapter – explicitly adopts the motif in relation to the final set of cases solved by the legendary, one might even say 'mythical', detective Hercule Poirot. Given his diminutive stature, his obsession with his perfectly clipped moustache and his fastidious attention to his attire, Poirot's resemblance to his mighty namesake is anything but physical. ('What was he,' exclaims Poirot, 'but a large muscular creature of low intelligence and criminal tendencies!') The similarity lies elsewhere: in a series of analogies deliberately devised by Poirot to disprove the assertion by a fusty old Oxford Classics don that 'Yours aren't the Labours of Hercules.' The last case – the equivalent of the Cerberus Labour – involves Poirot enduring the *enfer* of the London Underground, after which the plot turns on a hell-themed nightclub guarded by 'the largest and ugliest and blackest dog Poirot had ever seen!'[76]

Christie's re-imagining of the Labours is ingenious and engaging, but no more profound than that. More thought-provoking is a series of visualizations of the Labours by the New Zealand artist Marian Maguire. A set of her lithographs (2007–8) explores Heracles' role as an archetypal settler – a tamer of the land. But, by a complex set of cultural changes, the land in question is New Zealand, complete with the Maori people who inhabit it; Heracles is imagined as having included the South Pacific on his extraordinarily extensive set of travels. The pervasive visual framework is provided by ancient Greek black-figure vase painting, but it is supplemented by images evoking the colonized land to which Heracles has supposedly come. He retains his doughty heroism as he attempts to impose order, in spite of occasional despondency, but his adversaries retain every ounce of their dignity: there is nothing simplistic about the ethical balance. Of the scene envisaged in *Herakles Writes Home* (see pl. XIII) – note the lion skin draped casually over the back of the chair – the classicist Greta Hawes, herself a New Zealander, has brilliantly written: 'To whom does Herakles write from this outpost in the South Pacific? To his murdered wife and children? His absent father? His ever-hostile stepmother? Where would be "home" for him? Maguire's Herakles fits into New Zealand's colonial history as he fits in anywhere: he is a recognisable individual: eye-catching, solitary, larger than life, and always somewhat out of place.'[77]

One more aspect of Heracles' reception history needs to be mentioned: his beefy, quasi-gladiatorial role as the ultimate macho fighting hero. This trait has manifested itself in a lengthy career in films made for the cinema and television, as well in a colossal and ongoing participation in comic books and video games.[78] Among the movie actors whose physique has most famously qualified them for the role are Steve Reeves, Arnold Schwarzenegger and

Still from *Hercules: The Legendary Journeys*, 1995.

Kevin Sorbo (see opposite). Hercules' comic-book career took off in the 1960s in the pages of Marvel Comics and has never looked back. Throughout his exploits in the company of a host of other world-saving or world-threatening superheroes and supervillains, he has retained his superhuman, indeed godlike, strength (except when this is temporarily undermined by dastardly opponents). His combat skills include the traditional archery and wrestling, though they may also involve the use of more modern weapons such as assault rifles. As befits his ancient profile, he often acts alone; but equally often he participates in inconceivably powerful groups such as the Champions and the Avengers. If not exactly 'good to think with', the comic-book Hercules is surely good to fight with. In that respect – and in spite of encounters with highly untraditional characters such as Immortus, Baron Helmut Zemo and Kang the Conqueror – there remains a recognizable continuity with the man who, as the Greek myth-tellers narrated, started out by strangling the snakes that Hera had sent to attack him in his cradle, and ended up by making the transition to Olympus.

CHAPTER 8

Orpheus and Eurydice

One of the less well-known episodes in Heracles' career occurred when, as an adolescent, he received music lessons from a brilliant teacher by the name of Linos (a son, it was said, of one of the Muses). Fed up with Heracles' inadequate musicianship, Linos struck his incompetent pupil. Heracles retaliated and killed his mentor – according to one account, by bludgeoning him to death with his own lyre. The mythological character who takes centre stage in the present chapter seems in most respects the antithesis of Linos' unmusical pupil. Whereas Heracles dominated the natural world – especially the wild creatures it contained – by brute force, the miraculously gifted singer and lyre-player Orpheus literally entranced the environment around him: birds and other animals, trees, rivers, even rocks fell under the spell of his music. Yet the contrast between Heracles and Orpheus is not absolute. Like Heracles, Orpheus perished violently at the hands of women. Also like Heracles, he undertook a perilous journey to the Underworld and returned to tell the tale. But the experiences of the two heroes in that forbidding and gloomy place had little in common.[1]

Orpheus' parentage brought him close to the gods. His mother was the Muse Calliope, his father either the god Apollo or the Thracian king Oiagros, himself a son of the war god, Ares. But warfare was never one of Orpheus' preoccupations, nor did he feature in most of the collective enterprises in which the martial valour of other heroes was bloodily displayed. The exception is the adventure narrated in Apollonius' epic poem *The Voyage of the Argo*, in which Orpheus is one of the Argonauts who accompany Jason. But even on that testosterone-rich expedition, Orpheus' weapons of choice were not the spear or the sword, but the lyre and the voice. Already on the outward journey to Colchis, when a quarrel between two Argonauts looked like turning nasty, it was Orpheus who distracted and calmed the antagonists by singing of the primordial exploits of the gods, at a time when the universe was young.

> This was his song. He checked his lyre and his divine voice, but though he had finished, the others all still leaned forwards, ears straining under the peaceful spell; such was the bewitching power of the music which lingered amongst them.[2]

Later, on the return journey, he once more used his musicianship to further the success of the expedition, by neutralizing the potentially lethal danger posed by the Sirens. The tune he chose was lively and rapid; its notes blurred and blocked the Sirens' mellifluous voices, minimizing their seductive threat to the listening crew.[3]

It is no coincidence that we have begun our investigation of Orpheus with a passage from a work by Apollonius – a poet. Unlike those mythical episodes for which our main literary sources are the prose narratives of mythographers (Heracles' Labours are a prime example), the career of Orpheus, steeped as it was in glorious musicality and entrancing song, was above all a subject for poets. Apollonius was by no means the first. A fragment from the Archaic Greek lyricist Simonides evoked the compelling effect of Orpheus' music on the natural world: 'countless birds fluttered above his head, and fishes leapt up from the deep-blue sea at the sound of his lovely singing.'[4] Euripides, too, matched Orpheus' lyricism with his own.[5] Then there was a wistful epigram by the poet Antipater of Sidon (2nd century BCE):

> Never again, Orpheus,
> Will you lead the enchanted oaks,
> Nor the rocks, nor the beasts
> That are their own masters.
> Never again will you sing to sleep
> The roaring wind, nor the hail,
> Nor the drifting snow, nor the boom
> Of the sea wave.
> You are dead now.
> Led by your mother, Calliope,
> The Muses shed many tears
> Over you for a long time.
> What good does it do us to mourn
> For our sons when the immortal
> Gods are powerless to save
> Their own children from death?[6]

But these Greek musings are overshadowed by the contrastingly magnificent achievements of two Roman poets: Virgil and Ovid.

The whole of Book 10 of Ovid's *Metamorphoses*, and the beginning of Book 11, are dominated by the things done and suffered by Orpheus, and the songs that he sang. On the day of his marriage to the nymph Eurydice, Orpheus' bride was wandering in a meadow with her sister nymphs when a venomous snake bit her in the ankle and killed her. Tormented by grief, Orpheus descended to the Underworld via Cape Tainaron, just as Heracles had done, in order to plead his case before Hades and Persephone, pouring out his unbearable sorrow to the accompaniment of the lyre. Here is the gist of his complaint: 'I tried to master my grief, but Love was too much for me. It was Love that brought the two of you together; you know its power. Can you not rethink Eurydice's destiny? In the fullness of time she will come to you; grant her a temporary reprieve. If not, I have no wish to live: enjoy my death as well as hers.' The effect was extraordinary: the norms of existence in Hades were temporarily overturned. Even the eternal punishments meted out to legendary offenders were suspended:

> As Orpheus pleaded his cause,
>   enhancing his words with his music,
> he moved the bloodless spirits to tears.
>   For a moment Tantalus
> ceased to clutch at the fleeting pool,
>   Ixion's wheel
> was spellbound, the vultures halted
>   their pecking at Tityos' liver,
> the Danaids dropped their urns and
>   Sisyphus sat on his boulder.
> The Furies' hearts were assuaged by the
>   song, and the story goes
> that they wept real tears for the very
>   first time.[7]

Hades and Persephone, too, relented, giving permission for Orpheus to lead his beloved back into the light of the living. But there was one stipulation: he must not look back at her, otherwise she must remain for ever in the realm of death. Such a precondition, in the world of myth and folklore, is made to be broken. Yet the meaning of 'not looking back', in spite of its apparent familiarity, is unclear; it may be connected with the idea that 'what lies behind' is a sacred and uncanny place – a description that certainly fits the Underworld, from which Eurydice has just emerged and to which she is still closer than her husband.[8] In any case, what is vital to stress is that in Ovid's narrative there are no recriminations, just love and mutual understanding:

In deadly silence the two of them
  followed the upward slope;
the track was steep, it was dark and
  shrouded in thick black mist.
Not far to go now; the exit to earth and
  the light was ahead!
But Orpheus was frightened his love was
  falling behind; he was desperate
to see her. He turned, and at once she sank
  back into the dark.
She stretched out her arms to him,
  struggled to feel his hands on her own,
but all she was able to catch, poor soul,
  was the yielding air.
And now, as she died for the second time,
  she never complained
that her husband had failed her – what
  could she complain of, except that
  he'd loved her?
She only uttered her last 'farewell', so
  faintly he hardly
could hear it, and then she was swept once
  more to the land of the shadows.[9]

After a period of grief-stricken self-neglect, the Ovidian Orpheus withdraws to the unforgiving land of Thrace. He repels all contact with women; his erotic preference turns to young boys, a practice that he was said to have been the first to introduce to Thrace.[10] What does not change is the power of his music. The distraught poet sits down on an unsheltered hillside and begins to play his lyre. Soon he can enjoy shade in abundance, because tree after tree – oak, poplar, laurel, hazel, mountain ash and a dozen others – uproot themselves and move towards the source of the heart-rending melodies. All manner of wild creatures join the enthralled audience. To this motley, natural assembly, Orpheus narrates tales of doomed love: Apollo's ill-starred passion for the youth Hyacinthus; the grim fate of the Propoetides, whose denial of the divinity of Venus was punished when the goddess forced them into prostitution; the unnerving tale of Myrrha, who committed incest with her father and bore Adonis, himself destined to die early, bringing anguish to his divine lover Venus. Such melancholy songs sat well with Orpheus' own state of emotional devastation.

His concert over, Orpheus was espied by a group of Thracian women engaged in a wild maenadic ritual. Seeking vengeance for the poet's rejection of their sex, they hurled their trademark weapons at him – stones and tree branches, supplemented by agricultural implements abandoned by a group of petrified farmers. Orpheus' pleas for pity failed to move the frenzied women, and they tore his body apart. Even so, they could not stifle his music. His head and lyre, cast aside into the nearby river Hebrus, floated down to the sea, still intoning a plaintive refrain; eventually they were washed up on the isle of Lesbos. As for Orpheus' soul, this at last returned to the Underworld. There, a loving reconciliation with Eurydice took place, enacting a happy reversal of the act that had split them apart:

> At last the lovers could stroll together, side by side –
> or she went ahead and he followed; then Orpheus
>   ventured in front
> and knew he could now look back safely on his own
>   Eurydice.[11]

A generation earlier than Ovid, Virgil had composed his own version of the same myth in his fourth *Georgic*. The narrative anticipates Ovid's at many points; indeed, Ovid was consciously reworking his great predecessor. But there is one motif highlighted

by Virgil that Ovid ignores: a sequence of transgression and repara-
tory propitiation involving Aristaeus – as idiosyncratic a character
as Orpheus himself. The son of Apollo and the nymph Cyrene,
Aristaeus devoted himself to all manner of agricultural matters,
especially herding and beekeeping. But, in spite of his consummate
skill, one day his husbandry suffered a serious setback: his bees
inexplicably perished from disease and famine. On his mother's
advice, Aristaeus consulted the all-knowing sea god Proteus. The
culprit, Proteus explained, was Aristaeus himself. Once upon a
time he had pursued Eurydice in order to have sex with her; in her
haste to flee him, she failed to notice the poisonous snake at her
feet. In their grief and anger, Eurydice's sister nymphs punished
the guilty man by causing his bees to die. The way to propitiate
the nymphs was also the way to regenerate the bees: Aristaeus
slaughtered and exposed the carcases of some bulls and heifers,
from which a new swarm of bees miraculously emerged. As for
Orpheus, Virgil portrays his conduct less sympathetically than
Ovid would later do. Absent-mindedly (*immemor*) and in a moment
of madness (*dementia, furor*) he looked back at Eurydice – a motif
that may have been a Virgilian invention – fatally breaking his
agreement with the merciless god of the Underworld.[12] As in Ovid,
there follows the sequence of loss, lamentation, withdrawal, and
the tearing apart by the maenads. But there is no blissful ending
in the Elysian Fields – just the voice uttered by his river-borne
head, repeatedly crying 'Eurydice', as the banks of the stream echo
their plangent response.

For all the subsequent influence of the Virgilian and Ovidian
versions, theirs were not the only ways of telling the story; a
number of earlier myth-tellers had already had their say. A fascinating question, though one that is impossible to answer securely,
is how widespread was the variant according to which Orpheus
succeeded in bringing his wife back from the dead. Some lines from
Euripides' *Alcestis* (438 BCE) *might* carry that implication.[13] In a

Attributed to the Curti Painter,
Death of Orpheus, bell *krater*, c. 440–430 BCE.

Head of Orpheus, Attic red-figure *hydria*, c. 440 BCE.

passage from Plato's *Symposium* (early 4th century BCE), one of the speakers in the dialogue suggests that the gods gave Orpheus merely a phantom (*phasma*) of Eurydice to take back with him; this *probably* suggests the existence of a more mainstream version in which Orpheus brought back the real flesh-and-blood Eurydice.[14] But we have to wait till Hermesianax, writing in the 3rd century BCE, for a poem in which Orpheus *certainly* brings his wife back to the upper world.[15] Incidentally, Hermesianax called her Agriope (or Argiope), not Eurydice. This is just one of countless instances in Greek myth where names are variable, as if what was centrally important was not an individual's personal identity but simply their function within a narrative. The majority of such variable names, significantly, belong to women.

In visual art, Orpheus mostly kept a lower profile than he did in poetry. Four motifs stand out. The first is the poet's death at

Attributed to the Ganymede Painter, Orpheus playing his lyre
in the world of the dead, Apulian amphora, 330/320 BCE.

Orpheus with animals, Roman mosaic, Palermo, 3rd century CE.

the hands of the Thracian women, together with the image of the severed head (see pp. 233 and 234). The second is his presence in the Underworld in the absence of Eurydice; what is implicitly stressed is the general power of Orpheus' music in the realm of the dead, as opposed to its specific application in securing the rescue of his wife (see p. 235). Another group of images once more portrays Orpheus as musician, this time exercising calm dominance over a raptly attentive audience of animals; mosaics are a popular format for this scene (see opposite). Lastly, and more rarely, there are images of Orpheus, Eurydice and Hermes, most famously in Roman copies of sculptural reliefs whose Greek originals date back to the 5th century BCE. In one moving scenario, Orpheus has just turned around, while Hermes, as guide of the souls of the dead, places a hand on Eurydice as a prelude to guiding her back to the Underworld (see overleaf). In spite of such impressive representations, the bulk of the visual evidence suggests that scenes depicting Orpheus without Eurydice enjoyed greater artistic popularity than those that paired husband and wife.

One last aspect of the Orpheus of classical antiquity needs to be mentioned: his distinctive position at the intersection of religion and literature. As a singer whose penetration of the world of the dead gave him knowledge denied to ordinary mortals, he was credited with a large body of theogonical and eschatological poetry, whose contents diverged significantly from the traditions recorded by, for example, Hesiod. A particular focus of these poems was Dionysus, alleged to have been killed and eaten by the Titans, whom Zeus then punished by thunderbolting them. From the ashes sprang up not only humankind but a reborn Dionysus. Appropriately enough, such 'Orphic' texts were used by the followers of Bacchic mystery cults. As for eschatology, here, too, so-called 'Orphic' texts fed into real-world ritual practice. Priests known as Orpheotelestai ('Orphic initiators') went from door to door, persuasively equipped with imposing-looking examples of

Hermes, Eurydice and Orpheus, marble relief, c. 420 BCE.

'Orphic' literature. Their tactic was to promise favourable treatment in the next world to those who performed appropriate rites in this one. Such itinerant salesmen-of-the-hereafter were liable to arouse scorn. There is a particularly vitriolic example in Euripides' *Hippolytus*, where Theseus mocks what he sees as the hypocritically puritanical moral posturing of his son Hippolytus by associating him with the Orphics, that group of impostors who spent their energies on 'vaporous' writings, Bacchic rites and even, allegedly, vegetarianism.[16] In spite of such contemptuous dismissals, the existence of roving Orphics further confirms the considerable public profile of their mythical figurehead, in respects quite distinct from any connection with Eurydice.

From late antiquity to the Middle Ages[17]

There is a fundamental ambivalence about early Christian conceptions of Orpheus. On the one hand he can be seen as a sorcerer, capable of exercising a devilishly uncanny power over animals and the surrounding environment. Thus for the theologian Clement of Alexandria (2nd–3rd centuries CE), Orpheus and other musicians-cum-enchanters such as Amphion and Arion were nothing but deceivers

> who, corrupting life under the pretence of poetry,
> possessed by a spirit of cunning sorcery for purposes
> of destruction, committing crimes in their orgies, and
> turning human grief into the material of religious
> worship, were the first to entice men towards idols.[18]

Yet Orpheus also had about him a Christ-like quality. For one thing, both he and the Christian Saviour were believed to have gone down to the world of the dead: whereas Orpheus did so in order to rescue Eurydice, Christ was said by some to have descended to hell after the crucifixion in order to save the souls of the righteous (the so-called 'harrowing of hell', described by certain Christian writers). No less important was the analogy between the Orpheus who tamed animals and the Christian image of the Good Shepherd. The equivalence was frequently spelled out iconographically, especially through the presence of certain birds and animals (doves, sheep) that had particular significance in Christian ideology.

Late antique and medieval reflections on the Orpheus–Eurydice relationship display a rich variety of allegorical approaches. The straightforward moral drawn by Boethius (c. 477–524 CE) centres on the symbolic consequences of Orpheus' backward/downward look. If, Boethius concludes, while aiming for the upward path towards the light of day, you give in and look back towards the darkness, you risk losing everything.[19] More convoluted is the musical allegory developed by Boethius' contemporary Fulgentius.[20] Taking his trademark etymological route, Fulgentius maintains that Orpheus denotes the 'best sound (or voice)', while Eurydice represents 'deep judgment' – in other words, that which is needful in order to *understand* the mysteries of music. When Orpheus lost Eurydice, what he was actually deprived of was profundity of understanding – something that Aristaeus had been searching for. Incidentally, Fulgentius reads Aristaeus etymologically as 'the best (man)' – quite a compliment to pay a would-be rapist, and a startling demonstration of the distance between the narrative surface and the sense that the allegorist claims to have detected beneath.

Fulgentius' approach, which locates Orpheus' eloquent voice at the centre of his myth, persisted through numerous medieval interpretations. According to Boccaccio, Orpheus tried to bring Eurydice (= sexual passion) back from the depths to which she had fallen after fleeing Aristaeus (= virtue!); woe betide anyone tempted to look back upon (= give way to) what Eurydice represents, since the backward-looker's own pursuit of virtue might thereby be compromised.[21] More variants of the Aristaeus/Eurydice/Orpheus triangle are set out in Pierre Bersuire's 14th-century *Ovidius moralizatus*.

From one perspective, Orpheus stands for Christ, and Eurydice for the human soul tempted by the Devil (i.e. the snake that bites her).[22] Yet alternatively, Bersuire continues, the myth of Orpheus may be an allegory not of Christ but of a sinner who loses his own soul (Eurydice), only to regain it by repentance and prayer (represented by his singing). However, there are many who love their own soul too much through over-attachment to worldly things: 'They love their recovered wife [= soul] so excessively that they give way to her fleshly desires ... and so lose her once again, and hell takes her back.'[23]

Allegorical readings persisted well beyond the medieval period. The 15th-century Scottish poet Robert Henryson gave a splendidly vigorous account of the myth, as, for example, when Aristaeus, 'preckit with lust', pursued Eurydice:

> I say this be Erudices the quene,
> Quhilk walkit furth in to a May mornyng,
> Bot with a madyn untill a medow grene,
> To tak the air and se the flouris spring;
> Quhair in a schaw, neir by this lady ying,
> A busteous hird, callit Arresteuss,
> Kepand his beistis, lay undir a buss.
> And quhen he saw this lady solitar,
> Bairfut with schankis quhyter than the snaw,
> Preckit with lust, he thocht withoutin mair
> Hir till oppress – and till hir can he drawe.
> Dreidand for evill, scho fled quhen scho him saw,
> And as scho ran all bairfute on a buss,
> Scho trampit on a serpent vennemuss.[24]

The story culminates in a moral: Orpheus stands for the intellect, Eurydice for emotion (drawn now towards reason, now towards sensual pleasures), Aristaeus for 'gud vertew' (!), and the serpent for deadly sin.

Different again, but still figuring Orpheus in positive terms, is Francis Bacon's essay in Section 11 of his *Wisdom of the Ancients* (1609). This time Orpheus stands for two types of philosophy, correlated to the two kinds of audience that his music could attract. To the first kind – the powers of the Underworld – there corresponds natural philosophy (what we might call 'science'), which might preserve bodies from their state of physical corruptibility. To the second kind of audience – living creatures – there corresponds moral or 'civil' philosophy, which could induce people to set aside their passions and construct socially beneficial communities. Bacon added a misogynistic coda to the effect that Orpheus' ultimate rejection of womankind was a step in the right direction, 'because the indulgence of the married state, and the natural affections which men have for their children, often prevent them from entering upon any grand, noble, or meritorious enterprise for the public good'.[25] Not for the first or last time in its myth-history, the tale of Orpheus raises pressing questions about relationships between the sexes.

Chronologically concomitant with the allegorical method, and increasingly dominant at allegory's expense, were retellings that variously explored the resonances of the myth in de-allegorized form – sometimes with artistically stellar results. Two interrelated themes predominate: the lover's quest to rescue his beloved, and the magical power of music.

One of the most engaging of such retellings dates from the 14th century. The Middle English romance *Sir Orfeo* is a unique blend of the Greco-Roman with the Celtic, thus anticipating by more than half a millennium the countless modern comics, movies and video games that, in a boundary-crossing manner sometimes regarded as a characteristic of Postmodernism, exploit the same blend. *Sir Orfeo* tells the story of King Orfeo of Winchester (a city known at that time as 'Traciens', the poet points out). When his wife, Herodis, is abducted by the king of the Elves, Orfeo abandons his kingdom and sets out in forlorn pursuit. He spends ten years in the wilderness playing his harp and singing his laments to the animals that come to hear him. Then one day in the woods he spies Herodis among a group of fairy ladies. He follows them to the Elf King's palace, where he introduces himself as a poor, wandering minstrel. So delighted is the Elf King by the minstrel's music that he invites him to name his reward, promising to grant it. When Orfeo begs that his wife be restored to him, the request meets with a dusty response. An ill-matched couple *you* would make, the Elf King exclaims: whereas you yourself are thin and rough and sun-blackened, she, by contrast, is lovely and without blemish. But a promise is a promise, and the reunited couple head back to Winchester. When first he returns, Orfeo is an unrecognized beggar, in the manner of Odysseus on his homecoming to Ithaca. But eventually all is revealed: Orfeo and Herodis reign happily ever after, with no fatal, backwards look to mar their bliss.

Writers of the early modern period, including the very greatest of them, repeatedly describe the magical effect of Orphean music. In Shakespeare's *Two Gentlemen of Verona*, one of the title characters, Proteus, explains how poetical laments can be used to win the heart of a lady:

> For Orpheus' lute was strung with poets' sinews,
> Whose golden touch could soften steel and stones,
> Make tigers tame, and huge leviathans
> Forsake unsounded deeps to dance on sands.[26]

In *The Merchant of Venice*, it is not dancing leviathans but two enraptured human lovers who succumb to the enchantments of music. In the garden at Belmont, where musicians play by moonlight, Lorenzo woos his beloved Jessica:

> Therefore the poet
> Did feign that Orpheus drew trees, stones, and floods
> Since naught so stockish, hard, and full of rage

But music for the time doth change his nature.
The man that hath no music in himself,
Nor is not moved with concord of sweet sounds,
Is fit for treasons, stratagems, and spoils,
The motions of his spirit are dull as night,
And his affections dull as Erebus.
Let no such man be trusted.[27]

In the visual arts, too, there appeared numerous representations of Orpheus as an irresistibly effective musician. A joyous example is a relief sculpture set in a hexagonal panel by Luca della Robbia, created for the exterior of Giotto's Campanile in the Piazza del Duomo in Florence. Birds and wild beasts alike have fallen under the spell of the singer and his lute (see opposite). Even more fetching is Jacob Hoefnagel's vision of a group of concert-goers – lion and hedgehog, porcupine and leopard, and all their large and small friends – listening dreamily side by side (see p. 246). But darker contexts for Orphean musicianship are represented too. Jan Brueghel the Elder showed an isolated Orpheus gamely playing before Hades and Persephone, surrounded by an assorted public of ghoulish creatures (see pl. XIV). (There is a striking parallel with the same artist's *Christ's Descent into Limbo*, done in collaboration with Hans Rottenhammer; the analogy between Orpheus and Christ is by no means restricted to the medieval period.) Differently dark is Albrecht Dürer's drawing *The Death of Orpheus*, in which the poet is being beaten to death by stick-bearing women while his lyre lies abandoned at his feet (see p. 247). The banner displayed at the top of the image reads: 'Orpheus the first sodomite'. Orpheus' ancient reputation as one who renounced women and introduced a version of male homoeroticism to Thrace has rarely had a more uncompromising visualization.

For all the attention paid to Orpheus by artists and especially by poets, there is one other medium in which, in the early modern

Luca della Robbia, *Orpheus, c.* 1337–39.

Jacob Hoefnagel, *Orpheus Charming the Animals*, 1613.

period, his presence surpasses that of all other mythological characters: opera. Works by a series of Italian composers such as Jacopo
Peri, Claudio Monteverdi, Luigi Rossi and Antonio Sartorio were
eventually overshadowed by the melodically tremendous, radically innovative and triumphantly successful *Orfeo ed Euridice* by
Christoph Willibald Gluck, first performed in Vienna in 1762.
The key figure is Amore, god of love. In Act 1, set at the tomb of
Euridice, he responds to Orfeo's moving laments by granting that
the bereft poet may descend to the Underworld to reclaim his wife,
provided he does not look back. All goes smoothly till the moment
during the upward journey when Euridice, mystified by Orfeo's
refusal to explain what is happening, pesters him so much that he
turns to look at her. Losing her for a second time, he expresses
his grief in an aria that remains one of the summits of the entire
operatic repertoire: 'Che farò senza Euridice?'. Amore intervenes

Albrecht Dürer, *The Death of Orpheus*, 1494.

for a second time, dissuading Orfeo from suicide and definitively restoring Euridice to life. It all sounds simple; in a sense, it *is* simple. The secret lies – as it lay for Orfeo himself – in the music.

As we follow Orpheus towards modernity, a number of trends in his reception can be discerned. Re-imaginings of the poet's capacity to entrance the environment continue, perhaps most memorably in a work by the most romantic Romantic of them all, Percy Bysshe Shelley. His 'Orpheus' (c. 1820), conceived as a fragment of a Greek tragedy, dramatizes a dialogue between the Chorus and a Messenger. When first he lost Eurydice, reports the Messenger, the forlorn harp-player 'chose a lonely seat of unhewn stone/Blackened with lichens, on a herbless plain'; there he poured out 'the tempestuous torrent of his grief'. But in time the plain became herbless no longer, as all manner of trees and flowers migrated 'to pave the temple that his poesy/Has framed'. And not just vegetation:

> near his feet grim lions couch,
> And kids, fearless from love, creep near his lair.
> Even the blind worms seem to feel the sound.
> The birds are silent, hanging down their heads,
> Perched on the lowest branches of the trees;
> Not even the nightingale intrudes a note
> In rivalry, but all entranced she listens.[28]

Less transparent and more enigmatic than Shelley's 'fragment' are literary explorations of Orpheus as a spiritual mystic; writers in German and French, from Goethe to Rainer Maria Rilke and Stéphane Mallarmé, took the lead. In art, too, Orpheus can appear as a figure of mystery, as in a pastel drawing by Odilon Redon (c. 1903–10; see pl. XV); the poet's violent decapitation has been transmuted into a coolly tranquil blend of blues and mauves, in which singer and lyre are symbolically united.

But there was yet another side to Orpheus: not everyone took him seriously. Jacques Offenbach's comic opera *Orphée aux enfers* was first staged in Paris in 1858, reworked in a much-revised version in 1874, and replayed countless times ever since (see overleaf). The scene is the countryside near Thebes, where the marriage of Orphée and Eurydice is in big trouble. Orphée, a fiddle teacher, is having an affair with a shepherdess, while Eurydice is in love with her neighbour, the shepherd Aristée (who is actually Pluto/Hades in disguise). Worst of all, Eurydice cannot bear Orphée's music: 'Your violin is a bore, like your verses.' The plot thickens when it emerges that Orphée and Pluto have conspired to kill Eurydice, so that the god of death can have her all to himself. Eurydice duly dies from a snakebite and descends *aux enfers* to join her regal beloved. Unfortunately for Orphée, a character called 'L'Opinion publique' pressurizes him into trying to rescue his wife. He heads first for Olympus, where he plays a snatch from Gluck's 'Che farò senza Euridice' to gain divine sympathy. The scene then shifts to the Underworld where, among other developments, Pluto is no longer the ardent lover and is keeping Eurydice locked up at home; Jupiter too takes a fancy to her; and all the gods come down to Hades to have a party, the show-stopper to which is the 'galop infernal' (better known as the 'can-can'). Offenbach gleefully exploits some familiar classical storylines, including 'Don't look back'; in this case, what causes Orphée to break the prohibition is a thunderbolt hurled by Jupiter. Before the final curtain, Orphée, Pluto and Jupiter all manage to rid themselves of Eurydice, who ends up as a bacchante.

Over the *longue durée* since antiquity, Eurydice has rarely suffered such a poor write-up as she is given by Offenbach. Nevertheless, even when she is presented in a positive or idealized light her role is almost always passive – a junior partner, and very often a silent one, in the Orpheus-and-Eurydice relationship. She frequently appears as a serial victim, whether of male pursuit (by Aristaeus) or of male control (by Orpheus, and sometimes by Hades/Pluto). Sometimes she is almost literally torn apart by these conflicting

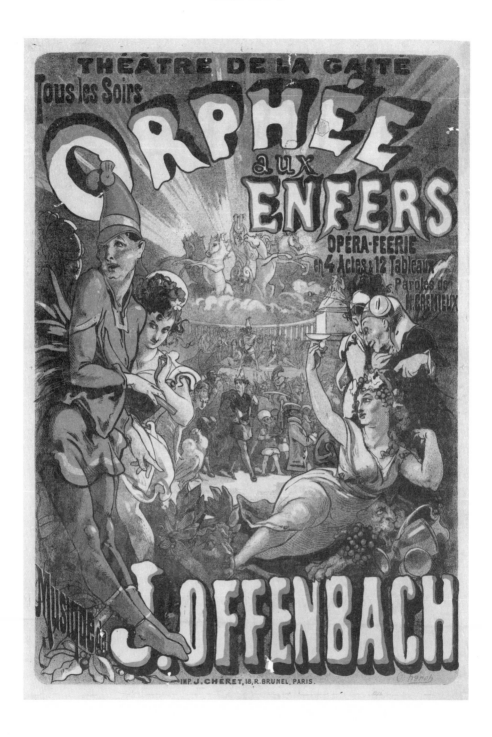

Jules Chéret, poster for Jacques Offenbach's *Orphée aux enfers*, 1878.

claims by men. However, several myth-tellers in the 20th and 21st centuries, particularly women, have at last given Eurydice a resonant voice. One of the earliest poets to do this was 'H.D.' (Hilda Doolittle), in whose 'Eurydice' (1917) the now-back-in-hell wife rails at her thoughtless, still-living husband:

> So you could have swept me back,
> I who could have walked with the live souls
> above the earth,
> I who could have slept among the live flowers
> at last;
> so for your arrogance
> and your ruthlessness
> I am swept back
> where dead lichens drip
> dead cinders upon moss of ash ...[29]

Yet, for all that, H.D.'s dead Eurydice claims to have 'more fervour' and 'more light' than the living Orpheus.

Nearly a century later, in her own 'Eurydice' (1999), Carol Ann Duffy created a knowing, funny and ego-puncturing putdown of Orpheus, expressed through the voice of his long-suffering wife. What really enrages Eurydice is not the music but the poetry – and Orpheus' absurdly high regard for it:

> Orpheus strutted his stuff.
> The bloodless ghosts were in tears.
> Sisyphus sat on his rock for the first time in years.
> Tantalus was permitted a couple of beers.
> The woman in question could scarcely believe her ears.
> Like it or not,
> I must follow him back to our life –
> Eurydice, Orpheus' wife –
> to be trapped in his images, metaphors, similes,

octaves and sextets, quatrains and couplets,
elegies, limericks, villanelles,
histories, myths ...

Duffy's Eurydice was, she suggests, thinking of stealing Orpheus'
poem from his cloak when at last inspiration struck her. She
stopped when Orpheus was a little way in front of her, and, with
a tremor in her voice, uttered the ultimate praise he was hankering
after: 'Orpheus, your poem's a masterpiece'. Irremediably hooked
by her apparent adulation, the Great Poet smiled modestly and –
how could it be otherwise? – turned round to look at her. Duffy/
Eurydice's conclusion plunges home the rhetorical stiletto with
deadly accuracy:

I noticed he hadn't shaved.
I waved once and was gone.[30]

Feminist-revisionist deflations of macho-heroic Greek heroes
have by now moved from the margin into the mainstream. But
when expressed in the most gifted voices – voices like Duffy's,
or that of Margaret Atwood, in her 'Orpheus 1', 'Eurydice' and
'Orpheus 2' – such deflations chart new emotional territory,
employing a glittering verbal music matching that more traditionally associated with Orpheus himself.

Almost exactly contemporary with Duffy's 'Eurydice' is Salman
Rushdie's extraordinary novel *The Ground Beneath her Feet* (1999),
an exuberant, sprawling, virtuoso exploration of – among many
other things – some implications of the Orpheus/Eurydice myth:
'music, love and life-death: these three'.[31] Rock music, with all the
urban-cool jargon that goes with that world, occupies the centre
(or one of the multiple centres) of the plot, alongside variants
on the idea of *katabasis*, the descent into the Underworld. The
three central characters are Ormus Cama, from an old Bombayite
family; Vina Apsara (father Indian, mother Greek–American); and

Rai Merchant, another Bombayite, who becomes a renowned photographer as well as being Vina's would-be and sometimes actual lover. But the twin foci are Ormus and Vina. They meet when she is an impossibly precocious 12-year-old, and he an impossibly handsome 19. In due course their explosive personal relationship accompanies and underpins their metamorphosis into global musical superstars – until rock diva Vina is fatally taken down into the earth during an earthquake in Mexico. At times Ormus certainly sounds like Orpheus: 'He was a musical sorcerer whose melodies could make city streets begin to dance and high buildings sway to their rhythm, a golden troubadour the jouncy poetry of whose lyrics could unlock the very gates of Hell; he incarnated the singer and songwriter as shaman and spokesman, and became the age's unholy unfool.'[32] But the novel plays as much with discrepancies as with overlaps. In spite of Vina's ultimate, seismic Mexican *katabasis*, quite un-Eurydice-like is *her* musicality: 'Ormus had the vision, but Vina had the voice, and it was the voice that did it … '[33] After her death, numerous Vina-impersonators spring up – another kind of return from the Underworld. As for Ormus' own deathward transition, he is shot with a handgun fired by a mysterious, lone woman. The police put it down to the act of 'a random crazy' (a Maenad, then); but Rai – perhaps tongue in cheek, as so often – has another theory: that the killer was Vina herself.[34]

At times, Rushdie demonstrates effortless familiarity with the classical and postclassical history of the myth, from Virgil to Rilke (whose *Sonnets to Orpheus* provide the epigraph). Yet one critic has argued that 'the alert reader has no choice but to ask whether Rushdie's vaunted "rewriting" of the Orpheus myth is in the end little more than a forced, arbitrary and far-fetched set of doubtful part-analogies.'[35] Part-analogies aplenty there certainly are, which often take the form of paradoxes and inversions. For example, when Ormus's coma looked like being terminal, he puts his recovery down to hearing Eurydice's voice.[36] However, rather than calling the analogies forced or far-fetched, we would do better to relish them for what they are, as when Rai and Vina play a language game, invoking, like a pair of supersmart children, such improbable figures as Endomorpheus, Ectomorpheus, Waldorpheus Astorpheus (god of hotels) and Hans Castorpheus (the magic mountaineer).[37]

Rushdie is a master of many moods, and outrageous humour is one of them. But more serious matters constantly intrude. In this respect, not the least pertinent sentence is the first one in the book, which announces that Vina met her seismic end on 14 February 1989 – the day the *fatwa* calling for the killing of Rushdie was issued. The starting date of the author's own nomadic journey 'underground' coincided, then, with that of Vina Apsara. The relationship between a writer's life and his/her imaginative creations is never straightforward, but it might not be a complete coincidence that the greatest of all portrayers of a descent into the Underworld – Dante Alighieri, the author of *Inferno* – spent the last two decades of his life in political exile from Florence, forbidden to return home on pain of death. To have the experience of being underground is at least one route towards imagining it.

Orpheus and Eurydice show no sign of loosening their grip on the contemporary imagination. Neil Gaiman's *The Sandman* fantasy comic books (1989 onwards), and Simon Armitage's BBC radio drama *Eurydice and Orpheus* (2015), are contrastingly imaginative ventures by English authors.[38] In the 21st century, the name 'Orpheus' has been variously used to designate a music research centre in Belgium and a brewery in Atlanta, Georgia; to provide one of the themes for a climate-change-aware Broadway musical; and as the title to an album by an Australian gothic rock band. All this is absolutely typical, not only of the enduring power of this constellation of myths, but also of the evocative potential of all the classical myths discussed in the present book – and of many other Greco-Roman stories that we have not had space to investigate.

The Legacy of Greek Myths

The tale I have been telling has involved a number of sub-plots. In describing the way the myths were told in classical antiquity, I have constantly sought to stress both their embeddedness in ancient life and their astonishing capacity to explore social and individual issues of profound significance. Themes I have highlighted include the family, that which is strange or monstrously alien ('other'), origins, politics, choice, and relationships between humans and gods. The family – and particularly its disruption – figures centrally in the myths of Medea and Oedipus, as well as those of Orpheus and Eurydice, and Daedalus and Icarus. The notion of 'otherness' underpins tales about the Amazons, and appears at every turn in the catalogue of monsters defeated by Heracles. The origins of both the cosmos and humanity are explored in myths about Prometheus. Political issues are perhaps less fundamental to the present selection of myths than to some others (the classic case is the myth of Antigone); but Oedipus' successive interactions with Creon (in *Oedipus Tyrannus*) and Theseus (in *Oedipus at Colonus*) are rooted in the idea of life in the ancient Greek city-state. The Judgment of Paris is the ultimate exploration of the theme of choice. As for relationships between humans and gods, there is not a single one of our chosen myths that does not invest significant intellectual and moral capital in examining this idea.

Each of the preceding chapters devotes at least half its time to the post-classical reception of the myths. The examples chosen – inevitably just a few out of a vast set of data – are designed to demonstrate the sheer diversity of the retellings. 'The classical tradition' has not, of course, been without its critics, and has at times been pilloried for its elitism and its culturally ostrich-like stance. Against that criticism, I have wanted to show how retellings of the myths can possess vibrancy, unruliness and unpredictability; sometimes there is a sense of raucous fun, and often a sense of menace. All that has been part of *my* tale.

To say that the Greek and Roman myths 'shape the way we think' is far from being mere market-driven hyperbole: that much, at least, should have become clear in the course of this book. The 'we' in 'we think' is the crux. 'We' have never been more diverse and more numerous. The individuals who 'receive' Greco-Roman mythology no longer belong to a homogeneous, exclusive club whose members share a knowledge that depends on access to high-status schooling in ancient languages. One need only recall the colossal, global movie-going public that has enjoyed cinematic re-imaginings of several of the myths discussed in previous chapters, and contrast it with the tiny numbers of those who have the chance to learn Greek and/or Latin at school and university. That there is an ever-widening set of frameworks within which the ancient myths have been reformulated is something at which to rejoice. Yet it would be desperately short-sighted to focus exclusively on such wide-spectrum reformulations, while sidelining the study of the stories in their ancient contexts and with their ancient meanings. There is – there *must* be – room for Sophocles as well as Berkoff, Virgil as well as Rushdie, Pompeian murals as well as Paolozzi collages, metopes from Olympia as well as lithographs by Maguire.

Any given contemporary reader or viewer will find some of the ancient mythical texts and images more attractive and inspiring, or alternatively more disturbing, shocking or even distasteful, than others. Ideologies change, and so do perceptions about (for example) gender, political values and human relations with the environment. Not every story told in antiquity bears a message or rests on assumptions that coincide with modern preferences. But that is inevitable, and is not – or should not be – a problem. A person who reads only those books whose contents s/he finds perfectly congenial is like a person whose favourite pastime is to gaze for hours into a mirror or, like Narcissus, into a tranquil pool reflecting his own adorable self-image. The best stories – and Greco-Roman myths are some of the very best stories ever told – have a unique power to shake us up – to challenge us to feel, to ponder, to question. Truly, these stories have shaped, and continue to shape, the way we think.

List of Abbreviated References

Aguirre/Buxton, *Cyclops*	M. Aguirre and R. G. A. Buxton, *Cyclops: The Myth and its Cultural History* (Oxford, 2020)
Bartel/Simon, *Medea*	H. Bartel and A. Simon (eds.), *Unbinding Medea: Interdisciplinary Approaches to a Classical Myth from Antiquity to the 21st Century* (London, 2010)
Bremmer, *Oedipus*	J. N. Bremmer, 'Oedipus and the Greek Oedipus Complex', in Bremmer (ed.), *Interpretations of Greek Mythology* (Beckenham, 1987), 41–59
Bull, *Mirror*	M. Bull, *The Mirror of the Gods: Classical Mythology in Renaissance Art* (London, 2005)
Burkert, *GrRel*	W. Burkert, *Greek Religion: Archaic and Classical* (Oxford, 1985)
Burkert, *Structure*	W. Burkert, *Structure and History in Greek Mythology and Ritual* (Berkeley, 1979)
Buxton, *Imaginary*	R. G. A. Buxton, *Imaginary Greece: The Contexts of Mythology* (Cambridge, 1994)
Dougherty, *Prometheus*	C. Dougherty, *Prometheus* (London, 2006)
Fletcher, *Underworld*	J. Fletcher, *Myths of the Underworld in Contemporary Culture: The Backward Gaze* (Oxford, 2019)

Fowler, *EGM*[2]   R. L. Fowler, *Early Greek Mythography*, vol. 2:
                         Commentary (Oxford, 2013)

LIMC   *Lexicon Iconographicum Mythologiae Classicae*
                         (Zurich and Düsseldorf, 1981–2009)

Mayor, *Amazons*   A. Mayor, *The Amazons: Lives and Legends*
                         of Warrior Women across the Ancient World
                         (Princeton, 2014)

Miles, *Classical Mythology*   G. Miles (ed.), *Classical Mythology in English*
                         Literature: A Critical Anthology (London, 1999)

Moog-Grünewald, *Reception*   M. Moog-Grünewald (ed.), *The Reception of Myth*
                         and Mythology (Brill's New Pauly, Supplements 4;
                         Leiden, 2010)

Morse, *Medieval*   R. Morse, *The Medieval Medea* (Cambridge, 1996)

PMG   D. L. Page (ed.), *Poetae Melici Graeci* (Oxford,
                         1962).

Raggio, *Prometheus*   O. Raggio, 'The Myth of Prometheus:
                         Its Survival and Metamorphoses up to the
                         Eighteenth Century', *Journal of the Warburg and*
                         Courtauld Institutes, vol. 21 (1958), 44–62

Reid, *ClMyth*   J. D. Reid, *The Oxford Guide to Classical Mythology*
                         in the Arts, 1300–1990s, 2 vols. (Oxford, 1993)

Renger, *Oedipus*   A.-B. Renger, *Oedipus and the Sphinx*
                         (Chicago, 2013)

Rushdie, *Ground*   S. Rushdie, *The Ground Beneath her Feet*
                         (London, 1999)

Segal, *Orpheus*   C. Segal, *Orpheus: The Myth of the Poet*
                         (Baltimore, 1989)

Stafford, *Herakles*   E. Stafford, *Herakles* (London, 2012)

ThesCRA   *Thesaurus Cultus et Rituum Antiquorum*
                         (Los Angeles, 2004–14)

Warner, *Monuments*   M. Warner, *Monuments and Maidens: The Allegory*
                         of the Female Form (London, 1985)

Notes

INTRODUCTION

1   P. Larkin, *Required Writing: Miscellaneous Pieces 1955–1982* (London, 1983), 69.
2   Clement of Alexandria, *Protrepticus*, ch. 2.
3   J. Addison, *Spectator*, no. 523 (30 October 1712); B. de Fontenelle, on the opening page of his *De l'origine des fables* (Paris, 1724).
4   See Buxton, *Imaginary*.
5   Pausanias, *Description of Greece* 3.24.10.

CHAPTER 1

1   See Buxton, *Imaginary*, 212–13.
2   See e.g. M. Griffith, *The Authenticity of 'Prometheus Bound'* (Cambridge, 1977).
3   Aeschylus, *Prometheus Bound* 64–70, trans. P. Vellacott (London, 1961).
4   Ibid. 248–51, trans. P. Vellacott (adapted).
5   e.g. Pindar, *Isthmian Ode* 8.
6   Ovid, *Metamorphoses* 1.82–86.
7   Aesop, *Fables* 516; cf. Dougherty, *Prometheus*, 17.
8   Dougherty, *Prometheus*.
9   Tertullian, *Apologeticum* 18.2.
10 Lactantius, *Institutiones divinae* 2.11.
11 Augustine, *De civitate Dei* 18.8.
12 Petrus Comestor, *Historia scholastica*, ch. 86.
13 Boccaccio, *Genealogia deorum gentilium* 4.44; cf. Servius on Virgil's *Eclogue* 6.42, Fulgentius, *Mythologiae* 2.6.
14 Natale Conti, *Mythologiae* (Paris, 1583), IV.6.

15   Raggio, *Prometheus*, 56–57 with fig. 8b.

16   Hartmann Schedel, *Liber Chronicarum* (Nuremberg, 1493), fol. xxviii recto; cf. Raggio, *Prometheus*, fig. 7a with 52–53; Moog-Grünewald, *Reception*, 558.

17   Servius on Virgil's *Eclogue* 6.42; Hyginus, *Astronomica* 2.15.

18   *On Discovery*, ed. B. P. Copenhaver (Cambridge, Mass., 2002), 2.21 (pp. 323–29).

19   Woodcut illustration to manuscript of Cicero, *Tusculan Disputations* (Venice, 1510) II, discussed by Raggio, *Prometheus*, 53, with fig. 7f.

20   For comparable versions of the tortured Prometheus in 16th- and 17th-century art, see plates 9 and 10 in Raggio, *Prometheus*.

21   *Goethes Werke*, ed. E. Trunz (Munich, 1998), vol. I, 44–46 (my translation).

22   Letter to John Murray, 12 October 1817; see A. González-Rivas Fernández, 'Aeschylus and *Frankenstein, or The Modern Prometheus*, by Mary Shelley', in R. F. Kennedy (ed.), *Brill's Companion to the Reception of Aeschylus* (Leiden, 2017), 292–322, at 299.

23   *The Works of Lord Byron*, ed. E. H. Coleridge (London, 1901), vol. IV, 48–51.

24   M. Shelley, *Frankenstein*, ch. 5.

25   See A. Griffin, 'Fire and Ice in *Frankenstein*', in G. Levine and U. C. Knoepflmacher (eds.), *The Endurance of 'Frankenstein': Essays on Mary Shelley's Novel* (Berkeley, 1979).

26   Dougherty, *Prometheus*, 114.

27   K. Marx, *Werke, Artikel, literarische Versuche bis März 1843* (= vol. I of the *Marx-Engels-Gesamtaufgabe*, Berlin, 1975), 15; J. Bentley, 'Prometheus versus Christ in the Christian–Marxist Dialogue', *Journal of Theological Studies*, N.S. vol. 29 (1978), 483–94; Th. Ziolkowski, 'Aeschylus in Germany', in R. F. Kennedy (ed.), *Brill's Companion to the Reception of Aeschylus* (Leiden, 2017), 225–42, at 230–31.

28   See V. Riedel, 'Wandlungen des Antikebildes in der Literatur der DDR', *International Journal of the Classical Tradition*, vol. 1 (1994), 105–16, at 107.

29   Well discussed in Dougherty, *Prometheus*, 124–41; also E. Hall, 'Tony Harrison's *Prometheus*: A View from the Left', *Arion*, vol. 10, no. 1 (2002), 129–40; H. Morales, *Classical Mythology: A Very Short Introduction* (Oxford, 2007), 36–38.

30   T. Harrison, *Prometheus* (London, 1998), 62.

31   Ibid. 55.

32   https://prometheus.io/docs/introduction/overview/#features (accessed 23 April 2021).

33   www.prometheusgroup.com (accessed 1 October 2019).

34   Discussed by N. Catellani-Dufrêne, 'Mythes antiques et humour dans *The Last Hero* de Terry Pratchett', in M. Bost-Fievet and S. Provini (eds.),

L'Antiquité dans l'imaginaire contemporain: fantasy, science-fiction, fantastique (Paris, 2014), 421–35.

35   T. Pratchett, *The Last Hero* (London, 2001), 174.

36   https://www.philamuseum.org/exhibitions/821.html?page=2 (accessed 2 January 2021).

CHAPTER 2

1   Apollonius of Rhodes, *Argonautica* 3.844–68.

2   See e.g. Book 10 of Homer's *Odyssey*.

3   Apollonius of Rhodes, *Argonautica* 3.648–51, trans. R. L. Hunter; see R. G. A. Buxton, 'How Medea Moves: Versions of a Myth in Apollonius and Elsewhere', in Bartel/Simon, *Medea*, 25–38, at 26.

4   Apollonius of Rhodes, *Argonautica* 3.756–60.

5   Ibid. 3.766–69, trans. R. L. Hunter.

6   Apollodorus, *Bibliotheca* 1.133.

7   Brief moments of control and stillness: e.g. the Talos episode. See Buxton, 'How Medea Moves'.

8   Apollodorus, *Bibliotheca* 1.143; Diodorus Siculus 4.50.1; the *hypothesis* to Euripides' *Medea*, citing lines from the epic poem *Nostoi*, from the fragmentary Epic Cycle; Ovid, *Metamorphoses* 7.162–63, 251–93.

9   See especially the narrative in Ovid, *Metamorphoses* 7.350–92, describing her flight through Greek airspace in her serpent-powered chariot.

10   Eumelos, *Korinthiaka* fr. 3a Davies (as reported by Pausanias, *Description of Greece* 2.3.10); scholia to Pindar, *Olympian Ode* 13.74. See E. Griffiths, *Medea* (Abingdon, 2006), 16.

11   Scholia to Euripides, *Medea* 264.

12   Edith Hall has acutely pointed out that, in Euripides' *Medea*, it is only after Medea has seen the psychological damage that childlessness causes to Aegeus that she understands the pain that childlessness will bring to Jason (E. Hall, 'Medea and the Mind of the Murderer', in Bartel/Simon, *Medea*, 16–24, at 21).

13   Apollodorus, *Bibliotheca* 1.147.

14   Ibycus fr. 291 in *PMG*; Simonides fr. 558 in ibid.

15   Excellent remarks on this by Morse, *Medieval*, 10–11.

16   Seneca, *Medea* 1026–27.

17   Ovid, *Tristia* 2.526.

18   See M. Carucci, 'The Representation of Medea in the Roman House', in Bartel/Simon, *Medea*, 53–65, at 62–63.

19 See C. Léglu, '"A New Medea" in Late Medieval French Narratives', in Bartel/Simon, *Medea*, 68–79, at 69–71.

20 *The Book of the City of Ladies*, trans. R. Brown-Grant (London, 1999), 63 and 174–75 (adapted).

21 See E. Kepetzis, 'Changing Perceptions: Medea as Paradigm of the Ideal Marriage', in Bartel/Simon, *Medea*, 80–93.

22 Illustrated as plates 3, 5 and 6 in Morse, *Medieval*.

23 See Morse, *Medieval*, 148–84, esp. 173.

24 Ibid. 160–61.

25 See the list in Reid, *ClMyth*, s.v. 'Medea'.

26 See B. Arkins, 'Three Medeas from Modern Ireland', and D. Cavallaro, 'Giving Birth to a New Woman: Italian Women Playwrights' Revisions of Medea', in Bartel/Simon, *Medea*, 186–94 and 195–208 respectively.

27 See Arkins, 190 and 193 n. 35.

28 I gratefully borrow here from the analysis by Arkins, 191.

29 See Cavallaro, 199–202.

30 Translation taken from Cavallaro, 200.

31 P. E. Easterling, 'The Infanticide in Euripides' *Medea*', *Yale Classical Studies*, vol. 25 (1977), 177–91.

32 Hall, 'Medea and the Mind of the Murderer', 16–17.

CHAPTER 3

1 Diodorus Siculus 1.61.3.

2 Ovid, *Ars amatoria* 2.25–28; Hyginus, *Fabulae* 40.

3 Homer, *Iliad* 18.590–92.

4 Virgil, *Aeneid* 6.14–33.

5 On Daedalus in Pausanias, see G. Hawes, *Rationalizing Myth in Antiquity* (Oxford, 2014), 207–12.

6 Diodorus Siculus 4.77.8–9, trans. C. H. Oldfather (London, 1939) (adapted).

7 Ovid, *Ars amatoria* 2.43–47, trans. P. Turner, *Ovid: The Technique of Love and Remedies for Love* (London, 1968) (adapted).

8 Ovid, *Metamorphoses* 8.203–34, trans. M. M. Innes, *The Metamorphoses of Ovid* (London, 1955).

9 Ovid, *Metamorphoses* 8.259.

10 Apollodorus, *Epitome* 1.14–15.

11 Lucian, *Somnium sive Gallus* 23; *Imagines* 21.

12 Lucian, *De astrologia* 14.

13 Lucian, *Navigium* 42–46.

14 Lucian, *Icaromenippus* 12, trans. H. W. and F. G. Fowler (Oxford, 1905). The quotation ends with a phrase familiar from Homer.

15 *LIMC*, 'Daidalos et Ikaros', vol. III, p. 317, no. 23a.

16 Ibid., p. 316, no. 15.

17 J. E. Nyenhuis, *Myth and the Creative Process* (Detroit, 2003), 38.

18 *LIMC*, 'Daidalos et Ikaros', vol. III, p. 318, no. 38.

19 Ibid., no. 36.

20 *LIMC*, 'Pasiphae', vol. VII, p. 196, no. 11.

21 *LIMC Supp.* 2009, add. 5.

22 Plato, *Meno* 97–98.

23 B. Greiner and J. Harst, 'Daedalus and Icarus', in Moog-Grünewald, *Reception*, 202–9, at 202.

24 *Ovide moralisé* 8.1819–24.

25 In *The Works of Francis Bacon*, vol. VI: *Literary and Professional Works* i, ed. J. Spedding, R. L. Ellis and D. D. Heath (Cambridge, 2011; first published 1858), p. 754.

26 C. Ginzburg, 'The High and the Low: The Theme of Forbidden Knowledge in the Sixteenth and Seventeenth Centuries', in Ginzburg, *Myths, Emblems, Clues* (London, 1990), 60–76.

27 Erasmus, as cited in Ginzburg, ibid. 60–61 with n. 6.

28 Thomas à Kempis, *The Imitation of Christ*, Book 1, ch. 2.

29 Alciati, *Emblemata* 104.

30 Fig. 5 in Ginzburg, 'The High and the Low', 72; Virgil, *Aeneid* 7.308.

31 Trans. by Niall Rudd in C. Martindale (ed.), *Ovid Renewed: Ovidian Influences on Literature and Art from the Middle Ages to the Twentieth Century* (Cambridge, 1988), 40.

32 See K. Kilinski II, 'Bruegel on Icarus: Inversions of the Fall', *Zeitschrift für Kunstgeschichte*, vol. 67, no. 1 (2004), 91–114.

33 Theatre: Frank Ceruzzi's play *Round Went the Wheel* (2019). Poetry: W. H. Auden, 'Musée des Beaux Arts' (1938); William Carlos Williams, 'Landscape with the Fall of Icarus' (1960). Sci-fi cinema: *The Man Who Fell to Earth* (1976). Rock music: the Titus Andronicus song 'Upon Viewing Brueghel's "Landscape with the Fall of Icarus"' (2008).

34 See K. Kilinski II, 101–2.

35 J. Collins, *Eduardo Paolozzi* (Farnham, 2014), 285.

36 See M. Aguirre Castro, 'Tecnología convertida en mito: la obra artística de Eduardo Paolozzi', *Icono 14*, vol. 15 (2017), 204–30.

37 See P. Boitani, *Winged Words: Flight in Poetry and History* (Chicago, 2007).

38 J. E. Nyenhuis, *Myth and the Creative Process*, xvii.

39 See F. Esposito, 'Icarus Rising: D'Annunzio, the Flying Artificer of Myth', in Esposito, *Fascism, Aviation and Mythical Modernity* (Basingstoke, 2015), 80–114; M. G. di Paolo, 'D'Annunzio's Icarian Mythopoiesis', *Forum*

Italicum vol. 44, no. 2 (2010), 287–300; L. Hughes-Hallett, *The Pike: Gabriele D'Annunzio – Poet, Seducer and Preacher of War* (London, 2013).

40   Gabriele D'Annunzio, *Prose di romanzi*, ed. A. Andreoli and N. Lorenzini (Milan, 1988–89), vol. II, 566 (my translation); cited by di Paolo, 'D'Annunzio's Icarian Mythopoiesis', 290.

41   M. Ayrton, *The Maze Maker* (London, 1967), 282.

42   M. Ayrton, *The Testament of Daedalus* (London, 1962), 14.

43   Ayrton, *The Maze Maker*, 63.

44   https://www.artspace.com/magazine/art_101/book_report/icarus-prometheus-pandora-10-famous-contemporary-artworks-based-on-myth-55374 (accessed 18 March 2021).

45   https://www.google.com/search?q=iron+maiden+icarus+flight+lyrics&rlz=1C1VASU_enES560ES560&oq=iron+maiden+icarus&aqs=chrome.2.69i59j4 6j0l5.7708j0j7&sourceid=chrome&ie=UTF-8 (accessed 18 March 2021).

46   D. Miller, *The Icarus Paradox* (New York, 1990).

47   https://www.icarus-ag.com/about-us/t1163 (accessed 25 May 2020); https://www.icarusjet.com/ (accessed 25 May 2020).

CHAPTER 4

1   Diodorus Siculus 2.45, trans. C. H. Oldfather (London, 1935).

2   Strabo 11.5.

3   Mayor, *Amazons*, 85–86.

4   Fowler, *EGM*², 291. See also J. H. Blok, *The Early Amazons: Modern and Ancient Perspectives on a Persistent Myth* (Leiden, 1995), 21–37.

5   Mayor, *Amazons*, 87–88.

6   I. Sluiter, 'Ancient Etymology: A Tool for Thinking', in F. Montanari, S. Matthaios and A. Rengakos (eds.), *Brill's Companion to Ancient Greek Scholarship*, vol. II (Leiden, 2015), 896–922; Aguirre/Buxton, *Cyclops*, 194, with refs. in n. 2.

7   A weaker form of the same motif, reported by Apollodorus (*Bibliotheca* 2.98), allowed the Amazons to have their cake (maternity) and eat it (warfare): they constricted (rather than cauterized) the right breast, leaving the left free for breast-feeding.

8   Strabo 11.5.1.

9   Herodotus 4.110–17.

10   Ibid. 4.114.

11   Apollonius of Rhodes, *Argonautica* 2.990–91.

12   See Fowler, *EGM*², 290.

13   Quintus of Smyrna 1.24–25.

14   Apollodorus, *Bibliotheca* 2.98.

15   Apollonius of Rhodes, *Argonautica* 2.966–69.

16   Apollodorus, *Bibliotheca* 2.101–2.

17   Homer, *Iliad* 6.186.

18   See Fowler, *EGM*², 485–86; Mayor, *Amazons*, 259–70.

19   Plutarch, *Life of Theseus* 26–27.

20   Pausanias, *Description of Greece* 1.2.1.

21   Virgil, *Aeneid* 7. 806.

22   Ibid. 11.655–63.

23   Ibid. 7.812–17.

24   Diodorus Siculus 2.44.2, trans. Oldfather.

25   Fowler, *EGM*², 486–87; Mayor, *Amazons*, 271–86.

26   Plutarch, *Life of Theseus* 27.

27   Lysias, *Funeral Oration* 4–6, trans. W. R. M. Lamb (London, 1930).

28   See Moog-Grünewald, *Reception*, 58–59.

29   Tertullian, *Adversus Marcionem* 1.1, trans. E. Evans (Oxford, 1972) (adapted).

30   Vv. 14524 and 14779; see C. Brinker-von der Heyde, 'Ez ist ein rehtez
      wîphere: Amazonen in mittelalterlicher Dichtung', *Beiträge zur Geschichte
      der deutschen Sprache und Literatur*, vol. 119, no. 3 (1997), 399–424, at 421–22.

31   See Brinker-von der Heyde, 411.

32   *The Book of the City of Ladies* 1.34; see Warner, *Monuments*, 203.

33   See the translation of *The Book of the City of Ladies* by R. Brown-Grant
      (London, 1999), sections 1.4, 16–19.

34   *The Travels of Sir John Mandeville*, trans. C. W. R. D. Moseley (London, 1983),
      116–17.

35   *The Discovery of the Amazon according to the Account of Friar Gaspar de
      Carvajal and Other Documents*, ed. H. C. Heaton (New York, 1934), 214.

36   Sir Walter Raleigh, *The Discovery of Guiana* (London, 1887), 42–43, and at
      https://archive.org/stream/discoveryofguian00rale iala#page/42/mode/2up
      (accessed 22 March 2021).

37   J.-F. Lafitau, *Moeurs des sauvages amériquains, comparées aux moeurs des
      premiers temps* (Paris, 1724); https://books.google.it/books?id=5EgY-FiwHY0
      C&printsec=frontcover&source=gbs_ge_summary_r&cad=0#v=onepage&
      q&f=false (accessed 22 March 2021).

38   Canto 36; see the translation by G. Waldman (Oxford, 1983), 438.

39   Canto 18; see also Canto 19 (pp. 206 and 226 in Waldman).

40   Canto 26 (p. 316 in Waldman).

41   Ibid. (pp. 310, 316 in Waldman). Cf. J. C. Bateman, 'Amazonian Knots:
      Gender, Genre, and Ariosto's Women Warriors', *MLN* [*Modern Language
      Notes*], vol. 122, no. 1, Italian Issue (2007), 1–23.

42   Warner, *Monuments*, 278.

43   See S. Poeschel, 'Rubens' "Battle of the Amazons" as a War-Picture. The
      Modernisation of a Myth', *Artibus et Historiae*, vol. 22, no. 43 (2001), 91–108.

44 In my account I follow the insightful comments of S. Georgoudi, 'Creating a Myth of Matriarchy', in P. Schmitt Pantel (ed.), *A History of Women in the West*, vol. I: *From Ancient Goddesses to Christian Saints* (Cambridge, Mass., 1992), 449–63.

45 E.g. the American suffragist Elizabeth Cady Stanton; see H. Morales, *Antigone Rising: The Subversive Power of the Ancient Myths* (London, 2020), 161–62, n. 17.

46 Excerpts from *Das Mutterrecht* (1861) are translated in Ralph Mannheim (ed.), *Myth, Religion, and Mother Right: Selected Writings of J. J. Bachofen* (Princeton, 1967); the passage quoted is at 150–51.

47 Burkert, *GrRel*, 351, n. 22; cf. S. Pembroke, 'Women in Charge: The Function of Alternatives in Early Greek Tradition and the Ancient Idea of Matriarchy', in *Journal of the Warburg and Courtauld Institutes*, vol. 30 (1967), 1–35. For a critique of feminist approaches to Bachofen, see C. Eller, *The Myth of Matriarchal Prehistory* (Boston, Mass., 2000), and *Gentlemen and Amazons: The Myth of Matriarchal Prehistory, 1861–1900* (Berkeley, 2011).

48 Mayor, *Amazons*.

49 See e.g. S. D. Goldhill in the *Times Literary Supplement* (6 March 2015) and J. R. Porter, https://www.academia.edu/37418474/Review_of_Adrienne_Mayor_The_Amazons_Lives_and_Legends_of_Warrior_Women_across_the_Ancient_World_Princeton_Oxford_Princeton_University_Press_2014_Pp_xiv_519_ISBN_9780691147208 (accessed 22 March 2021).

50 J. Wyndham, *Consider Her Ways and Others* (London, 2014).

51 E.g. Helen Diner and Monique Wittig. See the entry on 'Amazons' by D. G. Crowder in C. J. Summers, *The Gay and Lesbian Literary Heritage*, revised edn (Abingdon, 2013), 21–23.

52 J. Russ, *The Female Man* (New York, 1975), beginning of Part I.

53 Warner, *Monuments*, 175.

54 Ibid.

CHAPTER 5

1 Homer, *Odyssey* 11.272–80, trans. R. Lattimore (New York, 1965) (adapted).

2 Apollodorus, *Bibliotheca* 3.53.

3 Sophocles, *Oedipus Tyrannus* [*OT*] 219–20.

4 Ibid. 264.

5 Ibid. 362, 366–67.

6 Ibid. 432–41.

7 Bremmer, *Oedipus*, 45.

8   Ibid. 54–55: Oedipus cannot have a complex about Jocasta, since the
      woman he was raised by was his foster mother, Merope. Nevertheless,
      there *is* evidence for a 'Greek Oedipus complex'. As Jocasta says in *OT*:
      'Many mortals have slept with their mother in dreams' (981–82); cf. also
      the long discussion about such dreams in Artemidorus, *The Interpretation
      of Dreams* 1.79. Bremmer argues that, from the 5th century BCE onwards,
      upper-class children were looked after closely at home by women,
      rendering the possibility of an Oedipus complex more likely from the
      standpoint of the family situation.

9   *OT* 1014–16.

10   Ibid. 1051–53.

11   Ibid. 1142–45.

12   Ibid. 1171–72.

13   Ibid. 1182–85.

14   Ibid. 1186–96.

15   Ibid. 1368.

16   Ibid. 1369–74.

17   Ibid. 1529–30.

18   Aristotle, *Poetics* 1452^{a}32–33.

19   Scholia to Euripides, *Phoenician Women* 26.

20   Euripides fr. 541; Fowler, *EGM*^{2}, 408. For a detailed discussion, sceptical
      about the fragment's attribution to Euripides, see V. Liapis, 'The Fragments
      of Euripides' *Oedipus*: A Reconsideration', *Transactions of the American
      Philological Association*, vol. 144, no. 2 (2014), 307–70, at 316–24.

21   Euripides, *Phoenician Women*.

22   See e.g. the (now fragmentary) epic poem *Oidipodeia* (fr. 1), quoted by
      Pausanias, *Description of Greece* 9.5.11; cf. Fowler, *EGM*^{2} , 404–5.

23   Seneca, *Oedipus* 15–27.

24   Ibid. 703–4.

25   Ibid. 857–59.

26   Tacitus, *Annals* 14.8, 14.2; cf. also Seneca, *Octavia* 366–72. See C. Star, *Seneca*
      (London, 2016), 85.

27   Sophocles, *Oedipus at Colonus* 1656–65.

28   Ibid. 1756–57 and 1769–72.

29   See C. Calame, 'Le nom d'Oedipe', in B. Gentili and R. Pretagostini (eds.),
      Edipo: Il teatro greco e la cultura europea (Rome, 1986), 395–407.

30   Bremmer, *Oedipus*, 44–45.

31   See Reid, *ClMyth*, vol. II, 754–62; Moog-Grünewald, *Reception*, 458–69; some
      additional bibliography in Renger, *Oedipus*, 91–92, nn. 3 and 5.

32   Translation adapted from *Bacon's Essays and Wisdom of the Ancients* (Boston,
      1884), available at https://www.gutenberg.org/files/56463/56463-h/56463-h.
      htm (accessed 4 May 2021).

33 Text available at https://archive.org/details/dipustyrannusorooshelgoog/ mode/2up (accessed 24 March 2021). For interpretation, see e.g. M. Erkelenz, 'The Genre and Politics of Shelley's *Swellfoot the Tyrant*,' *Review of English Studies*, vol. 47, no. 188 (1996), 500–520.

34 Act I, 3–10.

35 'PASTOR ET NUNTIUS.

    In monte reppertus est, a matre derelictus;

    In montibus repperimus.

    Laio Jocastaque natus!

    Peremptor Laii parentis!

    Natus Laio et Jocasta!

    Coniux Jocastae parentis!

    Utinam ne diceres, oportebat tacere nunquam dicere istud:

    a Jocasta derelictum in monte reppertus est.

    OEDIPUS.

    Natus sum quo nefastum est, concubui cui nefastum est,

    cecidi quem nefastum est.

    Lux facta est.'

36 A. W. Johnson and D. Price-Williams, *Oedipus Ubiquitous: The Family Complex in World Folk Literature* (Stanford, 1996), 3.

37 Renger, *Oedipus*, 55.

38 S. Freud, *The Interpretation of Dreams*, trans. and ed. James Strachey (New York, 2010), 280.

39 Cf. Moog-Grünewald, *Reception*, 468–69.

40 Renger, *Oedipus*, 48–49.

41 H. Morales, *Classical Mythology: A Very Short Introduction* (Oxford, 2007), 78.

42 In a private collection; see W. Spies and S. Rewald (eds.), *Max Ernst: A Retrospective* (New York, 2005), cat. no. 36, p. 141.

43 Cf. E. M. Legge, *Max Ernst: The Psychoanalytic Sources* (Ann Arbor, 1989), 36–39.

44 Act 1, scene 2.

45 Act 2, scene 2.

46 *OT* 1186–88.

CHAPTER 6

1 Hyginus, *Fabulae* 92.

2 Hesiod, *Works and Days* 11–26.

3 Hesiod, *Theogony* 226–30; Homer, *Iliad* 4.440–45.

4 Apollodorus, *Bibliotheca* 2.113.

5   See Stafford, *Herakles*, 47.

6   See C. A. Faraone, 'Aphrodite's ΚΕΣΤΟΣ and Apples for Atalanta: Aphrodisiacs in Early Greek Myth and Ritual', *Phoenix*, vol. 44 (1990), 224–43; *ThesCRA*, vol. VI, 92–93.

7   Lucian, *Dialogi marini* 7.1.

8   For another myth about an inscribed apple in an erotic context, see the tale of Acontius and Cydippe, recounted notably by Ovid in *Heroides* 20 and 21.

9   See for example *Cypria* fr. 1, in A. Bernabé (ed.), *Poetarum epicorum graecorum: Testimonia et fragmenta*, Part 1 (Leipzig, 1987); Euripides, *Helen* 36–41; *Orestes* 1639–42; Apollodorus, *Epitome* 3.1.

10 Hyginus, *Fabulae* 92.

11 L. Kahn, *Hermès passe ou les ambiguïtés de la communication* (Paris, 1978); Burkert, *GrRel*, 156–59.

12 Apollodorus, *Bibliotheca* 3.150.

13 Lucian, *Dearum iudicium* 1.

14 Apuleius, *Metamorphoses* 10.30, trans. P. G. Walsh, *The Golden Ass* (Oxford, 1994).

15 Euripides, *Cyclops* 182–84.

16 Basel, Antikenmuseum, BS 434 = *LIMC* 'Paridis iudicium', vol. VII, p. 178, no. 14.

17 *Cypria* fr. 4 Bernabé.

18 Lucian, *Dearum iudicium* 9.

19 Apuleius, *Metamorphoses* 10.31; trans. P. G. Walsh.

20 E.g. Euripides, *Trojan Women* 924–31; Lucian, *Dearum iudicium* 11–16; Apollodorus, *Epitome* 3.2; Hyginus, *Fabulae* 92.

21 Among other places, the story was told in Euripides' lost tragedy *Alexandros*; see the edition of the play by I. Karamanou (Berlin, 2017).

22 See for example the essays in D. B. Dodd and C. A. Faraone (eds.), *Initiation in Ancient Greek Rituals and Narratives* (London, 2003).

23 Homer, *Iliad* 3.390–94.

24 Apollodorus, *Epitome* 5.3.

25 See Quintus of Smyrna, *The Fall of Troy* 10.253–489.

26 Fulgentius, *Mythologiae* 2.1.

27 Dares Phrygius, *De excidio Troiae historia* 7.

28 Gower, *Confessio Amantis* 5.7408–19. 'nam' = 'brought'; 'dede me to wite' = 'caused me to know'; 'putt hem upon me' = 'entrusted themselves to me'. Full text at https://d.lib.rochester.edu/teams/text/peck-gower-confessio-amantis-book-5 (accessed 26 March 2021).

29 Bull, *Mirror*, 345.

30 F. Healy, *Rubens and the Judgement of Paris: A Question of Choice* (Turnhout, 1997), 125.

31 See https://www.rct.uk/collection/403446/elizabeth-i-and-the-three-goddesses (accessed 4 November 2020).

32 Marsilio Ficino, *Opera omnia* (Turin, 1959), vol. I, 920; cf. Bull, *Mirror*, 348.

33 *Merchant of Venice*, II. vii. 5–9.

34 *Merchant of Venice*, III. ii. 106.

35 *King Lear*, I. i. 53.

36 *King Lear*, I. i. 95.

37 *Merchant of Venice*, III. ii. 41.

38 Cf. Moog-Grünewald, *Reception*, 510.

39 https://www.museodelprado.es/coleccion/obra-de-arte/el-juicio-de-paris/0675c0f3-1701-4d2a-8cc5-a1db2612411f (accessed 26 March 2021).

40 Agatha Christie, *The Labours of Hercules* (New York, 1947).

CHAPTER 7

1 See G. K. Galinsky, *The Herakles Theme: The Adaptations of the Hero in Literature from Homer to the Twentieth Century* (Oxford, 1972); Stafford, *Herakles*; Burkert, *Structure*, 78–98.

2 Lucian, *Iuppiter tragoedus* 21.

3 Hesiod, *Theogony* 954–55; cf. Pindar, *Nemean Ode* 1.67–72.

4 Stafford, *Herakles*, 137–70.

5 Pindar, *Olympian Ode* 10.

6 See Fowler, EGM^2, 271.

7 Temple of Zeus: see Stafford, *Herakles*, 24–25. Cf. Theocritus, *Idylls* 24.80–81; Apollonius of Rhodes, *Argonautica* 1.1317–20.

8 10: Apollodorus, *Bibliotheca* 2.73; 1,000: Virgil, *Aeneid* 8.291–93; 10,000: Sophocles, *Trachinae* 1101; cf. Fowler, EGM^2, 272–73.

9 Homer, *Iliad* 19.95–133.

10 Ibid. 19.105.

11 E.g. Pindar, *Nemean Ode* 1.60–72; Sophocles, *Philoctetes* 1418–20; Theocritus, *Idylls* 24.77–83; Diodorus Siculus 4.10.7.

12 Apollodorus, *Bibliotheca* 2.72–73.

13 Ibid. 2.75.

14 Ibid. 2.77–80, trans. R. S. Smith and S. M. Trzaskoma (Indianapolis, 2007).

15 Diodorus Siculus 4.11.5, with Stafford, *Herakles*, 34.

16 Euripides, *Hercules furens* 375–79.

17 Pindar, *Olympian Ode* 3.25–32.

18 Apollodorus, *Bibliotheca* 2.81–82.

19 Ibid. 2.87.

20 Diodorus Siculus 4.13.3.

21   Apollodorus, *Bibliotheca* 2.88–91.

22   Ibid. 2.92; Diodorus Siculus 4.13.2; Hyginus, *Fabulae* 30.6; Pausanias, *Description of Greece* 8.22.4.

23   See, for example, the remarks of Jeremy McInerney at https://www.penn. museum/documents/publications/expedition/pdfs/53-3/mcinerney.pdf (accessed 30 March 2021).

24   E.g. Euripides, *Alcestis* 492–96.

25   Aguirre/Buxton, *Cyclops*, 40.

26   Diodorus Siculus 4.15.3.

27   Ibid. 4.15.4; Apollodorus, *Bibliotheca* 2.96.

28   Apollodorus, *Bibliotheca* 2.97.

29   See pp. 106–7 above, on the Amazons.

30   Diodorus Siculus 4.16.

31   See Stafford, *Herakles*, 42–45.

32   Apollodorus, *Bibliotheca* 2.106.

33   Ibid. 2.112.

34   For a richly detailed account of this episode, see Fowler, EGM^2, 291–99.

35   E.g. Diodorus Siculus 4.26.4.

36   Apollodorus, *Bibliotheca* 2.119-20, trans. R. S. Smith and S. M. Trzaskoma.

37   Apollonius of Rhodes, *Argonautica* 4.1432–40, trans. R. L. Hunter (Oxford, 1993).

38   E.g. Ovid, *Metamorphoses* 7.408–19; other references at Fowler, EGM^2, 305, n. 157.

39   Hesiod, *Theogony* 311–12.

40   Ibid. 770–73.

41   Virgil, *Aeneid* 6.126.

42   Ovid, *Metamorphoses* 7.407 and 409.

43   Homer, *Odyssey* 11.625–26.

44   Apollodorus, *Bibliotheca* 2.126.

45   See G. Hawes, *Rationalizing Myth in Antiquity* (Oxford, 2014), 37–91.

46   Palaephatus, *On Unbelievable Tales* 18.

47   Ibid. 38.

48   See Aguirre/Buxton, *Cyclops*, 22–28.

49   Stafford, *Herakles*, 124–29.

50   E.g. Arrian, *Discourse* 3.24.13; similarly in Cicero, *De natura deorum* 2.62.

51   Heraclitus, *Homeric Problems* 33, trans. D. A. Russell and D. Konstan (Atlanta, 2005).

52   Lucretius, *De rerum natura* 5.22–54, trans. R. E. Latham (Harmondsworth, 1951).

53   Tertullian, *Ad nationes* 2.14.

54   Lactantius, *Institutiones divinae* 1.9, trans. W. Fletcher, available at https:// www.newadvent.org/fathers/0701.htm (accessed 8 May 2021).

55   Justin, *First Apology* 21.

56 See B. Berg, 'Alcestis and Hercules in the Catacomb of Via Latina', *Vigiliae Christianae*, vol. 48 (1994), 219–34.

57 See G. Scafoglio, 'Dante's Hercules', in A. Allan, E. Anagnostou-Laoutides and E. Stafford (eds.), *Herakles Inside and Outside the Church: From the First Apologists to the End of the Quattrocento* (Leiden, 2020), 155–70.

58 Canto 6, 16–18, trans. D. L. Sayers (Harmondsworth, 1949).

59 Canto 17.

60 Dante, *Epistle* 7.6.

61 *Ovide moralisé* 9.475–77.

62 See Stafford, *Herakles*, 205, on Christine de Pizan.

63 G. Chaucer, *The Canterbury Tales* 2095–2112 and 2139-42; modern English version by Nevill Coghill (Harmondsworth, 1951), 208–10.

64 See J. Chance, *Medieval Mythography*, vol. 3: *The Emergence of Italian Humanism, 1321–1475* (Gainesville, Fla., 2015), 394–426.

65 See Stafford, *Herakles*, 205.

66 See e.g. R. O. Iredale, 'Giants and Tyrants in Book Five of *The Faerie Queene*', *Review of English Studies*, vol. 17 (1966), 373–81.

67 This whole topic has been superbly explored in Bull, *Mirror*, 86–140.

68 Boethius, *Consolatio* 4.7; cf. Bull, *Mirror*, 100–101.

69 See L. D. Ettlinger, 'Hercules Florentinus', in *Mitteilungen des Kunsthistorischen Institutes in Florenz*, vol. 16, no. 2 (1972), 119–42.

70 K. Lippincott and R. Signorini, 'The *Camera dello Zodiaco* of Federico II Gonzaga', *Journal of the Warburg and Courtauld Institutes*, 54 (1991), 244–47.

71 See C. R. Ligota, 'Annius of Viterbo and Historical Method', *Journal of the Warburg and Courtauld Institutes*, vol. 50 (1987), 44–56.

72 Tacitus, *Germania* 3.

73 Trans. by D. Hobbins as *The Life of Henry VII* (New York, 2011).

74 Diodorus Siculus 4.19.1-2; 5.24.1-3.

75 C. Vivanti, 'Henry IV, the Gallic Hercules', *Journal of the Warburg and Courtauld Institutes*, vol. 30 (1967), 176–97.

76 A. Christie, *The Labours of Hercules* (London, 2001); quotations at 16, 14 and 380 respectively.

77 https://www.marianmaguire.com/the-unsettled-settler---by-greta-hawes.html (accessed 30 March 2021). See also M. Johnston and T. Köntges, 'Of Heroes and Humans: Marian Maguire's Colonization of Herakles' Mythical World', in M. Johnson (ed.), *Antipodean Antiquities: Classical Reception Down Under* (London, 2019), 195–207.

78 See esp. Stafford, *Herakles*, 232–41.

CHAPTER 8

1   For accounts of Orpheus see Segal, *Orpheus*; F. Graf, 'Orpheus: A Poet
     Among Men', in J. N. Bremmer (ed.), *Interpretations of Greek Mythology*
     (Beckenham, 1987), 80–106; also the 65-item bibliography compiled by
     Berhard Huss in Moog-Grünewald, *Reception*, 493–94.

2   Apollonius of Rhodes, *Argonautica* 1.512–15, trans. R. L. Hunter (Oxford,
     1993).

3   Ibid. 4.905–9.

4   Simonides fr. 567 in *PMG*.

5   Euripides, *Hypsipyle* fr. 752g. 8–14.

6   *Anthologia Palatina* 7.8, trans. K. Rexroth, in P. Jay, *The Greek Anthology*
     (London, 1973).

7   Ovid, *Metamorphoses* 10. 40–46, trans. adapted from D. Raeburn (London,
     2004).

8   A typically nuanced account of the motif is given by Jan Bremmer, 'Don't
     Look Back: From the Wife of Lot to Orpheus and Eurydice', in Bremmer,
     Greek Religion and Culture, the Bible and the Ancient Near East (Leiden, 2008),
     117–32.

9   Ovid, *Metamorphoses* 10.53–63, trans. D. Raeburn.

10   See also Phanocles fr. 1.7–10, in J. U. Powell (ed.), *Collectanea Alexandrina*
     (Oxford, 1925), with Segal, *Orpheus*, 57.

11   Ovid, *Metamorphoses* 11.64–66, trans. D. Raeburn (amended).

12   Virgil, *Georgic* 4.488, 491 and 495.

13   Euripides, *Alcestis* 357–62.

14   Plato, *Symposium* 179d.

15   Hermesianax fr. 7.1–14 in Powell, *Collectanea Alexandrina*.

16   Euripides, *Hippolytus* 952–57; cf. also Plato, *Republic* 364e–65a.

17   See especially J. B. Friedman, *Orpheus in the Middle Ages* (Cambridge, Mass.,
     1970).

18   Clement of Alexandria, *Protrepticus* 1.

19   Boethius, *Consolatio* 3.12.

20   Fulgentius, *Mythologiae* 3.10.

21   Boccaccio, *Genealogia deorum gentilium* 5.12.

22   Pierre Bersuire, *Ovidius moralizatus* fols. 58r–59r in the 1509 (Paris) edn,
     reprinted New York, 1979. For the comparison between Boccaccio
     and Bersuire, see P. Cherchi, 'The Inventors of Things in Boccaccio's
     De genealogia deorum gentilium', in I. Candido (ed.), *Petrarch and Boccaccio:
     The Unity of Knowledge in the Pre-modern World* (Berlin, 2018), 244–69, at
     262–64.

23   Trans. by G. Miles in Miles, *Classical Mythology*, 91.

24 Henryson, 'Orpheus and Eurydice', in R. L. Kindrick (ed.), *The Poems of Robert Henryson* (Kalamazoo, Mich., 1997), lines 92–105. ['Buss' = 'bush'], available at https://d.lib.rochester.edu/teams/text/kindrick-poems-of-robert-henryson-orpheus-and-eurydice (accessed 13 April 2021).

25 Text available at http://www.gutenberg.org/files/56463/56463-h/56463-h.htm (accessed 13 April 2021).

26 *Two Gentlemen of Verona*, III. ii. 78–81.

27 *Merchant of Venice*, V. i. 79–88.

28 Percy Bysshe Shelley, 'Orpheus', 68–69; 81; 117–18; 118–24. In *The Works of Percy Bysshe Shelley*, ed. H. B. Forman (London, 1880), vol. IV, 56.

29 In H. D., *Collected Poems 1912–1944* (New York, 1986).

30 In Carol Ann Duffy, *The World's Wife: Poems* (London, 1999).

31 Rushdie, *Ground*, 22. See the thoughtful analysis of the novel by C. Rollason, 'Rushdie's Un-Indian Music: The Ground Beneath Her Feet', https://www.academia.edu/42007123/Rushdies_Un_Indian_Music_The_Ground_Beneath_Her_Feet (accessed 19 January 2021). Also Fletcher, *Underworld*, 173–85.

32 Rushdie, *Ground*, 89.

33 Ibid. 157.

34 Ibid. 571.

35 Rollason, 'Rushdie's Un-Indian Music', 11.

36 Rushdie, *Ground*, 322.

37 Ibid. 456.

38 On Gaiman, see Fletcher, *Underworld*, especially 47–52 and 64–86.

Illustration Credits

Roman numerals refer to colour plates. a= above; b= below; l= left; r=right

I Philadelphia Museum of Art. Purchased with the W. P. Wilstach Fund, 1950 **II** Musée des Beaux-Arts de Strasbourg. Photo Musées de Strasbourg/M. Bertola **III** Musée du Louvre, Paris. Photo RMN-Grand Palais (musée du Louvre)/Maurice et Pierre Chuzeville **IV** Courtesy Swann Auction Galleries, New York **V** Photo Manuel Cohen/Scala, Florence **VI** Musées Royaux des Beaux-Arts de Belgique, Brussels. Photo Superstock/A. Burkatovski/Fine Art Images **VII** Gaziantep Museum of Archaeology **VIII** British Library, London. Photo The British Library Board/Leemage/Bridgeman Images **IX** Kunstmuseum Basel **X** © Eleanor Antin. Courtesy the artist and Ronald Feldman Gallery, New York **XI** Courtesy the Penn Museum, Philadelphia. Object number L-64-185 **XII** The J. Paul Getty Museum, Los Angeles **XIII** Royal Museums Greenwich, London. © Marian Maguire **XIV** Palazzo Pitti, Gallerie degli Uffizi, Florence **XV** The Cleveland Museum of Art. Gift from J. H. Wade 1926.25

2 Liechtenstein, The Princely Collections, Vaduz–Vienna. Photo Liechtenstein, The Princely Collections, Vaduz–Vienna/Scala, Florence **27** Vatican Museums, Vatican City. Photo Bridgeman Images **28a** National Archaeological Museum, Athens. Photo De Agostini/Getty Images **28b** The J. Paul Getty Museum, Los Angeles. Gift of Stanley Ungar **29** Museo del Prado, Madrid **31** The British Museum, London. Photo The Trustees of the British Museum **33** Photo Universal Images Group North America LLC/De Agostini/Alamy Stock Photo **35** Auckland Art Gallery Toi o Tāmaki, purchased 1965 **39** Musée Carnavalet, Histoire de Paris **42** © God of Fire **49** Museo Archeologico Nazionale, Naples. Photo © Luciano Pedicini **51** The British Museum, London. Photo The Trustees of the British Museum **54** The State Hermitage Museum, St Petersburg. Photo The State Hermitage Museum **56** Museo Archeologico Nazionale, Naples **60a** Musée des Arts Décoratifs, Paris **60b, 61** Bibliothèque nationale de France, Paris **62** Birmingham Museum and Art Gallery/Birmingham Museums Trust **63** Palais des Beaux-Arts, Lille **67** Photo Teresa Isasi/Miramax/Canal+/Sogecine/Kobal/Shutterstock **68** Library of Congress, Prints and Photographs Division, Washington, D.C. **70** Photo Keystone Pictures USA/Shutterstock **77** Villa Albani, Rome. Photo Bettmann/Getty Images **78** The British Museum, London. Photo The Trustees of the British Museum **82** House of the Vettii, Pompeii **83** Museu Monográfico de Conimbriga-Museu Nacional/Direção Geral do Património Cultural **87** Stiftung der Werke von C.G. Jung, Zurich **89a** Museo

Acknowledgments

To write a book like this involves accumulating a whole heap of debts: generations of students taught and learned from, colleagues and friends mercilessly pestered for advice, library resources pillaged and their custodians badgered. To single out a few names from this band of co-workers seems like wilful favouritism, yet it has to be done, and it is a pleasure to do it. First I think of various individuals at Thames & Hudson. The peerless Colin Ridler originally commissioned the book; his successor, Ben Hayes, has been a tireless supporter of the project; Sam Wythe, Nikos Kotsopoulos, Jen Moore and Isabella Luta have contributed significantly to the final result with their editorial and pictorial professionalism. Then there have been the staff of several libraries, above all those at the University of Bristol, where I spent most of my career; they have never failed to respond with speed and goodwill to my persistent demands. When I had to look elsewhere, the Fondation Hardt in Geneva, in the person of its librarian, Sabrina Ciardo, supplied me with a wealth of material to keep me happy, at a time when – because of unprecedented global circumstances – physical travel between academic institutions had become a challenge that often proved insurmountable. Finally, on a more personal note, I thank Mercedes Aguirre, who, in our innumerable conversations, has illuminated not only the topic of Greek mythology, but also the profound human importance of storytelling.

Index

Page numbers in *italics* refer to illustrations;
Roman numerals refer to colour plates.